The First-Year Experience
Monograph Series No. 39

S0-BRC-730

Integrating the
First-Year Experience:

The Role of First-Year Seminars in Learning Communities

Jean M. Henscheid

Editor

NATIONAL RESOURCE CENTER FOR
THE FIRST-YEAR EXPERIENCE®
& STUDENTS IN TRANSITION
UNIVERSITY OF SOUTH CAROLINA, 2004

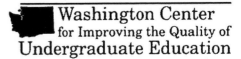

Washington Center
for Improving the Quality of
Undergraduate Education

Cite as:

Henscheid, J. M. (Ed.). (2004). Integrating the first-year experience: The role of learning communities in first-year seminars (Monograph No. 39). Columbia, SC: University of South Carolina, National Resource Center for The First-Year Experience and Students in Transition.

Sample chapter citation:

Murphy, S. K, & Gentile, S. (2004). Placing learning communities and first-year seminars at the core of general education reform. In J. M. Henscheid (Ed.), Integrating the first-year experience: The role of learning communities in first-year seminars (Monograph No. 39) (pp. 27-48). Columbia, SC: University of South Carolina, National Resource Center for The First-Year Experience and Students in Transition.

Additional copies of this monograph may be ordered from the National Resource Center for The First-Year Experience and Students in Transition, University of South Carolina, 1728 College Street, Columbia, SC 29208. Telephone (803) 777-6229. Fax (803) 777-4699.

Special gratitude is expressed to Jenny Anderson, Composition Assistant, for layout and design; to Kevin Kyzer, Editorial Assistant, Inge Lewis, Editor, Michelle Mouton, Editorial Assistant, and Alicia Phillip, Editorial Assistant, for copyediting and proofing assistance; to Tracy L. Skipper, Editorial Projects Coordinator, for copyediting and project management; and to Barbara F. Tobolowsky, Associate Director for Publications and Research for copyediting.

Copyright 2004, by the University of South Carolina. All rights reserved.
No part of this work may be reproduced or copied in any form, by any means,
without written permission from the University of South Carolina.

ISBN Number: 1-889271-47-0

The First-Year Experience® is a service mark of the University of South Carolina. A license may be granted upon written request to use the term The First-Year Experience. This license is not transferable without written approval of the University of South Carolina.

Integrating the first-year experience : the role of first-year seminars in learning communities / Jean M. Henscheid, editor.
    p. cm. -- (First-year experience monograph series ; no. 39)
    Includes bibliographical references.
    ISBN 1-889271-47-0 (soft cover)
    1. College freshmen--United States. 2. College student orientation--United States. 3. Interdisciplinary approach in education--United States. I. Henscheid, Jean M., 1961- II. Title. III. Series.
    LB2343.32.I58 2004
    378.1'98--dc22
                                2004016734

Contents

Mary Stuart Hunter, Jean MacGregor, and Barbara Leigh Smith

It is with great pleasure that the National Resource Center for The First-Year Experience and Students in Transition presents this 39th installment in our topical monograph series, which focuses on improving the college experience for students in the United States and beyond. This volume focuses on the integrative role of first-year seminars in learning communities, and the partnership with the National Learning Communities Project personifies the collaboration it advocates.

In recent years, two important educational initiatives, learning communities and first-year seminars, became widespread in colleges and universities across the country and around the world. Recent estimates indicate that more than 500 colleges and universities in the United States are using a wide variety of learning community structures (Smith, 2001). First-year seminars are even more prevalent, with more than 75% of institutions reporting one or more type of first-year seminar (National Resource Center, 2002). Many campuses are fusing these two initiatives. This monograph describes a number of exemplary programs that bring learning communities and first-year seminars together and demonstrate ideal partnerships for enhancing student learning and persistence in college. When co-registering students in two, three, or more courses within a learning community, institutions can create a more robust curricular platform for making intellectual connections, practicing active learning, and promoting student engagement than is normally found in a single course. Educators have greatly influenced how we think about the first year in college by arguing that academic success is a complicated subject that involves issues embedded in and beyond the formal curriculum. First-year seminars offer a flexible and adaptable framework for addressing first-year issues within the curriculum. Recognizing that joining a new community involves various transitional issues, building new relationships, and learning to navigate new structures and expectations, first-year seminar directors and instructors support and guide new students during the critical transition into the higher education culture.

First-year seminars and learning communities have deep historical roots, reaching back to the early 20th century. Both approaches stand out as early efforts to serve an increasingly diverse student population and create an educational milieu supportive of student learning and success. Over the years, other educational reform efforts have come and gone, but during the last two decades in which the postsecondary student population has doubled in size, both learning communities and first-year seminars have experienced an explosion of interest and a proliferation of designs. These efforts are important educational responses to today's new students who are more diverse in many respects and are often first-generation college students. Many institutions with large numbers of part-time and commuting students, as well as those with residential populations, now aspire to create challenging and involving academic environments. First-year seminar and learning community programs can respond successfully to such institutional needs.

The last 20 years' initiatives to reform undergraduate education (e.g., service-learning and civic engagement activities, outcomes assessment, collaborative/cooperative learning, multicultural education, and various uses of technology) have blossomed along with the emergence of a rich body of research on student learning and development. At

Foreword

the same time, our campuses are facing enormous financial stress. Campus leaders continue to search for ways to optimize learning in a time of increasingly limited resources. Part of the solution must be finding scalable approaches that serve large numbers of students, can be adapted to different institutional environments, and are cost effective.

As various educational reform efforts have grown and matured, it has become obvious that these reforms have much in common and that collaboration among these efforts can have incredible synergistic outcomes for the students they serve. The convergence of first-year seminars and learning communities demonstrates the benefits of cooperation as the effort draws upon each other's strengths and broadens the base of support.

Large-scale reform efforts typically face the challenge of maintaining quality as they expand. It is not an uncommon occurrence for education reforms to be co-opted by institutions and reshaped so that the original vision is lost or minimized. We believe that on many campuses both learning communities and first-year seminars are at that critical juncture where articulation of potential outcomes and communication of core practices are necessary.

Achieving a large enough scale to have a deep and broad reach is only one aspect of a successful reform effort. Promoting quality and excellence is equally important and requires explicit efforts to build a broad-based commitment to the innovation among staff and faculty. It requires making investments in faculty and staff development. It also requires situating these innovations in places that matter. The first year of college and general education is a prominent site for first-year seminars and learning communities for good reasons: These are the entry points to college and the place where academic expectations are set. It is also evident that the first year of college is critical in terms of student retention.

Through a series of case studies, this monograph offers much information about the design of educational programs and the practices that can make a difference in student success and retention. The range of examples demonstrates that learning communities and first-year seminars can take many different forms, yet through collaboration, can accomplish more than perhaps either can do alone. We assume you are reading this volume because you are interested in improving undergraduate education. We are confident that you will find considerable guidance from this book. As always, we welcome your comments and feedback.

Mary Stuart Hunter, Director
National Resource Center for The First-Year Experience and Students in Transition
University of South Carolina

Jean MacGregor, Co-Director
National Learning Communities Project
The Evergreen State College

Barbara Leigh Smith, Co-Director
National Learning Communities Project
The Evergreen State College

References

National Resource Center for The First-Year Experience and Students in Transition. (2002). *2000 national survey on first-year seminars: Continuing innovations in the collegiate curriculum* (Monograph No. 35). Columbia, SC: University of South Carolina, Author.

Smith, B. L. (2001, Summer/Fall). The challenge of learning communities as a growing national movement. *Peer Review*, 4-8.

Chapter 1

First-Year Seminars in Learning Communities:
Two Reforms Intersect

Jean M. Henscheid

Nearly all America's colleges and universities now offer their incoming students the opportunity to register for first-year seminars, courses of limited enrollment intended to ease the intellectual and social transition into higher education. The number of positive indications that these courses improve students' opportunities for success has shifted arguments from "should they be offered" to "what type should be offered." The typology of choices identified by the National Survey of First-Year Seminar Programs includes extended orientation seminars (emphasizing academic skills and introduction to campus resources), academic seminars with common content (skill development is taught in the context of a prescribed academic topic), academic seminars with variable content (skill development is taught in the context of an academic topic selected by the individual instructor), basic study skills seminars, and professional seminars (designed to prepare students for the demands of major or profession) (National Resource Center for The First-Year Experience and Students in Transition, 2002).

In recent years, first-year seminars of all types have taken on increasingly central roles in the undergraduate curriculum through their placement in curricular learning communities. These learning communities are defined by Gabelnick, MacGregor, Matthews, and Smith (1990) as the

> purposeful restructuring of the curriculum by linking courses that enroll a common cohort of students. This represents an intentional structuring of the students' time, credit, and learning experiences to build community, and foster more explicit connections among students, faculty, and disciplines. (p. 5)

A resurgence of interest in learning communities since the early 1980s, from ideas first formulated at the turn of the 20th century, is based on solid and growing evidence that this restructuring is linked to a variety of desired outcomes for students, including increased engagement in learning, greater satisfaction, improved grades, and increased retention (Matthews, 1993; Pike, 1997; Tinto, 1998; Tinto & Love, 1995; Zhao & Kuh, 2003).

The first-year seminar is appearing more often as one of the courses built into curricular learning communities as a strategy for synergizing the two educational approaches. In 1994, 17.2% of respondents to a national survey on first-year seminar programs indicated that their institution enrolled the same group of students together in a first-year seminar and in at least one other course. While only 14.1% of respondents reported such linkages in 1997, the percentage rose to 25.1% in 2000 (National Resource Center for The First-Year Experience and Students in Transition, 2002). Data gathered for the National Learning Communities Project's directory of institutional practices corroborates this growth (http://learningcommons.evergreen.edu). In addition, Randy Swing, co-director of the Policy Center on the First College Year, notes that among the hundreds of campuses the Center works with, he has seen an increasing interest in combining first-year seminars with learning communities (personal communication, May 22, 2003). Swing offers a detailed look at student perceptions of learning in these community structures in Chapter 2 of this volume.

The place at the learning community table for first-year seminars varies widely, according to an analysis of nearly 100 syllabi and program descriptions received from respondents to the 1997 National Survey of First-Year Seminar Programs (Henscheid, 2000). This analysis revealed nine non-mutually exclusive approaches first-year seminar instructors take in linking the seminar, in content or process, with other courses in the learning community.

1. The seminar serves as a "learning lab" for students to practice skills from other courses.
2. The seminar shares common readings, assignments, and projects with linked courses.
3. The seminar pulls together concepts from other courses.
4. The seminar serves as a place to process concepts from other courses and focus on metacognition, or learning about learning itself.
5. The seminar serves as a place for faculty members from other courses in the link to visit and discuss connections.
6. The seminar instructor and instructor(s) from other linked courses assign one grade for individual or multiple assignments or for the entire term.
7. The seminar serves as a place to review linked syllabi to keep students "on track."
8. Seminar discussions explicitly link personal and/or social concepts with concepts learned in the other course(s).
9. The seminar serves as a place to discuss process skills important to achievement in the other linked course(s).

In her extensive work with institutions throughout the country offering learning communities, National Learning Community Project co-director Jean MacGregor identified three additional roles first-year seminars play in learning communities (personal communication, February 14, 2003).

10. The seminar serves as a site for community building.
11. The seminar serves as a site for career exploration related to learning community themes and topics.
12. The seminar serves as a site for service-learning connected to learning community themes and topics.

These 12 roles can be collapsed into two metacategories: one in which the integration of learning across the learning community experience achieves primacy, and the other which foregrounds community building. Combinations of these two approaches are seen throughout the syllabi and program descriptions. At one end of the spectrum, first-year seminars carve out a central place for themselves as integrators of learning for linked courses. Assignments, activities, and assessments are tightly interwoven among the courses and disparate parts come together in the seminars. At the farthest end of the integration spectrum, a great deal of coordination between instructors takes place before the learning community is delivered, during the experience, and afterward for assessment and re-tooling purposes. These first-year seminars serve as the intellectual centerpiece of the learning community where students are assisted as they learn to integrate ideas from multiple sources and tasks from multiple masters. The integrative role is captured by Georgia State University (1999) in its description of Freshmen Learning Communities (FLC).

First-year college students deserve a formative, integrative academic experience on which to build lifelong strengths and perspectives. This experience should include not just the courses they take but the combination and sequence, and fit of those courses. The sections included in each FLC interest group were selected with those goals in mind. Each FLC course builds on the other by exploring unique yet related fields of knowledge. In combination, the courses in each interest-group cluster can provide you with opportunities for learning that will benefit you throughout your college days and beyond. (p. 1)

Explicit intellectual intersections occur throughout the courses in this institution's learning communities for first-year students and most overtly in GSU 1010, new student orientation.

At the other end of the spectrum are the majority of first-year seminars, linked to other courses in the learning community in ways that intend to increase interaction between and among faculty members and students but with no explicit role for the seminar as integrator of learning through linked assignments, activities, or assessments. According to the 2000 review of program descriptions and syllabi (Henscheid), students in these learning communities are likely to report building friendships and feeling supported as primary outcomes of their learning community experience. At this end of the spectrum, coordination of assignments, activities, or assessments among faculty members does not occur.

Which linked seminar approach is "best" is an open question, contingent on individual seminar and community goals. The First-Year Initiative Benchmarking Survey conducted in 2001 by the Policy Center on the First Year of College (Swing, 2003) suggests that seminars, of any kind, linked in learning communities seem to offer pedagogical strategies that engage students at higher levels than non-linked seminars. The initial analysis of these survey results did not isolate which kind of linked seminar offers the richest opportunities for engagement and which type of engagement—intellectual, communal, or a combination—is achieved. This refinement has been suggested for future study.

The thesis of this monograph is that first-year seminars linked in learning communities are perfectly positioned to serve as both community builders and chief learning integrators across all linked courses and beyond, to co-curricular activities, personal and social issues, and the students' future endeavors. First-year seminars are typically the smallest courses in the link, with 100% of the learning community students enrolled in them. Across seminar types, their function is to introduce students to the expectations of the academy, both intellectual and social. The authors' collective position is that the intellectual integration that can occur in the first-year seminar is fundamental to the kind of learning that will transcend the time and space of individual tests, assignments, courses, and academic terms. Through their case studies, the authors in this volume suggest that developers of first-year seminars in learning communities should not be asking "if" learning should be integrated in these courses, but "how." It is through these integrative learning activities that the community of learners is truly formed.

In their discussion, O'Connor and Oates (2001) concur with the thesis of this monograph, suggesting that the words "learning" and "community" are not receiving equal attention in learning communities or in higher education at large. For most of the academy, they note, community, when acknowledged at all, is built to serve learning. Many first-year seminar developers face the reverse issue, where community building serves as an end in itself, particularly in extended orientation courses, the most prevalent type of first-year seminars. These courses often emerge from orientation services, advising offices, or other non-classroom student service locations where communal activities are seen as central. By extension, developing support groups and orienting students to resources in the campus community are key goals of extended orientation seminars, as reported by respondents to the 2000 National Survey of First-Year Seminar Programs.

These survey findings and the 2000 syllabi analysis suggest that most first-year seminars are offering support for creation of community but may be missing a prime opportunity to serve as integrators for learning across all courses in a learning community. The powerful models show-cased in this monograph demonstrate this synergy. The architects of these seminars take seriously the central role these courses can play, both for enriching learning and for building community. They have designed experiences based on the best that is known about student learning. Equally important, they have committed to assessing outcomes and experiences and making improvements based on the results.

Each case study in this monograph begins with a brief description of the type of learning community in existence at the institution. Learning communities described in this monograph are generally one of the following types:

1. Students are co-enrolled in courses as part of the larger enrollment in at least one other course. They also enroll in a first-year seminar that is positioned in the learning community in one or more of the 12 ways listed above.
2. Learning community students comprise the entire enrollment in two or more courses. The linked seminar in this model is also positioned in the community in one or more of the 12 ways described above.

Each chapter presents a brief institutional description and rationale for the type of learning community offered. The cases provide details on administration of the programs, including instructor selection and professional development, funding, coordination, curriculum design, student recruitment, and typical pedagogical approaches. The section of each chapter on intersections familiarizes the reader with the assignments, activities, and assessments that underpin the seminar's role as integrator of learning throughout the entire community experience.

Each case ends with a description of the processes and outcomes of learning assessment and program evaluations and the program's overall plans for the future. Learning outcomes at these institutions are measured by portfolios, reflective writing, project development, and similar methods. Program evaluations are built from cost-benefit analyses, analysis of data on term-to-term and year-to-year retention rates, progress toward graduation, and student grades. Examples of program improvements driven by results of these analyses are also offered.

For this monograph, an attempt was made to select cases for program maturity, clarity of purpose, demonstrated role of the first-year seminar as learning integrator, and attention to learning assessment and program evaluation. Although a typical college or university does not exist, institutions with circumstances that would render their results difficult to replicate by others are not represented. Careful attention was also paid to offering examples across institution type. Four-year public institutions are overrepresented in the universe of first-year seminars embedded in learning communities and, thus, are somewhat overrepresented here. The hope, however, is that every reader is able to learn something from someone. A list of institutions and short summary of each case is offered here.

Chapter 3 – Appalachian State University – The authors offer a glimpse into the rich history of programs offered to the traditional age, residential students who make up the majority of their first-year undergraduate population. First-year seminars linked in learning communities are now at the center of these programs.

Chapter 4 – California State University, Hayward – Many institutions faced general education reform in the mid 1990s, including CSU, Hayward, one of the most ethnically diverse institutions in the California State System. A committee at Hayward determined that learning communities linked with first-year seminars could serve as the centerpiece of their general education reform efforts.

Chapter 5 – Community College of Baltimore County – For nearly 20 years, students who are part of what is now the Community College of Baltimore County have enrolled in an academic achievement course. That course has now expanded to include a slate of first-year experience offerings, including learning communities linking several courses and involving master learners.

Chapter 6 – Georgia State University – As Georgia's only urban research institution, GSU sets a standard for combining the research foci of its faculty with undergraduate teaching in a fast-growing metropolitan area. The first-year experience is anchored by a first-year seminar that integrates learning across a variety of courses and co-curricular experiences. These efforts enjoy a high level of faculty support and participation.

Chapter 7 – Iowa State University – This chapter is unique in that it does not describe a particular seminar and its uniform integrative role in learning communities. Administrators at ISU determined that the complexity and size of the institution necessitated the development of a broad range of learning communities and a wide variety of integrative approaches. While the models and approaches vary, all ISU learning communities share a commitment to integrating students' academic and social experiences in ways akin to those used in traditional first-year seminars.

Chapter 8 – Ripon College – The authors offer a description of an interlocking, multi-layered set of student experiences that begins with courses that introduce students to disciplinary thinking, moves them to interdisciplinary comparisons in multi-course seminar meetings and "mini conferences," and finally illuminates the meaning of a liberal arts experience in common meetings for all first-year students.

Chapter 9 – Slippery Rock University of Pennsylvania – Here, the authors offer a compelling case for the impact an integrated first-year experience may have on first-year student retention. Slippery Rock University, which serves a high percentage of at-risk students, moved from losing an unusually high number of its first-year students to building an impressive retention rate.

Chapter 10 – Temple University – Engaging commuter students is an issue faced by institutions of all sizes. At Temple, students are connected to campus, intellectually and socially, through learning communities that focus on a variety of important issues, including those of immediate relevance to students who live and learn in Philadelphia.

Chapter 11 – Texas A&M University-Corpus Christi – How does an institution design a first-year experience for an inaugural first-year class? Formerly an upper-division-only campus, Texas A&M-Corpus Christi chose learning communities and first-year seminars as the core of offerings for first-year students. The journey to successful integration of these offerings was not without its challenges.

Chapter 12 – University of New Mexico – This southwestern institution faces the challenge of meeting the increasingly diverse needs of a burgeoning student population. Similar to other large institutions, including University of Texas El Paso, University of Northern Colorado, and Iowa State, UNM has decided to meet the challenge by offering a variety of learning community/first-year seminar models to its new students.

Chapter 13 – University of Northern Colorado – UNC uses the creative energies of its faculty, staff, and administrators to tailor first-year learning communities to the interests and learning needs of a variety of student populations, including communities for pre-major and general interest students. A robust collection of methods has been used for several years to evaluate and improve UNC's efforts.

Chapter 14 – University of Texas at El Paso – A huge infusion of grant funding and interest in integrated learning opportunities diffused across the institution resulted in creation of successful, but separate, learning community/first-year seminar programs. A new administrative structure and support from the highest administrative levels for continuation of the programs have combined and strengthened efforts at UTEP.

Chapter 15 – Villanova University – The teachings of St. Augustine, who valued serious intellectual exchange as well as interpersonal relationships, underpin the learning community work at this Catholic institution. Teachings of the mind, body, and spirit are all integrated in courses linked in learning communities, including the required first-year seminar.

Chapter 16 – Washington State University – The centerpiece of this learning community program is the equal instructional partnership between peer facilitators, who lead the first-year seminars, and classroom faculty, who teach courses linked to the seminars in learning communities. Research, critical thinking, and intensive writing are the ties that bind these instructional teams together.

The institutions described in this volume are among the best in regard to the role the first-year seminars play in learning communities, but they are by no means the only models. Readers are enthusiastically encouraged to contact the editor to add their stories to the growing cache of information being gathered on the role of first-year seminars in learning communities.

This monograph is the result of collaboration between the National Resource Center for The First-Year Experience and Students in Transition at the University of South Carolina in Columbia and the National Learning Communities Project administered at The Evergreen State College in Olympia, Washington. These two entities share a common mission to improve understanding and facilitation of all students' learning and to affirm and support their place in the academic community. The likelihood is great that, if you selected this volume, you too share this mission. We congratulate you for your work on behalf of students and wish you well as you begin or continue to build an integrative role for the first-year seminar in your learning community.

References

Gabelnick, F., MacGregor, J., Matthews, R. S., & Smith, B. L. (1990). *Learning communities: Creating connections among students, faculty, and disciplines* (New Directions for Teaching and Learning, No. 41). San Francisco: Jossey-Bass.

Georgia State University. (1999). *Freshman learning communities*. Atlanta, GA: Author

Henscheid, J. M. (2000). [Responses to 1997 National Survey of First-Year Seminar Programs]. Unpublished raw data.

Matthews, R. (1993). Enriching teaching and learning through learning communities. In T. O'Banion (Ed.), *Teaching and learning in the community college*. Washington, DC: The American Association of Community Colleges.

National Resource Center for The First-Year Experience and Students in Transition. (2002). *The*

2000 national survey of first-year seminar programs: Continuing innovations in the collegiate curriculum (Monograph No. 35). Columbia, SC: University of South Carolina, Author.

O'Connor, J., & Oates, K. (2001, Summer/Fall). Developing the faculty we need. *Peer Review*, 9-13.

Pike, G. R. (1997). *The effects of residential learning communities on students' educational experiences and learning outcomes during the first year of college.* Paper presented at the annual conference of the Association for the Study of Higher Education, November, Albuquerque, NM. (ERIC Document Reproduction Service No. ED 415 828)

Swing, R. L. (2003, January). *What matters in first-year seminars: Results of a national survey.* Conference presentation at The First-Year Experience West Conference, Costa Mesa, CA.

Tinto, V. (1998). Colleges as communities: Taking research on student persistence seriously. *Review of Higher Education, 21*(2), 167-177.

Tinto, V., & Love, A. G. (1995). *A longitudinal study of learning communities at LaGuardia Community College.* Washington, DC: Office of Education Research and Improvement. (ERIC Document Reproduction Service No. ED 380 178)

Zhao, C., & Kuh, G.D. (2003, May). *Adding value: Learning communities and student engagement.* Paper presented at the 43rd Annual Association for Institutional Research Forum, Tampa, FL.

The Improved Learning Outcomes of Linked Versus Stand-Alone First-Year Seminars

Randy L. Swing

First-year seminars are found on the vast majority of American college and university campuses and have become a stable component of the first year of college. Because of their nearly ubiquitous presence in higher education and their proven record of success in supporting a number of outcomes also sought by learning communities, a logical step is to make first-year seminars one element of these communities. Data from the 2002 First-Year Initiative (FYI) Benchmarking Survey from Educational Benchmarking, Inc. (EBI) confirm that first-year seminars are being linked with other courses on a number of campuses. Authors writing in this monograph, and educators on many other campuses, base this linkage on the belief that, although first-year seminars have been shown to produce a number of learning outcomes, the synergy created by linking the seminar with at least one other educational component enhances these outcomes.

The analysis of data reported here confirms that, indeed, this assumption is correct. Linking first-year seminars with other components of the curriculum enhances learning outcomes for students who participate in these seminars over those who participate in stand-alone seminars. Students in first-year seminars linked in learning communities report statistically significant greater gains than students in stand-alone seminars on each of 10 measured learning outcomes. The largest gain (16%) in mean score was found in the factor that measures peer-to-peer connections. Impressive gains were also found in the impact of linked seminars on out-of-class engagement (9%), knowledge of wellness issues (7.5%), study skills (6%), and time/priority management (6%). Gains of 4 to 5% were also found in knowledge of campus policies, knowledge of academic services, critical-thinking skills, connections with faculty, and cognitive/academic skills. Given the overall positive impact of linking the seminar with another course, it is not surprising that students in the linked seminars also reported a 6% higher mean score on overall satisfaction with the college they are attending.

The analysis reported in this chapter is based on the First-Year Initiative Benchmarking Survey, which collects student data about seminar learning outcomes and matches them with the EBI Section Profile. This profile records section structures such as whether the seminar is linked to another course or is conducted as a "stand-alone" seminar. In the present case, the key question for review is: Are the learning outcomes of a first-year seminar enhanced by a linkage with another course?

The FYI Data

The First-Year Initiative Benchmarking Survey was created to evaluate seminars at the campus level and to provide insights to guide campus-level change. Analysis of these data also provide opportunities to study the impact of first-year seminars across institutions, although there are some limitations inherent in using data collected primarily for other purposes. For example, the FYI data have only one variable that identifies a section as being linked with another course. That variable is collected as a simple "yes or no" dichotomy; therefore, the extent of the linkage is not known. A "yes" may indicate that a group of students are simply co-enrolled in two courses or could signal a deep connection between the two courses. Because linked courses in the FYI data include sections that are linked at the lowest possible level, it is likely that the results of this study underestimate the value of more fully integrated course pairings. A second limitation is that campuses elect to participate in the FYI study; in fact, they pay a modest registration fee to be part of the study. Thus, the FYI data cannot be considered to represent a random sample of first-year seminars. Still the size of the dataset captures a large slice of American higher education and provides the best cross-institutional data available on first-year seminars, making this research valuable even though generalizations to all seminars must be made only with caution. Educators at two-year institutions should take special note that data were gathered from four-year institutions only because a two-year version of the FYI instrument was not available in 2002 (a two-year version of FYI was piloted in 2003).

The 2002 FYI data come from 1,961 sections of first-year seminars at 72 four-year institutions. In total, 41,294 students completed the FYI survey during the last two weeks of their seminar enrollment in fall 2002. Student responses were clustered into 15 assessment factors including 10 learning outcomes, three measures of the quality of the course delivery, and two measures of the overall campus experience.

In the FYI 2002 dataset, 75% of the sections ($n = 1,478$) were not linked to another course and 25% ($n = 483$) were linked. Of the 72 participating institutions, 46 (64%) had no linked first-year seminars, 12 (17%) linked all first-year seminars, and 14 (19%) had a mixture of linked and stand-alone courses.

Research Model

Evaluating specific aspects of any college course can be frustrating, because so many aspects of campus climate interact to influence outcomes. Selected structural elements, such as number of credit hours, grading format, and required or elective status and selected student characteristics, such as gender, high school grades, and student's residential status (i.e., on or off campus) can be statistically controlled so that the researcher can isolate other elements of interest. (In this study, controls were selected to isolate the course structural component of whether the seminar was linked or a stand-alone.) Still, in the absence of a true experimental design with random assignment of students to various treatments (which would require the unethical decision to restrict enrollments in some first-year seminars), the researcher must establish a nonintrusive method to form adequate control groups and ways to isolate the variables of interest.

To reduce the impact of variables outside the first-year seminar, the analysis reported here was conducted on a subset of the full FYI data built from 14 campuses that offered some linked and some stand-alone first-year seminars. Because the linked courses and stand-alone courses come from the same 14 campuses, many of the elements of campus climate are automatically held constant and the stand-alone seminars provide a naturally occurring comparison group for studying the outcomes of the linked courses. The reduced dataset is still quite large, including data from 484 sections of first-year seminars and responses from 7,059 students. These 14 institutions represent a large range of institutional characteristics. Ten are publicly controlled and four are privately controlled institutions. They range from very small undergraduate enrollments to large enrollment institutions (fewer than 2,000 students = 3 institutions; 2,000-10,000 = 3; 10,000 – 18,000 = 4; and over 18,000 = 4). Seven campuses enrolled fewer than 50% of their entering students in first-year seminars; three enrolled 51 to 90% in seminars, and four enrolled more than 90% of their first-year students. The campuses also varied in percentage of residential/commuter students. Four campuses housed fewer than 50% of their first-year students; three housed 51 to 75%, and seven housed more than 75% of their first-year students. Four campuses offered fewer than 20 sections of seminar; five offered 21 to 50 sections; four offered 51 to 100 sections, and one campus offered more than 100 sections in fall 2002.

Variation in Outcomes for Linked and Stand-Alone First-Year Seminars

Analysis of Variance (ANOVA) statistical tests were used to compare the mean scores for linked and stand-alone seminars on each of the 15 factors contained in the FYI Benchmarking Survey. Mean scores were derived from student responses to a set of questions using a seven-point scale with "1" indicating that the course had low or negative impact and "7" indicating that the course had a strong positive impact. For each ANOVA, data were used from the 298 stand-alone first-year seminars and 186 linked seminars from the 14 campuses that reported having both forms. Because there were only two levels of the independent variable, linked or stand-alone, no post hoc tests were required as differences could be immediately discerned from the ANOVA statistics.

The results reveal that across 13 of the 15 factors, linked courses had higher mean scores than stand-alone courses. While causation cannot be derived from a non-experimental research design, the consistency of evidence across multiple measures strongly supports the linked seminar to be a superior delivery structure.

Below are descriptions of each of the 15 FYI factors, the survey items that comprise each factor, mean scores for linked and stand-alone seminars, and ANOVA test statistics.

Learning Outcomes

Study Skills

The Study Skills Factor is formed from eight responses to questions about the degree to which the course improved the student's (a) understanding of academic strengths, (b) test preparation skills, (c) ability to find items through the library, (d) diligence in reviewing class notes before the next class meeting, (e) completion of homework assignments on time, (f) involvement in peer study groups, (g) note taking in class, and (h) ability to cope with test anxiety. Linked courses had a higher mean score (4.46) for the Study Skills Factor than stand-alone courses (4.20). The difference is statistically significant, $F(1, 483) = 16.91$, $p < .05$.

Academic/Cognitive Skills

The Academic/Cognitive Skills Factor is derived from five student self-evaluations of the degree to which the course improved the student's skills in (a) writing, (b) reading, (c) decision making, (d) computer usage, and (e) oral presentation. Linked courses had a higher mean score (4.17) for the Academic/Cognitive Skills Factor than stand-alone courses (4.02). The difference is statistically significant, $F(1, 483) = 4.150$, $p = .05$.

Critical Thinking Skills

The Critical Thinking Skills Factor is based on three response items about the degree to which the course improved the student's ability to (a) see multiple sides of issues, (b) identify solutions for complex problems, and (c) evaluate the quality of opinions and facts. Linked courses had a higher mean score (4.58) for the Critical Thinking Factor than stand-alone courses (4.41). The difference is statistically significant, $F(1, 483) = 5.329$, $p < .05$.

Connections with Faculty

The Connections with Faculty Factor contains responses to three items about the student's connection with faculty members in his/her other courses. The response items asked students to determine the degree to which the seminar had improved their (a) understanding of faculty expectations of students, (b) willingness to seek feedback from instructors, and (c) communications with instructors outside of class. Linked courses had a higher mean score (4.71) for the Connections with Faculty Factor than stand-alone courses (4.55). The difference is statistically significant, $F(1, 483) = 6.329$, $p < .05$.

Connections with Peers

The Connections with Peers Factor is based on three response items about the degree to which the course improved the student's (a) efforts to get to know students in classes, (b) ability to meet new people with common interests, and (c) ability to establish close friendships with peers. Linked courses had a higher mean score (5.35) for the Connections with Peers Factor than stand-alone courses (4.62). The difference is statistically significant, $F(1, 483) = 120.63$, $p < .05$. The linked structure had the greatest impact on this factor of any of the 15 studied—accounting for 20% of the variance in this outcome.

Out-of-Class Engagement

The Out-of-Class Engagement Factor is built from four response items about the degree to which the course increased the student's (a) participation in campus-sponsored organizations, (b) contributions to the success of campus-sponsored organizations, (c) time volunteered for worthwhile causes, and (d) attendance at campus cultural events. Linked courses had a higher mean score (3.98) for the Out-of-Class Engagement Factor than stand-alone courses (3.66). The difference is statistically significant, $F(1, 483) = 14.99$, $p < .05$.

Knowledge of Campus Policies

The Knowledge of Campus Policies Factor contains five response items about the degree to which the course increased the student's understanding of (a) college/university rules regarding academic honesty, (b) the grading system, (c) academic probation policies, (d) registration procedures, and (e) financial aid procedures. Linked courses had a higher mean score (4.83) for the Knowledge of Campus Policies Factor than stand-alone courses (4.62). The difference is statistically significant, $F(1, 483) = 8.359$, $p < .05$.

Knowledge of Academic Services

The Knowledge of Academic Services Factor contains four response items about the degree to which the course increased the student's understanding of (a) the role of the academic advisor, (b) how to obtain academic assistance, (c) how to obtain a tutor, and (d) available library resources. Linked courses had a higher mean score (5.13) for the Knowledge of Academic Services Factor than stand-alone courses (4.93). The difference is statistically significant, $F(1, 483) = 7.560$, $p < .05$.

Managing Time and Priorities

The Managing Time and Priorities Factor is derived from five response items based on the degree to which the course increased the student's (a) understanding of the impact of establishing personal goals, (b) likelihood of preparing for tests well in advance, (c) ability to establish an effective study schedule, (d) ability to set priorities to accomplish what is most important, and (e) ability to organize time to meet responsibilities. Linked courses had a higher mean score (4.65) for the Managing Time and Priorities Factor than stand-alone courses (4.40). The difference is statistically significant, $F (1, 483) = 12.016, p < .05$.

Knowledge of Wellness

The Knowledge of Wellness Factor is built on five response items based on the degree to which the course improved the student's understanding of (a) the impact of stress and how to deal with it, (b) college students' sexual issues, (c) the impact of alcohol consumption, (d) the impact of drug use, and (e) the impact of exercising regularly. Linked courses had a higher mean score (4.25) for the Knowledge of Wellness Factor than stand-alone courses (3.96). The difference is statistically significant, $F (1, 483) = 10.593, p < .05$.

Delivery of First-Year Seminars

FYI contains three measures of the quality of the delivery of the first-year seminar. Students evaluated the course readings, the level of engaging pedagogy, and the overall effectiveness of the seminar. Linked courses had a higher mean score for only one of the three course delivery factors.

Usefulness of Course Readings and Overall Course Effectiveness

The Usefulness of Course Readings Factor is composed of three response items where students evaluated the degree to which the course reading materials were (a) relevant, (b) interesting, and (c) helpful. The Overall Course Effectiveness Factor consists of five response items based on the degree to which the student reports that the course (a) included interesting subject matter, (b) contributed to the ability to succeed academically, (c) contributed to the ability to adjust to the college social environment, and (d) covered topics important to the student. The fifth item asks to what degree the student would recommend this course to other first-year students. Neither of these factors was significantly influenced by linking the seminar to another course.

Engaging Pedagogy

The Engaging Pedagogy Factor is derived from seven response items about the level at which the course included (a) a variety of teaching methods, (b) meaningful class discussions, (c) challenging assignments, (d) productive use of classroom time, (e) encouragement to speak in class, (f) encouragement for students to work together, and (g) meaningful homework. Linked courses had a higher mean score (4.87) on the Engaging Pedagogy Factor than stand-alone courses (4.67). The difference is statistically significant $F (1, 483) = 7.934, p < .05$.

Overall Experience

The FYI Survey investigates two measures of overall experience with the institution. Students evaluated the degree to which they feel a sense of belonging and acceptance, and the degree of their overall satisfaction with the college/university.

Sense of Belonging/Acceptance

The Sense of Belonging/Acceptance Factor is built on three response items about the degree to which (a) the student is accepted by other students at this college/university, (b) the student finds it easy to make new friends at this college/university, and (c) the student is able to identify other students with similar interests. Students in linked courses reported a higher mean score (5.61) for the Sense of Belonging Factor than students in stand-alone courses (5.36). The difference is statistically significant, $F\,(1, 483) = 26.099$, $p < .05$.

Overall Satisfaction with College/University

The Overall Satisfaction with College/University Factor is built from five response items. Students reported the degree to which they (a) want to return to this college/university for the next fall term, (b) would recommend this college/university to a friend, (c) believe their college experience was a high-quality learning experience, and (d) believe their college experience was a positive experience. In addition, students rated the value of the investment made in their education at their current institution. Students in linked courses reported a higher mean score (5.65) on Overall Satisfaction with the College/University than students in stand-alone courses (5.29). The difference is statistically significant, $F\,(1, 483) = 60.229$, $p < .05$.

Conclusions

Using the First-Year Initiative (FYI) Benchmarking Survey data from 14 institutions that employed a combination of linked and stand-alone first-year seminars provided a naturally occurring control group and made it possible to isolate the impact of the "linkage" on course outcomes. The results indicate that linked courses are associated with greater perceived improvements on 10 measured learning outcomes: (a) study strategies, (b) academic/cognitive skills, (c) critical thinking, (d) connections with faculty, (e) connections with peers, (f) out-of-class engagement, (g) knowledge of campus policies, (h) knowledge of academic services, (i) management of time/priorities, and (j) knowledge of wellness. These measures represent the goals of many first-year seminars, are consistent with the goals of many first-year learning communities, and are elements associated with success in the first year of college.

Linking the first-year seminar to another course had no significant impact on student perceptions of the assigned course readings or overall satisfaction with the seminar. This is an important finding because campuses that link the seminar may not see an increase in student ratings on traditional end-of-term course evaluations if these are largely focused on satisfaction with the teacher/course rather than on learning outcomes.

That students rated the pedagogy in the linked seminars as being more engaging is an important finding because the level of engaging pedagogy is a predictor of the other course outcomes. As Engaging Pedagogy Factor scores increase, there is generally an increase in the other FYI Factors. Since linked courses are positively correlated with higher Engaging Pedagogy scores, it would appear that linking the seminar is an effective way to improve the course delivery and, in so doing, improve a range of learning outcomes.

First-year seminars often have the twin goals of improving the academic achievement of students and increasing their chances of persistence at the institution by encouraging them to establish a bond with that institution. These data provide evidence that linked first-year seminars are associated with a greater sense of belonging and a more positive view of the whole institution as measured by the Overall Satisfaction with the College/University Factor. That factor includes response items about the student's intention to return to the same college for the following academic year. This analysis strongly suggests that linked first-year seminars outperform stand-alone seminars. More research is needed to determine the optimum level of linkage, but it appears that there is some gain even if the linkage is limited to simply co-enrolling students in two courses.

The most important aspect of these findings is that linking a first-year seminar to another course appears to improve the effectiveness of the seminar. Since institutions are already investing in first-year seminars to improve the first year of college, it is a logical step to maximize the outcomes of these existing structures. In other words, the linkage simply adds value to the investment already being made in the seminar. Given the large body of research that shows the positive impact of seminars on first-year students, maximizing seminar outcomes by creating purposeful linkages between the seminar and another course is both a fiscally and educationally sound use of resources.

A Century of Community: An Integrated First Year Continues a Long History of Learning Together

Joni Webb Petschauer, Rennie Brantz, Nikki Crees, and Beth Glass
Appalachian State University

Chapter 3

Appalachian State University is a regional, comprehensive university located in the heart of the Blue Ridge Mountains in Boone, North Carolina—a town with a year-round population of about 15,000 people. Enrollment for 2003-2004 was 13,350 students, of which 2,474 are experiencing their first year of college. First-year students hold an average Scholastic Aptitude Test (SAT) score of 1112. With instruction as its primary mission, the University has a stated commitment to excellence in teaching and fostering scholarship. As an academic community, it seeks to promote the intellectual, cultural, and personal development of its students by encouraging frequent faculty/student engagement.

Appalachian offers first-year students a range of programs to support their transition from high school to college. Among the oldest offerings is Watauga College, a residentially based, interdisciplinary program for approximately 200 first- and second-year students. Founded in 1972, amid a national upswing of experimental residential colleges, the program provided then, as it does now, team-taught, alternative core curriculum courses for small groups of students who live together. Most faculty members who teach in the college have offices in the residence hall and interact with the students throughout the day and evening. The success of this endeavor coupled with other efforts like several federally funded, pre-college preparation grant programs (i.e., Project Breakthrough, Upward Bound, and Student Support Services) demonstrated the potential need for targeted and, at times, intrusive programming for first-year students.

Freshman Seminar (U S 1150) grew out of these earlier projects. This three-hour, graded, graduation-credit course was first offered in its present form in 1987 and now serves as a foundational element in virtually every Freshman Learning Community (FLC) in General Studies. The FLC program, first piloted in 1998, presently enrolls approximately 60% of Appalachian's first-year students, on a voluntary basis, in an intentionally connective, academic experience. This chapter provides an overview of Appalachian State University's experience with first-year programming and especially the role of the Freshman Seminar as an anchor for Freshman Learning Communities in General Studies.

Institutional Background

Founded as Watauga Academy in 1899, Appalachian evolved into a state teachers' college, later broadened its mission to include the liberal arts, gained regional university status, and in 1971 became part of the University of North Carolina. Like many public universities, its particular curriculum, mission, and programming efforts reflect local responses to national trends and state expectations. Collaborative, supportive, and inviting first-year initiatives were implemented on the Appalachian campus, not because of a need to revise or reinvent the university, but because they supported the original values outlined by the first president. Long described as student friendly and academically supportive, Appalachian's challenge was not whether to implement new ideas, but how to select the ones that would ensure that academic rigor and excellence could be attained without losing the accessible and friendly nature of the campus.

The Appalachian First Year

Appalachian aspires to enhance intellectual and personal growth, develop academic and social connections with the University community, and improve learning for its first-year students. The institution has created structures intended to facilitate collaboration and coherence and wide acceptance of its mission. Communication is supported through a variety of informal and formal councils, committees, and task forces made up of individuals from throughout the campus. Efforts are made to include each of the academic colleges, many academic affairs and student development units, as well as individuals who are personally passionate about a particular effort. This has been especially important during the start-up phase of Appalachian's new initiatives. Not only has it helped raise the broadest level of campus awareness, but it has also increased the potential for long-standing campus processes to be modified to reflect these new ideas. Increases in retention, campus involvement, and improved graduation rates are believed to be the by-products of this type of engagement. It has taken solid support, over several decades, from senior administrators and teaching-focused faculty to create the many campus-based, first-year initiatives that exist at Appalachian. On-going faculty and staff development and comprehensive assessment support these efforts. This inclusiveness and campus-wide focus have also contributed to building a sense of academic and social community on the campus.

Central to Appalachian's first-year programming is the emphasis on academic community. This community is built by integrating faculty, curriculum, student development, and academic support services into an experience that shapes student learning and reflects the institution's core values. One way to engage the entire campus community is to connect them directly to courses. Freshman Seminar represents such an opportunity.

Freshman Seminar (U S 1150)

College Survival, a pilot course taught only for Student Support Services students beginning in 1984, was soon renamed the College Challenge and became part of a newly devised residential learning project called the Mountaineer Community (1985-1986), which drew upon the Watauga College model. Although the residential component of the Mountaineer Community proved unwieldy, the idea of an extended orientation course for first-semester students found a following and provided the foundation for Appalachian's current Freshman Seminar program. The national conversation about student success courses—led by John Gardner at the University of South Carolina—complemented campus conversations. Administered out of the General College and known as the College Experience (1987) and subsequently as Freshman Seminar (1988-present), U S 1150 has been a regular offering for almost two decades enrolling 14,474 students since that time.

Appalachian's current Freshman Seminar offers first-semester students a structured orientation to college, an introduction to academic and personal success strategies, and an opportunity for self-discovery and self-realization regarding their academic goals and the skills needed for success. It draws on national models and extensive research for much of its conceptual framework and is tailored to the unique needs of first-year students at Appalachian. The course acquaints students with the opportunities and demands of higher education through a mix of activities, lectures, discussions, and participation in community events. Small classes of 15 to 24 students build learning skills, practice time-management and other life skills; examine the purpose of higher education and learn to set goals for their first semester and beyond; and take time to volunteer in the community, eat meals together, and attend cultural events. The goals of this course complement and address specific aspects of Appalachian's mission.

Freshman Seminar supports the University goal of maintaining a strong sense of community while enhancing the undergraduate experience, with special attention to the first-year student. The course supports personal development through reflection papers about class discussions, films, or novels; feedback on communication skills; and supportive learning options in and out of class. Additionally, it assists students in making a successful transition to college through the discovery of resources and opportunities offered by Appalachian. Through strengthening learning skills, joining new organizations, attending performances, and viewing art exhibits, students are encouraged to move toward intellectual and individual independence. Based on early successes, the Freshman Seminar was selected to become a fundamental building block for the next phase of first-year programming at Appalachian—the development of new learning communities.

Freshman Learning Communities in General Studies

The national discourse calling for higher education to consider the powerful potential of learning communities resonated with Appalachian's traditions. Learning communities already existed on the campus, but historically these curricular programs served only small numbers of specially identified participants. Watauga College, Freshman Seminar, and Summer Preview allowed students to self-select as participants; but enrollment was limited. Honors, Student Support Services, and Teaching Fellows consisted of specially invited participants; Army ROTC fulfilled very specialized student interests. This meant that in any given year, approximately 400 to 500 out of 2,100 to 2,500 newly admitted students had access to a learning community experience (Figure 1).

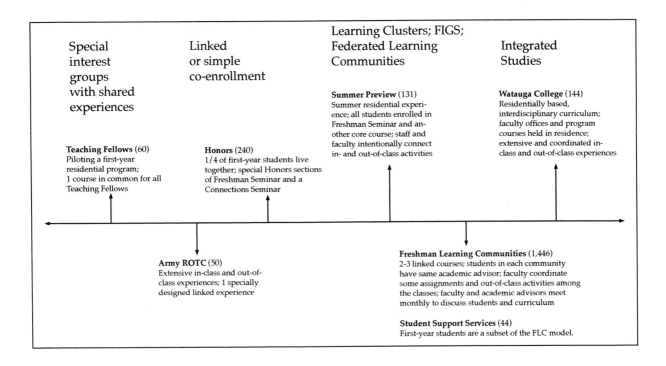

Figure 1. First-year learning community options at Appalachian State University. The numbers in parentheses indicate the number of students participating for 2003. More than 80% of first-year students participate in an intentionally connective academic experience, and 13.3% are enrolled in an academic, residential program.

In 1997, a small team was asked to seek out new models for implementation. In 1998, the provost created the Learning Communities Council and invited all first-year related program coordinators and directors to meet, identify what worked, and expand the learning community offerings available to Appalachian's first-year students.

The Pilot Project 1998-2000

Freshman Interest Groups (FIGs) were introduced in 1998 by the Office of General Studies and served as an intentionally connective, academic experience for entering students who were not eligible for or attracted to existing learning communities. Designed to co-enroll a cohort of students with similar career interests in three classes during their first semester, FIGs expanded the learning community concept on the University campus. The challenge was to identify additional models and processes that could be broadly replicated, potentially providing enough seats for the entire first-year class. A variety of cohort enrollments were put in place, from a single cohort comprising the total enrollment of three courses, to cohorts making up just a portion of larger course enrollments. Furthermore, the decision was made that the new offerings should not duplicate or compete with existing campus learning communities and should reflect the lessons learned from local and national efforts. Programmatic goals included enhancing the academic climate of the campus; improving first-to-second-year retention rates; and using current faculty, staff, co-curricular, and curricular offerings. The services and resources the planners considered connecting in this effort included admissions, orientation, the summer reading program, registration, advising, curriculum, residence life, learning assistance, career development, faculty development, leadership development, and Freshman Seminar.

During the initial project year, Appalachian offered four FIGs enrolling 82 students in one of the following groups: (a) Science/Pre-Med, (b) Business, (c) Communication/Pre-law, and (d) Exploring Majors. All FIGs provided students with nine hours of academic course credit and two of the FIGs—Science/Pre-Med and Business—also provided a residential component. Additionally, the Science/Pre-Med and Business groups participated in an experimental one-hour seminar, while the Communications/Pre-law and Exploring Majors groups enrolled in the three-hour Freshman Seminar. Because of the small number of participants, a test for statistical significance on outcomes was not possible. However, early trend data supported the continuation of the effort, particularly regarding the experience of the two non-residential and Freshman Seminar-anchored communities.

In fall 1999, the project sponsored five FIGs entitled Communication in the Business World, Foundations for the Legal Professions, Issues in the Helping Professions, Studies in Child and Family Development, and Applications in Design. Additionally, participants were also selected for another pilot learning community focused on technology called Project EXCEL. There were a total of 88 participants in FIGs and 59 in Project EXCEL during fall 1999, and 44 continuing students in Project EXCEL and 10 participants in a newly created GEAR UP (a federally funded pre-college program) FIG during spring semester 2000. During this period, all participants (FIGs and Project EXCEL) were enrolled in Freshman Seminar during their first semester. Owing to the success of residentially based learning communities on campuses elsewhere and Appalachian's experience with the Watauga College program, an attempt was made to house the technology-focused Project EXCEL cohort in one of the newly configured high-speed ethernet halls available to first-year students.

Fall 2000 served as the third and final pilot year for the learning community program and marks the year the project changed its name to Freshman Learning Communities (FLCs) in General Studies, which more readily allowed the program to initiate and administer more than one learning community model. In the beginning, the project attempted to co-enroll students based on specific majors or possible career interests; however, given the large proportion of undecided students entering Appalachian, this idea did not adequately address the needs of the entering class or the departments reserving seats in high-demand courses. Thus, a new model evolved using broad, general education themes and consisting of two linked courses, one of which was the Freshman Seminar and the other a core curriculum course. For fall 2000, the program assigned 335 students through an experimental registration process, prior to Phase 1 Orientation, to six traditional FIGs (Business—two groups of students, Forensic Science, Pre-Law, Design, and Religion/Sociology) and 12 thematically linked experiences, one of which was residential.

After three years of piloting several modifications to institution-wide processes and experimenting with various programmatic structures, FLCs in General Studies received the go-ahead for widespread implementation based on the most promising features discovered in the pilot period. Beginning in 2001, the program expanded greatly, enrolling 963 students into 52 FLCs of which 48 included the Freshman Seminar. This pattern of growth continued in 2002, with 1,326 students enrolled in 71 FLCs of which 63 included the Freshman Seminar. The expansion was facilitated by a new preliminary course registration process for all entering first-year students.

Freshman Learning Communities in General Studies, 2001 to Present

The role of Freshman Seminar proved to be a crucial element in the creation of Freshman Learning Communities in General Studies. The course served as a model for collaboration by connecting key co-curricular components such as service-learning, cultural affairs, campus computing, clubs and organizations, campus resources, and leadership training into its curriculum. Its success as a stand-alone experience raised the question of whether it was wise to modify its course offerings to facilitate the goals of the new learning community initiative. Studies by Appalachian's Office of Institutional Research, Assessment and Planning (IRAP) indicated that the self-selected students who enrolled in Freshman Seminar were not only retained from the first to second year at higher rates (Table 1) but also exceeded the non-Freshman Seminar cohorts' five-year graduation rates. IRAP has not controlled for the self-selection factor of these groups but has studied differences between the groups. Freshman Seminar students were similar in gender and race to non-Freshman Seminar students. However, measures such as predicted grade point average and SAT score were lower for Freshman Seminar students than for non-Freshman Seminar students (Langdon, 2001).

When interpreting these data, two points should be considered. First, these data show correlations between retention and enrollment in Freshman Seminar, but causation cannot be assumed. Second, since Freshman Seminar students volunteer to enroll, they are not a randomly selected group. Previous research has shown that the students who volunteer enter with academic skills and attitudes that correlate with non-persistence. As such, the positive retention rates from 1993-2000 show a surprising rate of persistence for students who enroll in the Freshman Seminar. The Freshman Seminar embraced its new role as the centerpiece in the much larger learning communities effort. Administrators believed this effort would provide a meaningful curricular base for students to process and connect a variety of components of their first-year experience.

The current FLC program design provides the opportunity for small groups of students (15-24) who share career aspirations or similar academic interests to take two to three classes together during their first semester of college. Virtually every FLC includes the Freshman Seminar as one of the classes, and an academic advisor works with each community. Student enrollment is initially determined by a preliminary course registration process that occurs prior to summer orientation. The early registration form asks students to identify the courses and experiences they hope to have in their first semester of college. Academic advisors use this information to develop a tentative schedule of classes with an appropriate learning community for each incoming first-year student prior to summer orientation. Additionally, this information helps academic departments adjust course seat

Table 1

One-Year Retention Rates, 1993-2000

	Year							
	1993	1994	1995	1996	1997	1998	1999	2000
All first-year students	84.3%	81.5%	83.2%	82.1%	82.9%	81.2%	84.2%	83.2%
U S 1150	87.7%	86.0%	87.4%	86.0%	86.4%	81.9%	87.29%	87.0%
Non U S 1150	82.6%	79.6%	81.7%	80.4%	81.1%	80.8%	82.27%	80.8%

$p < .05$

Note. Data from 1993-1997 prepared by Randy Swing. Data from 1998-2000 prepared by Heather Langdon, Beth Glass, and Dan Friedman. From *Freshman Seminar Annual Report to the Chancellor 2001-2002.*

availability based on the needs of students. Students finalize their schedules during summer orientation after meeting with an academic advisor and attending departmental meetings.

Freshman Seminar faculty members often tailor the course to their area of expertise, but each section is expected to deliver a core set of course requirements. The key to successfully linking Appalachian's Freshman Seminar to various other introductory-level and core curriculum courses was (and remains) the adoption, modification, and creation of elements that would support the learning goals of all involved. From the outset, this created the need for new and more fully coordinated faculty development and communication efforts. Faculty and academic support team members (i.e., course instructors, academic advisors, peer leaders, librarians) are prepared through extensive faculty development activities to integrate class material across the linked courses while supporting students in their efforts to make friends, discover resources, and explore various majors or potential career choices.

Several activities sponsored by various campus organizations and scheduled early in the semester are used to enhance connections among students, FLC faculty, and academic support team members. The Appalachian/Boone Community Walk for Awareness, University Convocation (featuring the Summer Reading author), Freshman Seminar Open House, and Campus Resource Tour traditionally occur in the first two to three weeks of classes, serving as standard course components in the Freshman Seminar. Now, in the context of learning communities, many FLC faculty and academic support team members share the responsibility for setting attendance and participation expectations through statements in their independent course syllabi (Freshman Seminar faculty and other course faculty), conversations with students (academic advisors), or e-mail messages to first-year students (peer leaders). Sometimes, the entire faculty and academic support team agree to attend one or more of these activities together with their students, demonstrating their own belief in the educational value of these experiences as well as signifying a commitment to one another as a teaching team.

Similarly, direct interactions with the academic support team occur within the classes during the first weeks of the semester. It is not unusual for the academic advisor and faculty members in linked courses to attend and be introduced to the students during the first class period of one or even both classes. Boundary breaking and name game activities are used widely in the first month and can be introduced in any of the classes. Furthermore, each course, though taught as an independent offering, contains in its syllabus information about the link (philosophy, goals, and shared assignments) and contact information for all faculty and academic support team members. This information is included whether the course is exclusive to FLC students or open to students not in the FLC.

Service-Learning as an Integrative Force

Since its inception, the Freshman Seminar has reviewed and reinforced many of the academic skills needed for success in college such as time management, reading, writing, note taking, test taking, and library research. Learning communities have proven to be a far more effective structure for connecting skill development to academic content than stand-alone Freshman Seminars. An example of this is one of the earlier Freshman Seminar and Introduction to Composition links. As part of a service-learning project connecting the two courses, students enrolled in this link composed and published the first newsletter for the local Watauga County Chapter of Habitat for Humanity. Identifying the stories, conducting the interviews, and writing the articles required the students and faculty to coordinate schedules, address issues of writing composition, and explore values in order to complete the assignment. Since both classes provided academic credit for various portions of the assignment, students understood the need to apply the lessons from one course to that of another, the faculty members found their work reinforced by that of other team members, and Habitat for Humanity received a high-quality and useful publication.

Another integration of service-learning in the context of a linked course experience is the GEAR UP learning community. Appalachian State University serves as a GEAR UP partner to the Ashe County Middle School. Since 1999, Appalachian first-year students expressing a desire to become middle school or high school teachers are invited to participate in one of the GEAR UP learning communities. Each GEAR UP link consists of a Freshman Seminar course and one of the following: Introduction to Composition and Grammar, Introduction to Math, World Civilizations, or Social Problems in American Society. Through the Freshman Seminar course, the first-year students receive support and academic credit for mentoring and tutoring the students attending Ashe County Middle School. First-year students are expected to keep a journal about their experiences as academic role models and explore how this activity reinforces their anticipated career goals. The connected course provides a specific area of expertise that can be applied in their tutoring or mentoring sessions. This particular learning community has proven effective in providing first-year education majors with an exploration of their intended major, which is valuable to first-year students who may not enroll in Reich College of Education courses during their first semester. Service-learning has demonstrated its usefulness as a tool for connecting academics to the needs and concerns of Boone and the surrounding local community.

Integrative Course Designs

Using a single activity to reinforce lessons in more than one class is a standard and strongly encouraged practice among linked courses. The following illustrates how shared course activities can create the time needed for deeper learning. The topic of learning and teaching styles is most often presented in the Freshman Seminar through the administration and discussion of the Myers-Briggs Type Inventory (MBTI). One of the Freshman Seminar and Introduction to Psychology links developed a series of activities and discussions focused on the MBTI. Rather than giving the inventory in the Freshman Seminar, the psychology professor administered it in the larger Introduction to Psychology class (Freshman Seminar students were only a subset of the total class enrollment), using it as part of a broader discussion of personality types and inventories. The Freshman Seminar instructor focused on the individual MBTI results for each student and led a discussion about how this information might be used to improve the success of different study groups. Students respond positively on end-of-course evaluations to this type of coordination and communication regarding learning goals by their faculty members.

Major and Career Decision Making

Through the years, three of the more popular FIGs have been the Business, Forensic Science, and Interior Design communities. Each of these groups have used a series of guest speakers, field trips, and applied learning activities to introduce first-year students to various career paths available through a specific course of study. The Freshman Seminar often provides a neutral meeting ground for different disciplinary voices to be heard and for students to feel secure questioning their commitment to a particular department. The academic advisor can play a pivotal role in these discussions and be a resource for students seeking to commit to, or step away from, a particular course of study.

Freshman Seminars in the FLC program have also been instrumental in advancing the University's Advisor in the Classroom model. Developed by the Academic Advising Center, this project directly connects the academic advising function to the classroom setting and supports the teaching role advisors play in the lives of first-year students. All students in a specific learning community share the same academic advisor. Academic advisors visit each Freshman Seminar class a minimum of three times in the first semester in order to disseminate information about academic policies and procedures, prompt questions and thinking about academic planning, explain schedule adjustment processes, and facilitate community building. They also encourage students to make individual appointments in order to discuss academic progress reports (a component of the institution's academic support process) and to plan their academic course of study. Providing several opportunities for first-year students to hear from their advisor in more than one venue has increased contact between advisors and students and enhanced the role of Freshman Seminar.

Implications for Faculty and Staff Development and Assessment

Faculty and staff development opportunities abound in the learning community context. Workshops, conferences, and collaborative teaching opportunities encourage an ongoing conversation about teaching and learning. Academic support team members including peer leaders, librarians, academic advisors, and student development professionals, are accessible and can address specific student concerns that may detract from the academic focus of the classroom. Furthermore, the academic support teams have defined groups (via classroom participation) and an academic context with which to direct resources and assistance. Finally, faculty members have been able to explore their disciplines in a cross-disciplinary context and with colleagues outside of their departments. To foster collaboration and shared responsibility, each FLC team is expected to meet monthly to discuss the progress of their students. Since a minimum of two faculty members, one peer leader, and one academic advisor make up the FLC team and share responsibility for each group of 15 to 24 students, the program is well positioned to provide the majority of first-year students on the Appalachian campus personalized attention, particularly during their first semester. This intentional reorganization and refocusing of existing resources allows individuals from throughout the campus to become involved in the learning enterprise.

Results of Assessment

Freshman Learning Communities in General Studies support the notion of continuous assessment to inform programmatic change. Throughout the three-year pilot project, several aspects of the program (e.g., recruitment of students, selection of courses, selection of faculty, registration processes, advising) were evaluated through qualitative and quantitative processes. Student and faculty satisfaction surveys, student retention studies, and evaluations of faculty and staff development activities were used to determine what types of learning community models could best be implemented and supported on the Appalachian campus.

Table 2 provides some insight into persistence and academic achievement for students involved in the Freshman Learning Communities Program. Studies conducted by Appalachian's Office of Institutional Research, Assessment and Planning (IRAP) indicated that from 1998 to 2001 FLC participants were retained from their first to sophomore year at higher rates than students who did not participate in the program.

IRAP also conducted studies on the predicted grade point average (PGPA), first-semester grade point average (GPA), and first-year GPA for FLC cohorts and non-FLC cohorts from 1998

Table 2
One-Year Retention Rates and Predicted GPA versus GPA for Freshman Learning Communities in General Studies, 1998-2001

	1998 Cohort[a]		1999 Cohort[b]		2000 Cohort[c]		2001 Cohort[d]	
	FLCs ($n = 81$)	Non-FLC ($n = 2,238$)	FLCs ($n = 148$)	Non-FLC ($n = 2,061$)	FLCs ($n = 335$)	Non-FLC ($n = 2,220$)	FLCs ($n = 963$)	Non-FLC ($n = 1,349$)
Percent Retained	86.4	81.0	89.9*	83.8	87.8*	82.3	85.0*	79.2
Predicted GPA	2.61	2.60	2.58	2.50	2.60	2.66	2.65	2.75
First-Semester GPA	2.71	2.62	2.89	2.72	2.85	2.78	2.90	2.74
First-Year GPA	2.63	2.68	2.83	2.82	2.81	2.83	2.86	2.87

* $p < .05$

Note. From the Office of Institutional Research, Assessment and Planning, Appalachian State University.
[a]Students self-selected and applied. Students attended a special Orientation session and met with academic advisor.
[b]Students self-selected and applied.
[c]Students were selected by academic advisors based on middle range SAT verbal (must place in English 1000) and math skills; first-semester schedule was developed by academic advisors prior to Orientation; students attended Orientation as a special population; met with academic advisor and some faculty during Orientation. Students were not Honors/Watauga College/Summer Preview/Teaching Fellows; avoided students with Advanced Placement credit.
[d]Students registered for learning communities during Summer Orientation.

through 2001. The PGPA formula is an objective instrument used to determine initial eligibility for admissions. The formula, derived from a validity study prepared by The College Board, consists of a regression analysis with predictors that include standardized test scores and high school academic measures. The study showed that each cohort of FLC students achieved a higher GPA at the end of their first semester than non-FLC cohorts. However, by the end of the first year, there was little difference in the GPAs of FLC participants compared to non-participants.

In 2000, the FLC program went from self-selection to institutional placement based on student academic needs. The "middle range" student was purposefully targeted for the FLC program and, therefore, the PGPA was lower for the 2000 and 2001 cohorts of FLC students. One interesting finding indicated that these students had lower predicted levels of academic performance before entering college, but they closed the GPA gap on their non-FLC counterparts by the end of their first year. The differences in size of the FLC and non-FLC cohorts has made tests of statistical difference with regard to academic performance difficult. Following several years of dramatic growth, we anticipate that the number of students participating in the FLC program will remain relatively constant over the next few years, which will allow for better analysis of statistical significance with regards to student GPA.

Specific areas received focused attention at different times based on available evaluation instruments and current student needs. The evaluation process is particularly useful in shedding light on potential future directions for the program. For example, experience and evaluation reminded us that students' living and learning together is a powerful aspect of the college experience. Therefore, identifying timelines and procedures that connect the residence hall assignment process to the preliminary course registration process is an important future direction for the FLC program.

In preparation for the Southern Association of Colleges and Schools Accreditation visit in 2002, Appalachian's first-year programs and, specifically, its seminars and learning communities were listed as evidence of "the concerted efforts of the faculty, staff, and administration to create an intimate atmosphere and personalized attention for students, especially first-year students, despite the size of the University" (Appalachian State University, 2002, pp. 17-18). Each generation of faculty, staff, and students at Appalachian have brought new ideas that are integrated into old traditions. New programs have found partnerships with proven practices. The Freshman Learning Communities Program builds on the long-standing Appalachian tradition of creating environments for effective individual and community learning.

References

Appalachian State University. (2002). *2000-2002 Appalachian State University SACS self-study executive summary.* Boone, NC: Author.

Langdon, H. (2001). *Institutional Research, Assessment and Planning August 2001 selected findings on first-year students.* Boone, NC: Appalachian State University.

Placing Learning Communities and First-Year Seminars at the Core of General Education Reform

Sally K. Murphy and Skye Gentile
California State University, Hayward

California State University, Hayward (CSUH) introduced mandatory yearlong learning communities for first-year students in fall 1998. The faculty created first-year and sophomore learning communities to reform the lower-division general education curriculum while simultaneously providing a more consciously designed academic experience for first-year students. CSUH's first-year learning communities are composed of a series of thematically linked courses (Appendix A), including courses meeting requirements in science, humanities, social science, composition (both remedial and baccalaureate), oral communication, information literacy, and a three-quarter first-year seminar. The first-year seminar—General Studies (GS) 1011, 1012, and 1013—helps students integrate perspectives on the theme explored in each of the learning community courses and supports development of skills for academic success and community building. Descriptions of the University, the evolution of the General Studies curriculum, and its central role in building community among first-year students in learning communities follow. This chapter includes results from five years of assessment of the first-year learning communities including their impact on enrollment, student retention, and academic success, as well as specific assessments of the GS seminar. Assessment results include national standardized measures of student preparation in subject areas, responses to national surveys and homegrown evaluations, and data from focus groups. The data have been the driving force in the evolution of the content and structure of the first-year seminar. Feedback from the GS faculty to the faculty in the learning community has often resulted in greater integration across courses in the learning community and changes in the way all learning community faculty support student learning.

Institutional Background

Student Population

California State University, Hayward is one of 23 campuses of the California State University (CSU) system. It is an urban, commuter campus situated in the East Bay hills overlooking the city of Hayward and the San Francisco Bay. The University is composed of four colleges: Arts, Letters, and Social Sciences (ALSS); Business and Economics; Science; and Education and Allied Studies. All four colleges offer courses in sophomore learning communities; ALSS and Science offer courses in first-year learning communities.

CSUH is a comprehensive university enrolling approximately 9,700 undergraduate and 4,100 graduate students. The student body is highly diverse with no single racial or ethnic group comprising the majority of students. Women constitute 64% of the student body. Hayward's diversity stretches beyond national boundaries, having the highest percentage of international students in the CSU system. Approximately 70% of the undergraduates are adult transfers or returning students—the average age of undergraduates is 27. The first-year class comprises about 7% of the enrollment; the average age of first-year students is just over 18 and a half.

General Education: A Context for Reform

During the academic year 1995, faculty, students, and administrators undertook a major revision of the general education program at CSUH. Dissatisfied with the inconsistent approach that had characterized general education in the past, the faculty was determined to create a more coherent program that would provide an obvious complement to a student's major. The Academic Senate appointed a special committee, composed of faculty, administrators, and students, and asked the committee to submit new general education models. Early in the revision process, the committee focused its attention on learning community models for first-year students, partly because of a desire for a coherent general education program. Learning communities also helped address additional goals: (a) creating community for a small, traditionally aged class of first-year commuter students and (b) creating learning environments specifically for young adults. The relatively small size of the first-year class, approximately 750 to 775 full-time students, made restructuring the first-year general education curriculum feasible.

As CSUH faculty debated the form of general education reform, discussions were complicated by a new CSU Chancellor's office policy that required many students who enter a California State University to enroll in developmental work in mathematics or English composition. Beginning fall 1998, students needing developmental work would be required to enroll in the appropriate preparation course upon matriculation and achieve college-level competence in the first year. Failure to reach college-level skills in a year would mean that developmental students could not continue in any state university until they demonstrated college preparedness. With approximately 60% of CSUH first-year students in need of some developmental instruction in composition,[1] the committee for a revised general education program developed a first-year learning community structure that included remedial and baccalaureate composition courses.[2]

As the learning communities took shape, the faculty approved a three-quarter first-year seminar—General Studies (GS) 1011 (fall), 1012 (winter), and 1013 (spring)—that carries one unit of general education credit per quarter. All first-year students enroll in one learning community. Each learning community requires first-year students to take the one-unit GS course and four to nine additional general education units each quarter of their first year.[3]

Learning Community Administration and Faculty Development

Administration

The Office of the Associate Vice President of Academic Programs and Graduate Studies oversees general education. The Office of General Education has two staff members: the general education coordinator and the program assistant. The general education (GE) coordinator, a faculty member with a full-time assignment to direct the general education program, coordinates all general education learning communities, chairs the general education subcommittee, lobbies for support from the college deans, coordinates learning community classes with department chairs, guides the assessment of the general education program, enforces the campus remedial policies, and serves as department chair for General Studies. As chair of General Studies, the coordinator teaches a GS class, recruits and hires GS faculty, and supervises their training. The Executive Committee of the Academic Senate appoints the coordinator for a two-year period. The program assistant oversees scheduling of learning community classes; manages the budget and administrative issues; coordinates GS faculty and activities for GS classes; maintains the general education web site; manages student records, tracking, and registration issues; assists with remedial policy enforcement; and advises students. In addition, the office employs a General Studies lead instructor to support the work of instructors in GS 1011, 1012, and 1013. The GS lead instructor teaches GS classes, develops curriculum, oversees the GS faculty, advises students, provides faculty training, and works with the GS faculty to develop strong connections on campus, and between the campus and the wider community. The provost provides a general fund for the GS courses and the learning communities to cover costs for integrative activities and materials, which departments offering courses in the learning community clusters would not normally fund.

Faculty Development

The summer before courses are offered, each learning community faculty team (i.e., three faculty members teaching the humanities courses, the lead composition instructor, librarian, communication instructor, and GS instructor) participates in a week-long workshop. Topics in the workshop include active learning, teaching first-year students, interdisciplinary teaching, and designing learning assignments. These faculty members receive a stipend upon delivery of syllabi and narrative descriptions of how the courses will be integrated with each other and how learning outcomes will be met and assessed. In-service training for GS faculty members on the content and instructional strategies of GS 1011, 1012, and 1013 has expanded over the years from informal training in the first year to a two-day formal training workshop prior to the opening of the new school year and required workshops during the term. Learning community faculty also access resources relevant to their work on the institution's course management system (i.e., Blackboard), on the general education web site, and through discussion at brown bag lunches. Instructors who teach GS 1011, 1012, and 1013 share office space where they can talk about pedagogy, difficult student situations, interesting assignments and activities, connecting first-year students to the campus and to faculty, and strategies for working collaboratively with the other faculty in their cluster(s). The GS faculty members receive very small stipends for the training sessions and, as described below, serve as primary content integrators and community builders within their course clusters.

Instructor Selection

The majority of GS instructors are graduate students. Graduate students sometimes have a better sense of the needs of entering first-year students than senior faculty do. They are often struggling with demands similar to those of first-year students and have energy and enthusiasm to work closely with such students on the skills needed for academic success. The key to selecting effective faculty, in our case, is to find a good fit between the instructor, the theme, and disciplinary content of the learning community in which he or she will be teaching. The students often turn to their GS instructor for advice about how to balance their complicated lives: 80% of the first-year students work, almost a third are first in their family to attend college, and a third are non-native speakers of English. Many have family obligations beyond work and school, and many find little understanding at home about the demands of being a serious college student. The GS class is intended to be a supportive community and an academic safety net; the GS faculty needs to have the sensitivity and concern to fulfill the multiple roles the students and course require of them (i.e., instructor, mentor, unofficial advisor, and role model).

Experience proved that the best GS instructors are those who remember what it means to struggle and succeed. They must be empathetic to the first-year student who may feel insignificant on a campus that generally caters to adult learners. The best GS instructors model effective communication, flexibility, and collaboration. Because it is difficult to identify ahead of time those candidates who have the required skills to make interdisciplinary connections, those who do not provide such support for their students do not continue as GS faculty. Instructors must also be comfortable with technology and willing to learn and use it. Moreover, they must teach first-year students about CSUH's online course management system, presentation software, campus e-mail, and other resources.

Evolving Integration of the First-Year Seminar in Learning Communities

First Class

In fall 1998, when CSUH enrolled its first class in the learning communities, the GS course had the least developed curriculum of all the courses in the clusters. The faculty imagined General Studies as an intensive orientation to the University and an academic support course with a large dose of skills development. The GS faculty members focused on helping students succeed in the linked courses in their learning community. During the program's first year, GS was an intensive tutorial with academic skills training and orientation to campus resources. One term of that kind of support was plenty for many first-year students, and they were not shy about providing feedback. The first assessment report about the program summarized the issues this way:

> While a number of students thought GS well connected to the curriculum, and close to 100 percent of a few sections agreed with the statement that the course expanded and enriched their understanding of what they were learning in their other cluster courses, a much larger number of students voiced complaints about the course. In course evaluations, a substantial number commented that three quarters of GS was far too much. Comments complaining about the lack of "substance" and structure were numerous, as were comments that much of the material was covered elsewhere. While the instructors were perceived as trying to be helpful, the purpose of the course was obscure to most students. (Cowen, 1999, p. 45)

Reflecting on that feedback, the general education coordinator and the director of assessment and testing determined that the purpose of the GS 1011, 1012, and 1013 should be made clearer to both instructors and students. To accomplish that, a common curriculum was developed for all sections of GS, making connected knowing primary and explicit to all students. (See Appendix B for a yearlong list of GS topics and a sample syllabus that demonstrates how one GS course adapts the topics to the specific cluster theme.)

Developing a Purpose and Common Curriculum

Over the last four years, the curricula of the General Studies courses has changed significantly. Review of all the assessment data from the first year indicated that some of the faculty teaching linked courses in the learning community clusters were not adapting their content or pedagogy to meet the goals of the new general education program. The GS class, therefore, took primary responsibility for building a strong sense of community and modeling collaborative, active, connected learning for first-year students. GS adopted a yearlong curriculum and set a goal of assisting first-year students in becoming self-motivated, reflective learners. It also embraced the following general education learning outcomes in addition to academic and technological skill development, orientation, and advising:

- Enhanced sense of community among first-year students and between first-year students and their faculty
- Improved ability to work well with a diverse group of other students

- Improved ability to see connections among disciplinary approaches to topics and between higher education and active citizenship (i.e., integrated knowing)
- Increased awareness of issues of cultural, racial, ethnic, and gender diversity

Each academic year, the lead GS instructor, working with the program assistant and General Education coordinator, spends the summer researching and developing program enhancements to improve the GS curriculum and increase integration among linked cluster courses. All GS faculty now use a common text and yearlong syllabus—both of which provide common topics for all GS sections while requiring adaptation to the needs of particular learning communities. While still offering extensive orientation, academic skill development, and study support throughout the year, each quarter now includes instruction in and practice with technological skills that a successful student needs and extensive general advising prior to registration for the next quarter. Most important, the GS courses now have clear learning goals for the year and learning outcomes. Each quarter of GS has its own theme, while active learning pedagogies support the student's learning experience in these courses.

Typical Pedagogies, Assignments, and Activities

Pedagogies and Assignments. Faculty teaching GS model collaboration for their students by working closely with other faculty who are teaching in the learning community cluster. They attend lectures or class discussions in other learning community courses, team-teach some classes with other learning community faculty, act as co-managers of each other's Blackboard sites, design GS activities and field trips used to illustrate and integrate learning in the other learning community courses, and collaborate with their students to adapt the GS content to meet the students "where they are." When an instructor finds a student with very good skills in one academic area, he or she will offer that student an opportunity to become a peer teacher on that topic. Students work in collaborative study groups to prepare assignments and assessments in their linked courses. The group work reinforces students' ability to listen to and respect others' ideas, work well, disagree respectfully, and recognize the benefit of collaborating with others.

GS faculty members also provide feedback to the faculty teaching in other courses in their learning community cluster to improve the quality of student learning. In The Search for Spirituality learning community cluster, for example, the GS instructor noted that the students did not understand the way in which the three humanities courses in the learning community were integrated. The GS instructor worked with other cluster faculty members to help them make these connections explicit to students in the fall quarter, modeling for students the integration they wanted the students to achieve for themselves.

Activities and Assessments. All GS classes include either field trips or end-of-year culminating experiences linking the learning community themes to the world beyond the classroom. For example, when the learning community The Search for Spirituality explores Hinduism, the GS instructor takes the students to an area Hindu temple. Here, they talk with the priest and see and hear the art and music of that faith. At year's end, the GS instructor collaborates with the faculty teaching the linked courses to present a workshop with leaders from each of the religious traditions the students have studied. Students report in the end-of-year learning community assessment that meeting with the religious leaders and hearing them debate the role of faith in the contemporary world was a powerful synthesizing activity.

The Individual and Society learning community takes a field trip each year through the neighborhoods of San Francisco. On their Collaborative Photo Scavenger Hunt, students explore the socioeconomic divisions in the city and record their observations for later reflection and writing on how society affects the individual. The day ends with lunch in San Francisco's China Town.

At year's end, The Ancient World learning community sponsors a daylong conference on the relevance of the ancient world to modern day, where a noted scholar presents the keynote speech, and students and faculty present papers. The conference has gained some regional recognition, and two faculty members from universities in neighboring states presented papers last year. The GS students organize and manage almost all aspects of the conference.

Service-Learning. For those learning communities that do not plan a culminating activity for the spring, GS instructors design and organize service-learning experiences for their students. Like the culminating activities and field trips, service-learning extends the yearlong strategy of engaging students in their own learning and provides an opportunity for them to see that even their first year of education helps them have a positive impact on their communities. The lead GS instructor works with the service-learning coordinator each year to bring local non-profit organizations to campus to connect with cluster students seeking volunteer opportunities, faculty interested in incorporating or expanding service-learning in their courses, and non-cluster students looking for volunteer or internship placements.

Each GS instructor designs the service assignment to make the strongest connections possible with the learning community theme. The common elements include a minimum of 10 hours of community service and 10 hours of class discussion to process the experience of service and make connections between the students' service and their learning community through reflective writing.

The GS instructor in The Individual and Society cluster, working with the GS lead instructor, arranged for CSUH to sponsor a major community service effort in San Francisco. The CSUH "Helpers from the Hill" worked collaboratively on a number of daylong projects in San Francisco neighborhoods. Dividing themselves into workgroups, they painted fences for elderly residents, weeded community gardens, or cleaned public school yards. They wrote and talked about how their projects increased their understanding of the way individuals shape society and how societies shape individuals.

The GS instructor for the Gender in the Arts, Literature, and Society cluster approaches service differently. His students volunteer at a wide range of local agencies. He asks the students to view their service-learning experience through the lens of gender, and they write several reflective essays describing their observations. While most of the students describe the personal value of their service, they also realize the relevance of the learning community theme when they notice the many gender issues that permeate their daily interactions.

Student reflections are the primary source for assessing service-learning, field trips, and culminating activities. Reflections take different shapes depending on the needs of the particular learning community. The range of assessments includes online group discussions, personal journals, dialogue journals, double-entry journals, essays, classroom discussion, and group presentations. Students enter and provide summary comments on their reflective assignments in the yearlong portfolio required of all students enrolled in GS courses.

Learning Community Assessment

Assessment Instruments

Since the program began, CSUH has assessed correlations between learning community participation and the students' learning, persistence, and performance on general education outcomes. Evaluation of learning community classes is separate from standard course/instructor evaluations used in every CSUH course and focuses on general education learning objectives. Data come from both quantitative and qualitative measures including individual course/instructor evaluations; focus groups with learning community students and faculty; surveys of student perceptions of program goals and academic skills acquisition; standardized measures of students' competence; both first- and third-quarter surveys of student perceptions; and institutional data on enrollment, student grades, and persistence rates. (See Appendix C for a complete list of assessment instruments used.)

Building Community

CSUH is a commuter campus. The faculty designed first-year learning communities to build a community among students and between students and faculty. First-year students are considerably younger than the majority of undergraduates, most of whom are returning adult students. Faculty and administrators have long felt the need to help first-year students connect with each other, their faculty, and the campus.

Table 1 lists students' reports about the campus climate as reported on the College Student Experiences Questionnaire. Their responses suggest that the GS course, which takes primary responsibility for building community, has been successful in supporting connections among students and between students and faculty. CSUH students report higher levels of connection to peers and faculty than their national comparison group.

Table 1
Mean Rating of Campus Climate

	1998-99	1999-00	2000-01	2001-02	National
Students are friendly and supportive	5.50	5.70	5.60	5.70	4.90
Faculty are friendly and supportive	4.90	5.00	5.00	5.00	4.64

Note. Mean scores on a scale where 1 = hostile and alienating and 7 = friendly and supportive. From the College Student Experiences Questionnaire.

CSUH students report that they recognize the connections they have formed with their peers and with the faculty. They engage in behaviors that support building and maintaining community connections. In particular, they report positive relationships with faculty at levels above the national cohort on the College Student Experiences Questionnaire (see Table 2).

Participants' responses suggest that the GS course is successful in supporting students' connections to each other and to the campus. Faculty teaching in learning communities report that a higher percentage of first-year students attend class and turn in assignments in learning communities than in stand-alone courses.

Ability to Work With Others

One desired GS learning outcome is to help students develop skills to work effectively in groups. Faculty development initiatives include activities and assignments for GS instructors that support the development of students' ability to work with others. Student reports suggest these efforts have been successful (see Table 3).

Levels of Persistence

Data presented in this chapter are from assessments of student persistence from 1996 (prior to implementation of the learning community program) to 2002. Since 1996, the entry characteristics of first-year students have remained stable. In other words, the percentage of students requiring

Table 2

Student Experiences and Perceptions of Connections to Peers and Faculty

Creating Communities	1998-99	1999-00	2000-01	2001-02	National
Percent of students who agreed or strongly agreed that their GS course helped them to feel connected to other students	76	73	69	75	n/a
Percent of students who said they would remain friends with GS classmates beyond freshman year	94	92	93	91	n/a
Percent of students who reported they never discussed their academic program or course selection with a faculty member	21	16	18	14	n/a
Percent of students who reported they never discussed ideas for a term paper or other class projects with a faculty member	20	14	15	12	45
Percent of students who reported they never socialized with a faculty member outside of class	59	56	62	56	82

Note. From the College Student Experiences Questionnaire.

Table 3

Student Experiences and Perceptions of Gains in Ability to Work with Others

	1998-99	1999-00	2000-01	2001-02	National
Ability to work well with others in groups					
Percent of students who reported that they very often or often worked on a class assignment, project, or presentation with other students	60	71	71	72	n/a
Mean estimate of gain					
Ability to get along with different kinds of people	2.81	3.03	2.97	3.12	2.75
Ability to function as a team member	2.66	2.84	2.71	2.81	2.54

Note. Mean scores on scale 1 = very little and 4 = very much. From the College Student Experiences Questionnaire.

developmental work in composition and mathematics has shown little change, and high school grade point averages and entrance examination scores remain constant. Since the number of specially admitted students, those without academic qualifications for automatic admission to CSUH, has declined dramatically, Table 4 reports separately on the regularly and specially admitted students.

The first year of the learning community program and the first year of required remediation was 1998, and second-year persistence rates dip below previous rates in this year. Since 1998, persistence rates for regular and specially admitted students have increased slightly.

Table 4
Persistence Rates from First to Fourth Year, Fall 1996 to Fall 2001

	Cohort 1996 (N=707)			Cohort 1997 (N=753)			Cohort 1998 (N=770)		
	Reg (*n*=488)	Spec (*n*=219)	All	Reg (*n*=531)	Spec (*n*=222)	All	Reg (*n*=592)	Spec (*n*=178)	All
Second-Year Return Rate	81	70	78	77	79	77	78	59	74
Third-Year Return Rate	59	56	65	65	59	63	66	47	62
Fourth-Year Return Rate	60	46	57	62	54	59	62	49	59

	Cohort 1999 (N=737)			Cohort 2000 (N=710)			Cohort 1991 (N=716)		
	Reg (*n*=555)	Spec (*n*=182)	All	Reg (*n*=612)	Spec (*n*=98)	All	Reg (*n*=622)	Spec (*n*=94)	All
Second-Year Return Rate	82	72	80	81	69	79	82	73	81
Third-Year Return Rate	71	53	67	69	60	68			
Fourth-Year Return Rate	65	48	61						

Learning community students are also returning for their third year at slightly higher rates than students enrolled at CSUH before the program began. CSUH allows students with the greatest developmental needs six quarters in which to complete their developmental courses. Thus, the impact of the remedial requirement is felt fully in the third year.

While the impact of the learning community program on persistence is far from conclusive, there is reason to believe that both social and academic support from the learning communities has lingering positive effects that may translate into higher persistence across the four years of a student's tenure at the institution. Student comments about their learning community experience consistently note that the skills they learned in their first year and the friends they made in their learning communities were crucial to helping them succeed in their first two years.

Focus Group and Short Answer Data

In spring 2002, as part of a five-year program review, the director of assessment and testing conducted focus groups with current first-year students, upperclass students who had previously enrolled in the first-year learning communities, and faculty teaching in the program. A number of common themes emerged (Strait, 2002) (Table 5).

Those students who had complaints about the learning communities focused on the cluster scheduling, its lack of flexibility, and the amount of work required in the one-credit GS class. From the perspective of the learning outcomes, too few saw clear intellectual connections among their learning community cluster classes.

Table 5
Common Themes From Focus Group Data

Themes	Comments
Learning communities create a sense of community	• "Most of my friends are people in my cluster." • "I really miss the clusters and taking classes with people my age and people I know. I just don't see the connections among my classes that I did when I was in the clusters."
Students are able to enroll in classes they want.	• "I know that I wouldn't be able to enroll in most of these classes if it weren't for the cluster program." • "I had trouble with my financial aid and had to register late. Without the clusters I don't know what classes I'd have ended up with."
Students complete requirements efficiently.	• "I'm going to get through my general education requirements faster than any of my friends in non-learning community programs." • "I can't believe that I'm almost done with general education. None of my other friends [not at CSUH] are anywhere close to finishing GE."
Students have predictable schedules.	• "Since being a part of the cluster system, I have had less stress in scheduling and attending my classes than my peers in non-cluster system."
Students receive academic support.	• "I've really been able to see the positive influence of the cluster system. For me, all these benefits have made it much easier to maintain a good GPA and build strong friendships."

Note. From Strait, 2002.

Faculty as a whole found the first-year learning community clusters to be a positive experience. They particularly appreciated the stimulation that came from working with colleagues from other departments and other colleges. Faculty who teach second-year students noted that, since the inception of the cluster program, students are much better prepared. The faculty also experienced the social network provided by the first-year learning communities—for both students and themselves—as beneficial. Their major complaints focused on what they perceived as a lack of sufficient institutional support for the program, pointing to ballooning class size and substitution of lecturers for full-time faculty in the first-year program. Some faculty, particularly those who teach mostly upper-division classes, felt unprepared to deal with first-year students' classroom behavior, although many faculty members found the first-year students' energy stimulating.

Student feedback about GS activities supports the value of changes made over the past few years. Most spoke positively about the field trips and both career and major exploration activities. Their most positive comments were reserved for the service-learning projects in the spring. Most students completed a service-learning experience in spring 2003. The evaluations (Table 6) made it clear that service provides students with palpable benefits.

While not all students expressed their appreciation for the experience with the same enthusiasm, one student's comment captured what many said: "I can hardly believe my time with my organization is already over! It was one of the best experiences ever! I thank you very much for, in a sense, forcing us to do this service-learning project."

Table 6
Benefits of Service-Learning Experiences

Themes	Comments
Students' understanding of self and others increased.	• "My participation in this [service] activity has helped me become more aware of the often difficult circumstances people face, [and] I feel this has influenced my attitude towards life. I have learned to be content with what I have and who I am."
Students' sense of civic responsibility increased.	• "I will use my higher education not only for personal gain, but to contribute to society." • "We think of successful people as 'valuable members of society,' and a valuable member of society is not one who obtains many things, but a person who gives."
Students' teamwork skills improved.	• "The main benefit I found was that [service-learning] taught me more about teamwork."

Note. From Strait, 2002.

The Future of the Learning Communities and the First-Year Seminar

CSUH completed its program review of learning community clusters in spring 2003. The review underscored the value of this first-year program. The Academic Senate endorsed the continuation of the first-year clusters and the GS course, with some modifications, for the next five years. The Senate recommended that the funds budgeted for second-year learning community clusters be redirected to the first-year learning communities to provide for more enrichment activities in the GS classes. The Senate also recommended the colleges make renewed efforts to keep class sizes small, place the best faculty in the learning community classes, and offer more support for faculty development. In the face of dramatic budget reductions, it is unlikely that additional monies will go to the first-year learning communities. Nonetheless, the University's president has voiced a commitment to supporting the learning communities and will be creating a task force to explore ways to build on the foundation provided by the first-year learning communities.

Notes

[1] The vast majority of students requiring developmental work in composition and/or mathematics are, on paper, college-ready: They graduate in the top third of their high school class having completed the college preparatory course sequence, and their grade point average is above 3.0.

[2] We debated including mathematics in the learning communities but were not able to get approval for a single course (college algebra or statistics) to count for general education. The large number of quantitative reasoning courses required by majors and approved for general education made linking them to the first-year learning communities unfeasible.

[3] All levels of remedial and baccalaureate composition are linked in the learning communities. Each of the baccalaureate courses in the learning communities carries general education credit and each, whether remedial or baccalaureate, is linked to the others through a common theme.

References

Cowen, S. (1999). *California State University, Hayward, assessment of the new general education program.* Hayward, CA: California State University, Hayward, Available Institutional Research and Assessment.

Strait, M. (2002). *General education focus group report.* Hayward, CA: California State University, Hayward, Available Institutional Research and Assessment.

Appendix A
Learning Community Offerings

Sciences

Diversity of Life: Designed for majors in Biological Science, Environmental Science, and Biochemistry. Method: One science course a quarter, large lecture format.

Biology 1301 Fall	English 1001, 800s/900s	General Studies 1011
Biology 1302 Winter	Library 1010	General Studies 1012
Biology 1303 Spring	Speech 1000	General Studies 1013

Evolution: Explores the formation of the universe; the evolution of the earth, its oceans, and atmosphere; and the emergence and development of living things. Method: One science course a quarter, large lecture format.

Physics 1600 Fall	English 1001, 800s/900s	General Studies 1011
Geology 1001 Winter	Library 1010	General Studies 1012
Biology 1003 Spring	Speech 1000	General Studies 1013

Healthier Living: Explores chemical, biological, and psychological aspects of health and helps students learn to think, write, talk, and make decisions about healthier living. Method: One science course a quarter, large lecture format.

Chemistry 1601 Fall	Speech 1000	General Studies 1011
Biology 2010 Winter	English 1001, 800s/900s	General Studies 1012
Psychology 1000 Spring	Library 1010	General Studies 1013

How Things Work: Examines scientific explanations for everyday occurrences. Method: One science course a quarter, large lecture format.

Physics 1500 Fall	Library 1010	General Studies 1011
Biology 1005 Winter	Speech 1000	General Studies 1012
Geology 1001 Spring	English 1001, 800s/900s	General Studies 1013

Interdependence of Chemicals, Living Things, and Energy: Designed for majors in Chemistry, Geology, Physical Science, and Physics.

Chemistry 1101 Fall	Library 1010	General Studies 1011
Chemistry 1102 Winter	Speech 1000	General Studies 1012
Chemistry 1103 Spring	English 1001, 800s/900s	General Studies 1013

Humanities

The Ancient World: Increases cultural awareness by studying the commonality and diversity of human experience. Method: Two sections of a discipline course; different discipline each quarter.

History 1014 Fall	Speech 1000	General Studies 1011
Art 1014 Winter	Library 1010	General Studies 1012
English 1014 Spring	English 1001, 800s/900s	General Studies 1013

Gender in the Arts, Literature, and Theater: Examines the traditions and changing expectations of the genders in the arts, literature, and theater. Method: Semi-team taught; meets as whole learning community about five times per quarter. All other meetings in discipline classes.

Mod Lang & Lit 1104	English 1001, 800s/900s	General Studies 1011
Theater 1010	Library 1010	General Studies 1012
Philosophy 1101	Speech 1000	General Studies 1013

Language Culture and Literature: Offers students the opportunity to develop the ability to reason and communicate in another language.

Spanish 1201 Fall	Speech 1000	General Studies 1011
Spanish 1202 Winter	English 1001, 800s/900s	General Studies 1012
Spanish 1203 Spring	Library 1010	General Studies 1013

Search for Spirituality: Examines the spiritual origins of the multinational people that make up the University. Method: All three humanities classes integrated each quarter; meets as a whole learning community in large lecture.

Art 1011	English 1001, 800s/900s	General Studies 1011
Philosophy 1401	Speech 1000	General Studies 1012
Music 1014	Library 1010	General Studies 1013

Social Sciences

The Individual and Society: Explores the answers offered by psychology, sociology, and political science to questions related to the individual's role in society and society's shaping influence. Method: Mixed model variation 1: One course taught as large lecture for entire cohort during one term. The other two discipline courses taught in 45/45 sections, one discipline per quarter.

Psychology 1000 Fall	Speech 1000	General Studies 1011
Sociology 1000 Winter	Library 1010	General Studies 1012
Political Science 1000 Spring	English 1001, 800s/900s	General Studies 1013

Science, Technology, & Society: Explores the relationship between science and technology and the ways they affect daily life and society. Examines the moral and social questions raised by scientific and technological advances. Method: Mixed model variation 2: one course taught as 45/45; other two taught as 30, 30, 30 with two sections of one discipline and one of the other one term, and one-two the final term.

Science 1005 Fall	English 1001, 800s/900s	General Studies 1011
Philosophy 1103 W & Sp	Speech 1000	General Studies 1012
Sociology 1000 W & Sp	Library 1010	General Studies 1013

Viewing Diversity: Provides a critical overview of visual presentations of diversity regarding individual identity, culture, gender, race, ethnicity, nationality, and the global balance of political and economic power. Team-taught model: Cohort meets as large learning community for lecture one day a week and breaks into discipline discussion groups the other.

Anthropology 1006	Library 1010	General Studies 1011
Ethnic Studies 1005	English 1001, 800s/900s	General Studies 1012
Mass Communication 1005	Speech 1000	General Studies 1013

Appendix B
General Studies Course Plan and Sample Syllabus

Annual General Studies Course Requirements

Fall Areas of Focus

Technology assessment and orientation to campus technology
- Horizon e-mail
- Net ID
- Blackboard (e-learning)
- MY INFO
- E-portfolio

    Evidence of student learning: Core components for student e-portfolio (key artifacts)
    - Posted (to Blackboard) responses to exploration of personal values, goals, action plans, and self-assessment strategies; students download to CD-ROM at end of quarter
    - Technology assessment

Introduction and exploration of campus resources
    Evidence of student learning: Core components for student e-portfolio (key artifacts)
    - Photos from campus resource scavenger hunt
    - Notes from visit to at least three student support centers (e.g., University Advisement Center, Student Center for Academic Achievement, Counseling Center, Student Life, Peer-Mentoring Program, Honors Program, Financial Aid, Math Student Service Center)

Academic success skills
- At least three academic skills dependent on student needs and learning community demand: learning styles, time management and goal setting, reading, money management, and/or managing lectures
- Becoming a self-motivated learner
- Advising for winter quarter

    Evidence of student learning: Core components for student e-portfolio (key artifacts)
    - Learning styles inventory
    - Personal explorations and reflections
    - Winter course plan

Winter Areas of Focus

Extension of technology skills
- Blackboard (e.g., discussion boards)
- Maintaining MY INFO & e-mail
- PowerPoint (can be incorporated into presentations)

- Researching online
  Evidence of student learning: Core components for student e-portfolio (key artifacts)
  - PowerPoint presentation

Academic success skills
- Two or three academic skills: test-taking, note-taking, reading, and any chapter topics from fall not covered
- Advising for spring quarter

  Evidence of student learning: Core components for student e-portfolio (key artifacts)
  - Personal explorations and reflections
  - Spring course plan

Career and major exploration
  Evidence of student learning: Core components for student e-portfolio (key artifacts)
  - Written response to/reflection on career workshop
  - Written response to/reflection on major workshop
  - Interview: Faculty members, students and/or alumni in career of interest
  - Résumé and plan for success
    - Résumé will also be submitted for student leadership GS in spring
  - Research for either career or major component (choose one)
    - Research various careers, seeking information on qualities that make for a successful candidate
    - Research what to do with a degree from majors of interest

Spring Areas of Focus

Academic success skills
- Two or three academic skills as needed: love and relationships, health and wealth, becoming a mindful thinker and learner
- Second-year cluster advising

  Evidence of student learning: Core components for student e-portfolio (key artifacts)
  - Personal explorations and reflections
  - Second-year course plan

Service-Learning
- 10 hours of service, 10 hours in-class reflection and activities

  Evidence of student service-learning: Core components for student e-portfolio (key artifacts)
  - Student reflection and connection journal
  - Time log
  - Responsibility/liability release

- Student agency evaluation
- Agency student evaluation
- Visual representation of service-learning experience
- Presentation

Cluster integrative activity
- 10 hours of work on cluster integrative experience, 10 hours in-class reflection and activities

Evidence of student learning—culminating experience: Core components
for student e-portfolio (key artifacts)
- Student reflection and connection journal
- Time log
- List of activities and responsibilities for cluster conference, workshops, panels
- Performance assessment
- Visual display of learning experience
- Presentation General Studies: Fall 2003

Sample Syllabus

GS BIG SISTER

This class will be different from any other class you will take at CSUH. Instead of focusing on an academic subject (e.g., psychology, modern world history, calculus), this course will focus on you and your success! Like the cast of the CBS reality show *Big Brother*, you will meet new friends, form alliances, and encounter many challenges over three short months. Your general studies course is designed to give you the tools and resources to meet your first quarter college goals, and when things get tough, you can always count on...

Your Big Sisters!

Laura Kelley		Skye Gentile
WA LM 61	Office	**WA LM 57**
M & W 10:30-11:00, T 10-11:45a	Office Hours	**M & W 9-12, T 12-3**
lkelley@horizon.csuhayward.edu	E-mail	**sgentile@csuhayward.edu**

Make sure your full name is in body of e-mail

GS 1011 Catalog Description:
Orientation to the University and its services. Academic skills development in support of linked cluster course. Development of skills needed for success in college. Beginning development of students' portfolio. A-F grading only (p. 217).

Required Course Materials:
(You must bring these things to every class)
1. *Learning Success: Being Your Best at College and Life*, 3rd edition, Wahlstrom and Williams
2. Syllabus

Suggested Materials:
Weekly Planner (like the one you received at orientation)

Goals Your Big Sister Has for You

- Master CSUH computing tools (MY INFO, Blackboard, Horizon E-mail, & e-Sailer)
- Effectively format e-mails and documents
- Identify goals that are specifically important to you and the steps you need to take to achieve them
- Master your personal time-management style
- Learn to take notes efficiently, successfully process information, and study for exams
- Understand the different styles of learning and apply them to your study habits
- Be informed of the campus resources available to you
- Develop personal responsibility and accountability
- Make new friends and build new relationships

Classroom Decorum:
During class, we will talk, listen, read, and write together. Participation is critical. Since each one of you is a unique individual with different life experiences, you may have different views and opinions on issues that we discuss. It is crucial that we respect each other, and create a climate that is conducive for sharing our thoughts.

Academic Honesty:
Academic dishonesty is defined on pages 79-80 of the 2002-2004 University Catalog. Plagiarism can take shape in a variety of different ways by writers: verbatim copying without giving credit to the author, sloppy paraphrasing, recycling papers from other classes, and not including a works cited (to name a few). Please be certain that the work you turn in to me is your own, original, and that you give credit to theories, concepts, and ideas you used to prove your argument. Using MLA (or APA) style guide, cite your sources and include a bibliography for all major assignments.

Attendance Policy:
Congratulations. You currently have 100 attendance points in your CSUH academic learning account. If you do not miss any class sessions, you will receive 20 extra credit points. Every absence beyond one is a deduction of 10 points. You have no overdraft protection with this account. More than 3 unexcused absences could result in failing the course. What is an excused absence? An excused absence is a medical emergency, death in the immediate family, immigration, or circumstances beyond your control but verifiable with documentation.

Class Schedule (Subject to change, see Blackboard for current information):

Week	Class Activity	Homework/Highlights
September 30	Introduction to course: objectives, outcomes, purpose of course Student survey	Technology survey in class Icebreakers Meet in computer lab next week
October 7 Meet in computer lab WA B 01	Technology lab: web ID, Horizon e-mail, MY INFO, e-Sailer, formatting documents, e-mail	
October 14 Meet in computer lab WA LM B01	Technology lab: Blackboard, journal assignment/haystack (Psychology class terms)	Read *Learning Success* 1-11 (browse through rest of chapter). Complete Personal Exploration on p. 19 & 20. Post on discussion board your responses to the following: "Reflecting on what you said you value, do you think you have control over how you spend you time? Are there spaces in your life where you could devote more time to what you value?"
October 21 Meet in special room, then off to library for your Psych assignment	Guest Speaker Chapter 1-Developing Staying Power for Lifetime Success	Chapter 1 Discussion Board: Mid-term 1 test prep. Respond to Psych test preparation prompts (1-45). Also respond to non-test prompt: "Why are you in college?"
October 28	Campus Resources	Discussion Board: Respond to Psych mid-term 2 test preparation prompts.

Week	Class Activity	Homework/Highlights
November 4	Mid-quarter assessment Winter advising	Whalstrom Chapter 5 (Time Management as a Learned Skill) Discussion Board: "Does your time reflect your values?"
November 11 Meet in University Club	Guest Speaker Time Management & Goal Setting	e-portfolio Discussion Board: "How do you waste time? Do you find, after keeping a record of your time usage for three days, that you waste time in specific ways, such as watching too much T.V.? Do these time-wasting ways serve some other purpose in your life, such as alleviating stress or furthering relationships? Give some thought to how these needs might be addressed in some other ways so that you save more time for schoolwork."
November 18	Campus Resources revisited—tie things together	Discussion Board: "Has college met your expectations? What makes it different from HS?"
November 25	Ch 5-Managing Lectures, mindful learning THANKSGIVING WEEK	Discussion Board: "Identify things that have helped you deal with the demands of the 1st quarter. Identify things that have hindered success in the 1st quarter. Identify two areas, either personal or academic, in which you would like to make improvements. Formulate these as goals with specific action statements and steps designed to achieve them."
December 2	Evaluation of course Campus Resource online Presentations due	e-portfolio: Include materials in each category from your Psych and GS classes and from any other cluster classes that demonstrate your growing competencies.
Dec. 8-14	No scheduled classes	

Appendix C

Assessment Measures for General Education Learning Community Clusters

Time	Place	Instrument
First Year:		
Pre-instruction	Freshman Orientation Freshman Orientation	Entering Student Survey Academic Profile (*4 years of data: no longer given*) – Short Form
Beginning fall quarter	Composition Classes	Writing Skills Test: Analytic Essay Self-Perception of Writing Skills
As Soon As Possible	Linked Library Classes	Fundamentals of Info Literacy
Mid-quarter	GS Classes	Mid-Quarter Course Evaluation
End each quarter	Discipline Classes GS Classes All Classes	Course Evaluations Course Evaluations Course Grades
End spring quarter	Discipline Classes GS Classes	College Student Experiences Questionnaire Portfolio
Second Year:		
End fall quarter	Discipline Classes All Classes	Course Evaluations Course Grades
End winter quarter	All Classes	Course Grades
End spring quarter	All Classes	Course Grades College Outcome Survey
Third Year:		
Upon achieving junior status	Campus	Writing Skills Test

Growing Learning Communities at the Community College: Two Decades of First-Year Student Development Efforts

Alicia B. Harvey-Smith

Community College of Baltimore County

The last decade in American higher education has seen a shift from an emphasis on instructional approaches to a more focused examination of learning outcomes (O'Banion, 1997). As a consequence, colleges and universities of all types are seizing the opportunity to reshape and redefine themselves (Barr & Tagg, 1995; Eckel, Green, Hill, & Mallon, 2001; Flynn, 2000; Harvey-Smith, 2003b; O'Banion, 2000).

The Community College of Baltimore County (CCBC) has begun the process of consciously using this learning paradigm to innovate programs and practices in the first-year experience, learning communities, and student development courses. While CCBC is a multi-campus institution, the focus of this chapter will be services at the Catonsville campus—its orientation, First-Year Experience program, SDEV 101 (Student Development 101 course), and Innovative Communities of Learning. The chapter will provide an overview of services to first-year students, with a particular focus on SDEV 101 and learning communities.

The first-year seminar, SDEV 101, is offered to students new to the institution, typically during the first semester, although returning students may also enroll. A variety of different general education courses are linked to first-year seminars as a strategy to increase student participation in the learning communities. The courses selected to be linked in learning communities are requirements for all regularly admitted entering students and for students participating in developmental education courses. Because they are requirements, they are in high demand among first-year students.

Institutional Background

The Community College of Baltimore County (CCBC) has a reputation as a premier learning-centered, multi-campus public institution. In 1998, the Maryland General Assembly authorized the merger of three campuses—Catonsville, Dundalk, and Essex—which formerly served the county as independent colleges, and established CCBC. The new institution was recently named one of 12 Vanguard Learning Colleges in North America by the League for Innovation in the Community College. As a Vanguard College, CCBC serves as a model for other community colleges interested in sharpening the focus on student learning. CCBC has designed a "LearningFirst" environment, where students are encouraged to engage in their experiences at the College and to take primary responsibility for their own learning. The learning-centered nature of the College means ideas are freely exchanged and innovation is celebrated. Continuous improvement in delivery of programs and teaching practices is encouraged as are partnerships among students, faculty, and staff members.

More than 100 degree and certificate programs are offered in the arts and sciences, business, computer and information technology, environment and engineering technology, and health sciences and human services fields, with more than 50 non-credit programs offered through Continuing Education. Through its wide range of offerings, CCBC has become an important member of the larger community and a key provider of workforce training to support economic and community development efforts. In 2001-2002, the College enrolled 27,892 credit students and 47,168 non-credit students, which represented 68% of all county residents attending an undergraduate institution. In addition, 11% of those students resided in Baltimore City and 16% in other Maryland counties. Through online learning opportunities, CCBC offers "anytime anyplace" learning and training experiences intended to prepare Baltimore citizens for employment opportunities.

Maintaining a diverse learning environment is a key component of the College's strategic plan. CCBC is an open-admissions institution committed to providing credit-bearing and non-credit courses at a low cost for those who desire them. Students may enroll in any credit-bearing experience for $77 per credit. Non-credit courses are also available at a low cost. In order to make education and training available in all parts of the county and region, CCBC also maintains extension centers in several communities in the greater Baltimore area. All three campuses and the extension centers are accessible by bus, light rail, or subway.

Such a wide range of learning opportunities is critical, because CCBC enrolls a student population that closely reflects Baltimore County's rich diversity. In 2001-2002, 57% of CCBC students were women. The largest proportion of students (40%) were 40-to-59-year-olds. Thus, many first-year students at CCBC are adult learners. In spring 2003, out of the 18,333 students enrolled, 27% were African Americans; 5% were Asians; 60% were Caucasians; and 2% were Hispanic Americans. Over the past five years, there has been a 17% increase in the number of degrees awarded to African Americans and a 20% increase in the number of degrees awarded to Hispanic Americans.

A high percentage of entering students are admitted requiring at least one developmental course. For example, nearly 80% of all students enroll in a developmental reading course, and slightly more than half enroll in a developmental math course. Approximately one third of all students enroll in a developmental English course. Thus, remediation and moving students toward completion of general education requirements is a key goal of SDEV 101 and the learning communities program.

At CCBC, the infrastructure for students entering college includes an orientation program and support system used throughout the student's first year, the expansion of a student development course, and the opportunity for students to engage in a wide variety of learning communities.

The CCBC First-Year Experience

The Division of Learning and Student Development houses the First-Year Experience and Orientation programs. The Division also administers placement and instructional testing through the Student Success Center, tutoring services, Supplemental Instruction, a technology lab, disability services, day-care facilities, student services, library and media services, career services, and counseling and advising services. The First-Year Experience and Orientation mission statement and program objectives focus on student learning outcomes and academic success:

> The mission of the First-Year Experience is to provide quality services and activities that enable first-year students to pursue their higher education goals while simultaneously providing learning opportunities that will contribute to a positive college experience that engages, educates, and challenges students as members of the community of learners. (Harvey-Smith, 2003a)

During their work with academic advisors in the orientation program, students are encouraged to register for the SDEV 101 course for their first semester. This course is highly recommended to full- and part-time developmental studies students and all students considered to be at high risk academically. The course was coordinated through the Counseling Center until fall 2003; then administration became the joint responsibility of the Student Success Center and the Counseling and Advising Center.

Student Development 101

The SDEV 101 course is designed to support those student behaviors and attitudes that are most consistently identified with achievement of success in college (see Appendix A for a course outline). The significance of a college education is explored as are the specific ways the College can partner with students to achieve their goals. The course is typically a semester-long experience, although modified and accelerated six- to seven-week courses have been offered. During the course, students are exposed to the College community through a wide range of activities and are provided information regarding College policies and operating procedures. An emphasis is also placed on building study, career, and life skills and understanding individual learning styles. Students complete assignments that introduce them to critical and creative thinking, building positive relationships, conflict resolution, an appreciation of diversity, campus resources, the culture of higher education, and expected classroom behaviors. Topics also include time and stress management, communication skills, memory improvement, test taking, note taking, some reading and writing skills, and goal setting. Both cognitive and non-cognitive areas are integrated into the course and all first-year experience initiatives at the College.

A key principle adopted by CCBC in its effort to be a "learning college" is to assist students in taking responsibility for their learning. Central to the SDEV 101 course, then, is an opportunity for students to discuss how they are responsible for their experience in college. In the course, they are asked to describe ways they can create a successful and satisfying college experience for themselves. The course, taught at the Catonsville Campus of the Community College of Baltimore County for 19 years, was initially a one-credit course. Then it became a two-credit course as it was a pre- or co-requisite for the upper-level reading class (at the request of reading faculty). In fall 2001, three credits were given to students who completed it. Many non-developmental students elect to take the class, as do students preparing to transfer.

In the fall of 2001, 23 sections of the course were offered including special self-selected sections for students in a grant program for first-generation college students, African American men, and a skills development learning community. Eleven sections were offered in spring 2002, and 40 sections were offered between summer 2002 and summer 2003. Classes are offered in both summer and winter terms, and as many as 50 sections have run in an academic year. Between 80% and 85% of all incoming first-time, full-time students enroll in the SDEV 101 course within their first academic year. Participation numbers are considerably smaller in learning communities, including those described below. However, the Learning and Student Development Division is exploring ways to expand learning communities. CCBC also hopes to expand the connection of first-year seminars and learning communities to include honors learning communities, thereby creating more intentional connections between the SDEV 101 classes and general education.

Faculty Development, Compensation, and Program Marketing

Instructors of the SDEV 101 course are drawn from areas across campus and include instructional and counseling faculty, student services faculty and staff, continuing education administrators, and others. An all-day instructor training session is conducted in the summer. Mentoring and internships are offered to prospective teachers. Instructor training involves an examination of learning styles, teaching strategies, course content and methodology, and active learning strategies (see Appendix B for workshop outline). Instructors also meet during the semester to share ideas, challenges, and successes.

All instructors agree to abide by a set of general guidelines such as topics to be covered, common assignments, policies on participation and attendance, and testing and assessment approaches. Instructors are free to design their own syllabi within these guidelines. Incorporation of cooperative learning in the courses is also encouraged and the importance of individual learning and teaching styles is emphasized. SDEV 101 course instructors are compensated primarily through adjunct contracts, although some instructors have been compensated through overload and release time.

Faculty members interested in teaching new learning communities that integrate the SDEV 101 course formulate a proposal, which is submitted to the program coordinators who also assist with developing new learning communities. The proposals are informal and include a discussion of the rationale for linking the courses, the approach that will be taken (including themes to be emphasized), the identity and role of the master learner (described below), a list of assignments and tentative due dates, and the methods that will be used to market the learning community. Marketing efforts are developed with the coordinators in an effort to assure sufficient enrollment for the new learning community. Proposals receive preliminary approval from the coordinators. Final approval is granted by the dean of Learning and Student Development. Faculty members receive $1,000 for the development of new learning communities and an additional $1,000 if the college enrolls enough students for it to be offered.

Courses, learning communities, and all other support for first-year students are marketed through the orientation and advising programs, but they are also often recommended to students by their peers and faculty.

Innovative Communities of Learning

Two full-time Catonsville campus faculty members, compensated on overload and through release time, are responsible for coordinating learning communities through the Division of Learning and Student Development, which is a part of the College's Center for Learning and Teaching Excellence. The predominant learning communities model on the Catonsville campus enrolls students in multiple courses, often including the SDEV 101 course, and encourages faculty and staff to create intentional links between the courses. The intent is to increase student opportunities for a deeper understanding and integration of the material in the courses and to achieve greater interaction between students and between instructors and students.

Learning communities on the Catonsville campus have recently added a faculty member to serve as a master learner. This master learner model has also been used on the Essex campus with developmental learning communities. The master learner attends all classes, completes all class assignments, schedules discussions, helps students integrate material across courses, and holds private tutorials. In this model, master learners are reassigned time or receive a stipend and serve as part of the design team that creates the learning community. Master learners are selected from faculty members who elect to participate in courses or learning communities. Their primary function is to be a model of a college-level learner to students in the learning communities. The master learner should help all students, but is particularly valuable as a guide for students who are the first in their families to attend college.

Figure 1 shows examples of learning community clusters at CCBC. Courses in learning communities are linked by theme (e.g., differences in communication styles based on gender and ethnicity) or by common interest (e.g., a business course and an American history course examine the Great Depression and the changes made in the economy to protect against a reoccurrence). To build on the common theme or interest, faculty members from different courses will link their assignments. For example, an ethics course linked to a business communication course will explore common problems or scenarios demonstrating ethical dilemmas. In the cluster involving physical education, health, and lifetime fitness and wellness, students learn health concepts related to all three courses. In each course, they learn to apply health and wellness theory to their personal work on creating a healthy lifestyle. Similarly, in the art cluster, students are learning larger art concepts applicable to all three courses. In the cluster involving English and reading, students focus on applying academic skills, learned in the student development courses, to their work in reading and English. Linking skills courses in this way provides students with opportunities to apply newly acquired skills in diverse settings.

Fall 2000		
Physical Education 101	Health 101	Lifetime Fitness and Wellness 101

Fall 2000			
English 051	Integrated Reading and Writing Student Development 093	Reading 051	Student Development 101

Fall 2001		
Elements of Visual Thinking I Arts 102	Drawing I Arts 110	Sculpture I Arts 140

Figure 1. Sample learning community course clusters.

Assessment Methods and Results

To date, results on student academic achievement have been gathered as they relate to the SDEV 101 course, with plans now in place to conduct a comprehensive assessment of first-year programs, including learning communities, as described below. On anonymous evaluations, more than 90% of the students who take the SDEV 101 course, either alone or as part of a learning community, say they would recommend it to a friend. Retention data over several semesters indicate that between 80% and 91% of the students who pass the course in the fall, with a "D" or better, return to the institution in the spring, while the overall College fall to spring retention rate hovers around 60%. Retention among those students who enroll in the course from the spring of the first year to fall of the second is around 70%, higher than the general population's retention rate. The latest year for which statistics are available is academic year 2002-2003. In fall 2002, 82% of participants in the SDEV 101 course were retained at the institution for the spring, and 94.6%

of students who participated in the course in spring 2003 would recommend the experience to a friend. Collection of similar data for learning communities is planned as part of the college's comprehensive assessment process.

A formal college-wide outcomes assessment was launched in 2003 through SDEV 101 on all three campuses. On the Catonsville campus, this assessment process incorporated student learning portfolios. Program coordinators for both SDEV 101 and the learning communities are developing a strategy for using the results from the learning portfolios analysis to make program improvements.

Challenges and Solutions

CCBC joins many institutions in attempting to address the primary challenge of implementing a first-year experience program: securing adequate financial and human resources. The Division of Learning and Student Development on the Catonsville campus has used several strategies to ensure it has the resources necessary for program administration. These strategies include an increasing reliance on assessment and data-driven program improvement, as most recently demonstrated by a College-wide outcomes assessment effort. The division is also cross-training personnel to assist with core first-year experience and orientation services. For example, library staff members have facilitated new student workshops and assisted with advising during orientation. Student Success Center staff members have served as instructors in the SDEV 101 courses. The emphasis on partnerships across campus should solidify support across departments.

The Community College of Baltimore County acknowledges that the retention and success of students are major challenges and is confident that the First-Year Experience and Orientation program, including SDEV 101 and learning communities, are viable strategies for addressing these challenges.

Future Plans

Future plans for first-year seminars and learning communities include program expansion and links between the first-year seminar and a wider array of developmental and general education course offerings. Honors learning communities are being developed for implementation in fall 2004, as are the links among courses, co-curricular programming, and student clubs. The latter is an effort to integrate the students' academic and social experiences and support out-of-class learning in our learning communities.

References

Barr, R. B., & Tagg, J. (1995). From teaching to learning: A new paradigm for undergraduate education. *Change, 42*(7), 13-25.

Eckel, P., Green, M., Hill, B., & Mallon, B. (2001). *On change III. Taking charge of change: A primer for colleges and universities.* Washington, DC: American Council on Education.

Flynn, W. J. (2000). *The search for the learning-centered college. New expeditions: Charting the second century of community colleges.* Washington, DC: American Association of Community Colleges.

Harvey-Smith, A. B. (2003a, July). *Designing new learning models. Unpublished division report.* Baltimore, MD: The Community College of Baltimore County, Catonsville Campus, Division of Learning and Student Development.

Harvey-Smith, A. B. (2003b). A framework for transforming learning organizations: Proposing a new learning college principle. *Learning Abstracts, 6*(7). Retrieved June 7, 2004, from http://www.league.org/publication/abstracts/learnab_main.htm

O'Banion, T. (1997*). A learning college for the 21st century.* Phoenix: Oryx.
O'Banion, T. (2000). An inventory for learning-centered colleges. *Community College Journal, 71*(1), 114.

Author's Note

The author wishes to acknowledge the contributions made to the chapter by Mr. Fred Bartlett, Jr., Coordinator of The First-Year Experience and Orientation Program; Professor Judith Maisey, Counselor and Co-Coordinator of the SDEV 101 course; and Professors Patricia Rhea and Dan Sullivan, Co-Coordinators of Learning Communities on the Catonsville Campus.

Appendix A
SDEV 101 Achieving Academic Success: Common Course Outline

Description

Achieving Academic Success is designed to focus on those student behaviors and attitudes that are most consistently identified with achieving success in college. The significance of a college education is explored and the specific ways that the Community College of Baltimore County operates are discussed. Strategies for time management, test taking, memory and recall, communication, and personal success are included. 3 credits.

Overall Course Objectives

Upon completion of this course, you will be able to:

- Discuss how you are responsible for your experience in college
- Describe ways you can create a successful and satisfying experience in college
- Discuss college policies and procedures and be able to locate and use information in the college catalog to develop a personal academic plan
- List and describe specific methods to:
    - Improve your ability to recall information
    - Manage time more efficiently
    - Read a textbook with improved understanding and retention
    - Prepare for and take tests
    - Take effective notes
    - Listen, with comprehension, to a lecture
- Describe and use a model of communication that facilitates listening to, speaking with, and conflict resolution among peers, family members, and instructors
- Discuss several procedures for focusing attention on the task at hand when reading, listening, and taking notes and tests
- Assess your general health habits including diet, exercise, substance use, and methods for managing stress
- Locate resources (including academic advisement, library, career center, financial aid) both on and off campus to assist you in meeting your needs as a student at the Community College of Baltimore County
- Discover your individual learning style so you can draw on your particular strengths and adapt to and develop skills using other styles
- Develop decision-making skills for effective goal setting
- Learn tools for creating new ideas, problem solving, and thinking
- Strengthen skills to study, work, and live in a multicultural, diverse, and changing world

Major Topics

Self-Assessment – study skills, learning styles, self-monitoring
Time-Management Techniques
Memory
Reading
Note taking
Tests – test-taking skills, test anxiety

Diversity
Thinking – creative and critical thinking, problem solving
Relationships – listening, sending, communication, conflict management
Culture of Higher Education at CCBC
Attitudes That Promote College Success
Life Skills – stress management, self-responsibility, self-awareness
Personal Empowerment
Risk Taking / Involvement
Concentration

Course Requirements

Grading/exams: The College community is concerned that high standards of academic performance be met. Grading procedures will be determined by the individual faculty member but will include the following:

Participation and attendance	up to 25%
Exercises, projects, and quizzes	up to 50%
Mid-term exam	up to 25%
Final exam	10% to 33%

Writing: The individual faculty member will determine specific writing assignments and expectations.

Other Course Information

Text:	To be determined by each campus
Supplies:	To be determined by each instructor

Appendix B
SDEV 101 Achieving Academic Success Instructor Training Workshop:
Sample Workshop Agenda

Workshop Objectives

The purpose of the workshop is to provide SDEV 101 instructors with:

- A general overview of the course and how SDEV 101 fits into CCBC's educational mission
- An understanding of the SDEV 101 course content, requirements, and philosophy
- An introduction to the resources that support SDEV 101 instructors
- An exploration of SDEV 101 teaching strategies and an opportunity to begin using the text and manual
- A variety of exercises to help engage students
- An experiential introduction to understanding different learning styles using the Kolb Learning Strategies Inventory
- An explanation of how students are advised to take the class and of the wide variation in students' skills

Workshop Agenda

Introduction to Training
Preview (purpose, objectives)
Introduce participants
Overview of course (i.e., history, CCBC mission, topics, benefits)

Students to Reach
How they get into course (assessment, video orientation, academic advising)
What research says (national, campus-specific)
Pilot project – creating an academic plan

Learning Styles
Complete Kolb Learning Strategies Inventory
Interpret and discuss "Learning Styles Approach to Learning and Teaching"

VIP Exercise

Lunch

Power Processes

Course to Teach – exercise within exercise
Learning seven-part course structure in small groups using text and manual
Beginning to apply the seven-part course structure
Common course outline and learning outcomes assessment project

Diversity – beginning a conversation
Naming Exercise

Brown Exercise

Resources
People – mentors/buddies, monthly meetings, contact the unit secretary, ext. 4720
Materials – videos, 3 x 5 cards, two and three-part paper, library exercise, syllabi quizzes, CD
with PowerPoint slides
CSI. 1-800-528-8323, Student Success newsletter

Questions and intention statement

Evaluation

The First-Year Seminar: The Cornerstone of an Interdisciplinary Learning Community Program

William J. Fritz and Nannette Evans Commander

Georgia State University

Efforts to integrate curriculum are not new. In fact, they can be traced back to Spencer in the 1800s through national curriculum reforms in the 1930s and 1940s to Vars's (1993) supportive research of the 1980s. The reports and proposals during the last decade of the 20th century often urge more connection within the college experience. For example, *The Challenge of Connecting Learning* (Association of American Colleges, 1991) argues that students have a right to expect teachers and colleges to help them inquire, understand, and connect their knowledge. Connecting learning not only reinforces what is taught but also more closely resembles "real" life where the subjects typically interact and overlap. Interdisciplinary learning communities are one structure that help college students achieve these skills.

First-year seminar courses are increasingly recognized for the vital role they play in learning community programs. This is the case at Georgia State University, a large, urban research institution of more than 28,000 students located in the heart of downtown Atlanta, where each learning community includes the first-year seminar as a credit-bearing course. Four other core-curriculum courses are taught along with the seminar, which is required for all students enrolled in the community. The first-year seminar increases interaction between faculty and students, orients students to college, and is the central place for intentional integration of learning across disciplines. Because of the vital role the first-year seminar plays as the integrator of learning, it is identified as the "anchor" course of many learning communities and is considered one of the important highlights of Georgia State's program.

Another important highlight is the extent of faculty participation in the program, including senior research faculty. Those wishing to offer a course in the first-year learning community submit a proposal that is reviewed by a university-wide curriculum faculty advisory committee. Faculty members determine the best combination, sequence, and "fit" of the courses in the community and also participate in the design of the curriculum for the first-year seminar course. The result is a faculty-driven learning community program that focuses on delivering an integrative academic experience for students.

Perhaps the greatest highlight is the diverse academic environment that allows the learning communities to flourish. Georgia State has a large minority presence with 32% African Americans, 11% Asians, and a growing Hispanic/Latino population. The diversity in the learning communities has been equal to or greater than the diversity of the University at large. Ranked as first among traditionally White institutions in the nation (and seventh when including historically Black colleges) in granting degrees to African Americans, Georgia State provides a rich milieu for communities of learners. With more than 51% minority representation in the undergraduate student body, first-year students are able to interact with students from every state in the nation and from more than 148 countries. Thus, the diversity supports a community setting that broadens perspectives, develops critical thinking skills, and challenges stereotypes.

This chapter begins with a brief introduction to Georgia State, followed by a description of the first-year seminar course, GSU 1010: New Student Orientation. Additionally, a program for engaging faculty in the process of integrating the curriculum is described along with three sample learning communities that have a mature integrated curriculum. Finally, assessment data and lessons learned are presented for others interested in designing programs where the first-year seminars emphasize interdisciplinary learning.

Institutional Context

As the only urban research university in the state, the overarching goal of Georgia State is to achieve a front-rank position among the nation's premier state-supported universities located in urban settings. The University offers more than 200 degree programs with strong disciplinary-based departments and a wide array of problem-oriented interdisciplinary programs. When the state of Georgia adopted a tiered system of higher education in the mid-1990s, the institution was designated as a research university. This required the discontinuation of learning support and a sharp increase in entrance requirements. As a result, somewhat planned and somewhat accidental, Georgia State became much more traditional with respect to its student population, with the number of traditional age first-year students quadrupling since 1992 and doubling since 1996. Other issues including poor retention, low graduation rates, small percentage of alumni giving, and inadequate student services further complicated the picture. In response to these challenges and the change in student population, the University initiated the Freshmen Learning Community (FLC) program in 1999 to establish what the Boyer Commission (1998, p. 34) called a "purposeful place of learning" and a much needed sense of community for entering students. Along with other initiatives, including writing across the curriculum, a new core curriculum, and new facilities, Georgia State designed FLCs and the first-year seminar course to address specific problem areas, such as advising, retention, and degree completion. Student advisement is a part of the first-year seminar course. Because 40% of all students in America who start at a four-year college fail to earn a degree and 57% of all dropouts from four-year institutions leave before the start of their second year (Tinto, 1996), the FLC program is an integral part of Georgia State's retention efforts. In fact, prior to the initiation of the FLC program, 70% of all entering students failed to earn their degrees from Georgia State. The FLC program and the first-year seminar course are credited with positively impacting this percentage.

Georgia State's program is based on the Federated Learning Communities model described by Gabelnick, MacGregor, Matthews, and Smith (1990). The learning communities are best described as "learning clusters" where cohorts of 25 students enroll in a first-year seminar and four courses in which the learning is connected around a central theme (Appendix A provides a list of possible themes). Students register for the FLC theme of their choice and are then assigned to each of the sections in the course cluster. All FLCs are designed with general education core curriculum courses that apply to any major. As noted above, faculty members submit proposals reviewed by a university-wide faculty advisory committee for the creation of the FLCs. Since the FLC program's inception, more proposals have been submitted annually than are accepted. The proposal's merit is judged by the rationale for the community, the courses to be linked, and the interconnectedness of the community. Funding at Georgia State is highly dependent on credit generation. The FLC program represents a vehicle for accomplishing this since the first-year seminar course counts as one course in the faculty member's workload. Thus, faculty members have an incentive for submitting proposals.

The program has tripled over the past three years from 275 students enrolled in 11 learning communities to an enrollment of approximately 800 students in 33 learning communities for fall 2003. Currently, 40% of first-year students at Georgia State voluntarily enroll in an FLC. Students are primarily recruited through a brochure mailed to all accepted first-year students and through the new student orientation program called Incept. The orientation program consists of one-day sessions during fall, spring, and summer where students receive group academic advising and register for classes. The FLC program is explained to students in detail as an initiative designed to support their success, offering the best schedules of classes at the best times. While not required, entering first-year students are strongly encouraged to enroll.

GSU 1010: New Student Orientation

Although faculty members propose and design the learning communities by including various courses, the required first-year seminars share common goals to ensure a similar student experience across learning communities. Comparable to most first-year seminar courses, GSU 1010 is designed to help students make a successful transition to university life (Appendix B offers a general syllabus). Information is provided about the academic demands of the University and its rules, procedures, and resources for academic success. Instruction is focused on four areas: (a) Self, (b) Self and Others, (c) Academic Environment, and (d) Community, with certain topics identified as essential for inclusion in every GSU 1010 course (Appendix C contains a list of topics for each focal area).

GSU 1010 is a three-hour elective course, primarily taught by academic faculty members. Based on student performance, a letter grade is awarded and computed in the student's grade point average. The topics prescribed as essential by the program designers provide a base for connecting students to one another, faculty, and the University; but GSU 1010 instructors are encouraged to build on this base with activities related to the overarching theme of their community. Approximately 60% of the first-year seminar course consists of prescribed curriculum modules integrated throughout the course as deemed appropriate by individual instructors. The theme of the community and the integration of the content areas from other courses in the community are directly addressed during the remaining 40% of the course. To deliver the prescribed portion of the curriculum, faculty receive support from student services representatives who make presentations in the first-year seminar on co-curricular issues such as diversity, financial aid, and alcohol awareness. Additionally, regular meetings are scheduled among GSU 1010 faculty to support their teaching activities.

Engaging Faculty in the Process of Integrating Curriculum

Bystrom (2002) describes interdisciplinary learning communities as "… a course of study designed by two or more faculty that includes work in different disciplines integrated around a particular issue or theme" (p. 68). Creating such a learning environment with curricular coherence requires strong collaboration among faculty. Thoughtful development of curriculum occurs after repeated reflection on whether the information presented matches the purposes of the curriculum and its content. Instructors must continually evaluate the way the curriculum is delivered and how students respond. It is a daunting challenge for faculty not only to teach their particular disciplines but also to teach material that synthesizes and integrates two or more subject fields.

The difficulty of the task is not the only barrier against efforts to integrate curriculum. The faculty reward system traditionally does little to validate teaching efforts. In response to this lack of support, and in response to one of the 10 recommendations of the Boyer Commission (1998) to "Remove Barriers to Interdisciplinary Education," GSU created a "bubbling-up" strategy that encourages faculty involvement. A summer stipend funded by the Office of the Provost to develop curriculum for interdisciplinary learning communities is available to GSU 1010 faculty. The program, entitled "The Freshman Learning Community Faculty Grants for Development of

Integrated Courses," was initiated in 1999. The purpose of the program is to reward faculty teams for work over the summer to develop FLC courses with an integrated curriculum. A linked model of integrated courses is described in the Request for Proposals as one in which the instructor is responsible for the content of his/her own course but works on integrating themes, assignments, and activities with the instructor of another course (or courses). The "call," with detailed information on the format of the proposals, takes place at the end of spring semester; and proposals are reviewed and rated for funding by a faculty committee. The ranking of the proposals considers the following: (a) justification for linked courses, (b) degree of proposed integration, (c) creative nature of integration, (d) demonstrated benefits to students, and (e) emphasis in curriculum on verbal and written communication.

The first-year seminar is often described as having a natural linkage to the learning community. Barefoot, Fidler, Gardner, Moore, and Roberts (1999) summarize the first-year seminar as what "…may be the most effective way to facilitate creation of bonds and connections across disciplines, students, and faculty. It is in the first-year seminar where faculty integrate new learning from several discipline-based courses into a coherent whole" (pp. 84-85). This natural linkage is evident in the proposals written by Georgia State faculty for integrating course content. Although the grant program does not dictate which courses in the learning community may be linked, 14 of the 16 funded proposals for 2003 link the first-year seminar, GSU 1010, with one or more of the other courses.

Analysis of data collected on FLCs where faculty received summer funding for integrated learning (IL) suggest that a significant academic advantage exists for participating students when faculty members are given additional support to integrate learning across their linked courses. The data indicate significant differences in student grade point averages over the years 2001 and 2002. In fall 2001, 213 FLC students were in an FLC that received summer funding for IL; 359 students were in FLCs that had not received summer funding. The fall 2001 GPA of the IL students (3.06) was significantly higher ($p < .01$) than that of the other FLC students (2.91). In the 2002 fall term, 192 FLC students were in an FLC that received summer funding for IL compared to 485 students who were in FLCs not receiving funding. The fall 2002 GPA of the IL students (3.12) was significantly higher ($p < .001$) than that of the other FLC students (2.83). These preliminary data suggest that when the first-year seminar supports interdisciplinary efforts, it enhances the positive impact of learning communities on student achievement. While many campuses have decreased or cut funding for these programs due to budget constraints, support for these faculty grants has steadily increased over the past five years (Appendix D).

FLCs with Mature Integrated Curriculum

A joint report by the American Association for Higher Education, the American College Personnel Association, and the National Association of Student Personnel Administrators (1998) identifies 10 principles about learning and strategies for strengthening it. First among these is that learning is fundamentally about making connections. The report notes, "Rich learning experiences and environments require and enable students to make connections…through curricula integrating ideas and themes within and across fields of knowledge and establishing coherence among learning experiences…" (p. 3). The following describes three FLCs, with mature integrated curriculum, which have been successful in making such connections. FLCs with mature integrated curriculum are those that have been offered multiple times and that the faculty review committee has confirmed are evolving in terms of integration across courses and continuous development of the curriculum. All three of the descriptions demonstrate the importance of the first-year seminar course in its role as the anchor course of the FLC where reflection and integration of material takes place. Examples of joint assignments are included.

African-American Culture and History

Designed for students interested in understanding the role of people of African descent in contributions to the arts, sciences, and humanities, this FLC prepares students to take their places as leaders in an increasingly multicultural United States and world. The African-American Culture and History FLC integrates the curriculum of the first-year seminar course (GSU 1010), English composition (ENG 1101), and Introduction to African-American Studies (AAS 2010) through assignments and discussions. For example, AAS 2010 requires a service-learning project. GSU 1010 introduces the definition, purpose, and benefits of service-learning and assigns a library and Internet exercise to research the background and population served by various community organizations or agencies. GSU 1010 supports assignments in AAS 2010 by facilitating study skills for reading, writing, and test taking that are applied to the AAS 2010 content. GSU 1010 also supports ENG 1101 through various assignments that monitor timely paper completion and required readings. Journal entries in the form of reflection papers in GSU 1010 allow students to reflect on class discussions from both ENG 1101 and AAS 1020.

Economic Policy Issues in the Global Economy

This FLC focuses on both domestic and international economic and business policy issues. Courses focus on current issues, including economic forecasting, tax reform in Russia, and the impact of environmental costs on the business community. Activities integrate the curriculum of GSU 1010 and Principles of Microeconomics (ECON 2106). For example, the media and government policy assignments are the basis for an oral presentation and some short written assignments in GSU 1010. This provides students with extra experience in undertaking economic assignments, since first-year students are sometimes at a disadvantage in this area compared with the upper-class students in economics courses. GSU 1010 is also used to provide additional review of basic economic concepts expressed graphically and mathematically. The library research orientation session in GSU 1010 is used to focus on databases appropriate for studying economic and business issues.

Quantitative Sciences

This FLC is designed to introduce students to quantitative sciences and to demonstrate how mathematics can be used to solve problems. Students develop a greater understanding of mathematical ideas, learn to communicate mathematical ideas more effectively, and begin to relate mathematics to the entire curriculum. Assignments and activities integrate the curriculum of GSU 1010, ENG 1101, and Pre-calculus (MATH 1113). For example, GSU 1010 requires students to take a walking tour of the downtown area as a community building exercise. In this FLC, students prepare an essay and oral presentation on the geometric forms of the buildings they see during the tour. Students also select from a list of math problems in pre-calculus and write an essay for ENG 1101 explaining how to solve the equation. Another assignment in ENG 1101 requires an essay using communication principles learned in GSU 1010 to describe trigonometric functions presented in MATH 1113.

Assessment Data

The positive effect of first-year programs and learning communities on issues related to student retention has been well documented. Continued enrollment beyond the first year, grade point average, credit hours, student satisfaction, graduation rates, and student adjustment/

involvement were favorably affected by first-year seminars at 47 institutions according to research summaries compiled by Barefoot, Warnock, Dickinson, Richardson, and Roberts (1998). A review of research on learning communities in a variety of institutions (Shapiro and Levine, 1999) indicated favorable outcomes on student achievement and retention, intellectual and social development, student involvement, and classroom experiences.

Assessment data on Georgia State's program provides further support for the effectiveness of first-year seminars and learning communities. Students enrolled in FLCs for fall 1999, 2000, 2001, and 2002 achieved higher GPAs (Table 1) and were retained at higher rates than non-FLC students (Table 2). Predictions of academic performance at the time of college entry suggest that FLC and non-FLC participants have similar academic preparation. For the 1999 cohort of learning community students, 15.6% of the students graduated in Fall 2003. The four-year retention rate for this group is 56.9%. Among non-learning community students, 12.3% graduated in Fall 2003, for a four-year retention rate of 50.6%. The graduation rate for the entire cohort was 12.8%, with a four-year retention rate of 51.7%.

Furthermore, a study was conducted to evaluate the impact of FLC participation on grade point average and retention and address the issue of self-selection (Hotchkiss, Moore, & Pitts, 2003). Students who were predicted to have below average academic performance were more likely to participate in an FLC. Belonging to an FLC increased these students' GPAs over their predicted GPAs from about three quarters to one full letter grade, depending on the student's race and gender. The study also reports that the probability of African American men and women being enrolled one year after matriculation increased significantly for those who participated in an FLC during their first year.

Table 1

Earned Grade Point Average (GPA) for Students Enrolled in Learning Communities versus Non-Learning Communities Students, 1999-2002

	1999 Cohort		2000 Cohort		2001 Cohort		2002 Cohort	
	FLC	Non-FLC	FLC	Non-FLC	FLC	Non-FLC	FLC	Non-FLC
	($n = 295$)	($n = 1,465$)	($n = 432$)	($n = 1,650$)	($n = 572$)	($n = 1,570$)	($n = 677$)	($n = 1,882$)
Fall 1999 Term GPA	2.72***	2.38						
Fall 2000 Cum GPA	2.70*	2.61	2.87***	2.47				
Fall 2001 Cum GPA	2.79*	2.70	2.74**	2.63	2.96***	2.67		
Fall 2002 Cum GPA	2.86*	2.79	2.77	2.72	2.87**	2.78	2.91***	2.61

* $p < .05$

** $p < .01$

*** $p < .001$

Table 2

Percent of Students Retained, Learning Communities versus Non-Learning Communities, 1999-2002

	1999 Cohort (N = 1,760)			2000 Cohort (N = 2,082)			2001 Cohort (N = 2,142)			2002 Cohort (N = 2,559)		
	FLC (*n* = 295)	Non-FLC (*n* = 1,465)	All	FLC (*n* = 432)	Non-FLC (*n* = 1,650)	All	FLC (*n* = 572)	Non-FLC (*n* = 1,570)	All	FLC (*n* = 677)	Non-FLC (*n* = 1,882)	All
Fall 2000	78.6*	71.9	73.1									
Fall 2001	65.4	60.8	61.6	86.6***	77.9	79.7						
Fall 2002	60.0*	54.0	55.0	69.7**	62.4	63.9	86.5***	78.9	81.0			
Fall 2003	41.3*	38.3	38.9	64.1**	55.9	57.6	75.9***	67.5	69.7	96.6***	91.9	93.1

* $p < .05$

** $p < .01$

*** $p < .001$

Lessons Learned at Georgia State

The integrated activities, reflection, and synthesis of GSU 1010 is the mortar that holds the FLC together. Future plans include continuing to develop the first-year seminar as the keystone for building an interdisciplinary program. The institution hopes to increase faculty development efforts with continued emphasis on integration of the curriculum and is exploring the pros and cons of making the first-year seminar course and/or the FLC mandatory.

The efforts to build a program that weaves first-year seminars into learning communities have yielded important lessons that guide decision-making as the program evolves and grows. These lessons include:

1. *Encouraging academic faculty from various disciplines to teach the first-year seminar along with their content area course within the learning community.* This is important to broaden the base of support across campus and to increase the interdisciplinary nature of the FLCs themselves. At Georgia State, 24 of the 33 seminars (73%) in FLCs for fall 2003 were taught by academic faculty.
2. *Encouraging the instructor of the first-year seminar to serve in the role of advisor to other instructional members of the FLC.* The instructor of the first-year seminar is often the designer of the FLC and is most aware of how all courses in the community are contributing to the overall theme. Also, the instructor of the first-year seminar can encourage interaction among faculty in the community and foster a team approach to supporting student success.
3. *Creating forums to communicate the benefits to students participating in FLCs.* In particular, Georgia State emphasizes to faculty that the first-year seminar also serves as an excellent opportunity to introduce students to their discipline.
4. *Using a peer review process to encourage buy-in from the faculty.* Faculty members are generally familiar with the peer review process as applied to research publication and application of grants. The competitive nature of submitting proposals communicates rigorous standards and the degree to which the administration values participation in the program.
5. *Giving the first-year seminar the same weight as other courses in a teacher's work load.* Conveying the fact that teaching a first-year seminar is equal to teaching any course has been important.

6. *Providing faculty with a well-developed curriculum for the first-year seminar that they can easily supplement with their own materials and expertise.*
7. *Providing faculty with additional support through student services representatives who make presentations in the first-year seminar on co-curricular issues.*
8. *Conducting regular meetings for faculty of the first-year seminar to share successes and challenges and to facilitate involvement in the FLC program.*
9. *Encouraging instructors of the first-year seminar to participate in the process of integrating course curriculum through summer stipends or course releases.*
10. *Continually evaluating and assessing the effect of first-year seminars and FLCs with data that can be shared with the University community to encourage support of and participation in the program.*

The learning communities at Georgia State University have been institutionalized through a careful process of defining goals, understanding the needs of the institution's student population, encouraging widespread involvement of faculty members and staff, and evaluating and assessing multiple aspects of the program. A hallmark of the program is the first-year seminar as anchor and primary site of learning integration and community building.

References

American Association for Higher Education, American College Personnel Association, and National Association of Student Personnel Administrators. (1998). *Powerful partnerships: A shared responsibility for learning.* Washington, DC: Authors.

Association of American Colleges, Project on Liberal Learning, Study-in-Depth, and the Arts and Sciences Major. (1991). *The challenge of connecting learning.* Washington, DC: Author.

Barefoot, B. O., Fidler, D. S., Gardner, J. N, Moore, P. S., & Roberts, M. R. (1999). In J. H. Levine (Ed.), *Learning communities: New structures, new partnerships for learning* (Monograph No. 26) (pp. 77-86). Columbia, SC: University of South Carolina, National Resource Center for The First-Year Experience and Students in Transition.

Barefoot, B. O., Warnock, C. L., Dickinson, M. P., Richardson, S. E., & Roberts, M. R. (Eds.). (1998). *Exploring the evidence: Reporting the outcomes of first-year seminars, Vol. II* (Monograph No. 25). Columbia, SC: University of South Carolina, National Resource Center for The First-Year Experience and Students in Transition.

Boyer Commission on Educating Undergraduates in the Research University. (1998). *Reinventing undergraduate education: A blueprint for America's research universities.* Stony Brook, NY: State University of New York at Stony Brook.

Bystrom, V. (2002). Teaching on the edge: Interdisciplinary teaching in learning communities. In C. Haynes (Ed.), *Innovations in interdisciplinary teaching* (pp. 67-93). Westport, CT: Oryx Press.

Gabelnick, F., MacGregor, J., Matthews, R. S., & Smith, R. S. (1990). *Learning communities: Creating connections among students, faculty, and disciplines.* (New Directions for Teaching and Learning No. 41). San Francisco: Jossey-Bass.

Hotchkiss, J. L., Moore, R. E., & Pitts, M. M. (2003). *Freshmen learning communities, college performance, and retention.* Unpublished manuscript, Georgia State University.

Shapiro, N. S., & Levine, J. H. (1999). *Creating learning communities: A practical guide to winning support, organizing for change, and implementing programs.* San Francisco: Jossey-Bass.

Tinto, V. (1996). Reconstructing the first year of college. *Planning for Higher Education, 25,* 1-6.

Vars, G. F. (1993). *Interdisciplinary teaching: Why and how.* Columbus, OH: National Middle School Association.

Appendix A
Themes of Freshman Learning Communities—Fall, 2003

1. African-American Culture and History
2. Art and Design
3. Business and Technology
4. Business of Health Care
5. Business, Risk, and Society
6. Career Choices and Life Options
7. Chemistry: Introduction to the Natural Sciences
8. City Life: Exploring Atlanta
9. Communication, Culture, and Stereotypes
10. Conflict Resolution in the 21st Century
11. Crime: Society's Response
12. Emerging Leaders I
13. Emerging Leaders II
14. Exploring Diversity
15. Global Business and Society
16. Health Professional
17. Honors I
18. Honors II
19. Internet and the Information Age
20. International Business Practices
21. Introduction to Business and Finance
22. Language and International Business
23. Language and Intercultural Communications
24. Latin American and Latino Studies
25. Law and Society
26. Pre-Med
27. Promoting a Healthy GSU
28. Quantitative Sciences
29. Residential Emerging Leaders I: A Village Learning Community
30. Residential Emerging Leaders II: A Village Learning Community
31. Strategic Thinking and Learning
32. Understanding Social Change
33. Understanding Yourself and Others

Appendix B
Generic Syllabus—GSU 1010: New Student Orientation

Course Description:
GSU 1010 is designed to retain new students and help them make a successful transition to university life. The course will provide students with essential information about the academic demands of the University, its rules, procedures, and resources and will introduce students to academic, social, and personal survival skills that contribute to academic success. The course curriculum will encourage students to establish supportive relationships with peers and faculty and will help them become part of the academic community. Students will read and learn about study strategies, group dynamics, GSU history and policies, Atlanta history, nutrition, and urban pollution.

GSU 1010 is a three-hour course that will count as an elective and not as part of the 120-hour degree requirement. Based on student performance, a grade of A, B, C, D, or F will be awarded upon completion of the course. The grade for GSU 1010 will be computed in the student's Grade Point Average (GPA).

Course Goals:
1. To introduce students to the procedures and resources of the University and help them become proficient in using them
2. To teach academic, social, and personal survival skills which are essential to success at college
3. To provide students with a supportive community of peers who will assist them in their transition to college
4. To help students improve communication skills in both speaking and listening
5. To help students clarify their career objectives and provide guidance as they explore and select a major
6. To encourage student involvement in the extra-curricular intellectual, cultural, and recreational activities of the University
7. To encourage responsible citizenship in the local community
8. To provide students with a faculty mentor
9. To introduce students to the library and the Internet
10. To help students follow directions and complete projects in a timely manner using university resources
11. To help students strengthen writing skills in a variety of formats

Required Text:
Achieving Personal and Academic Success by Petrie, T. A., Pinkenburg Landry, L., and Bobinski Edwards, K. (1998)

Required Materials:
Notebook/Portfolio, GSU Catalog
Daily Planner/On Campus Student Planner

Class Attendance:
Hopefully, you will not miss a single GSU 1010 class. The absentee policy for GSU 1010 is very firm. Attendance is based on the entire period. Students accumulating more than two absences will be withdrawn from the course and will be assigned either a W, if the withdrawal is before

the midpoint, or a WF if the withdrawal is after the midpoint. Absolutely no exception to this attendance policy is envisioned. If an exception is requested, the instructor cannot make the decision.

Responsibility for Assignments:
Class time will not be used to distribute handouts from previous class meetings. Please obtain these from the instructor before or after class. Use e-mail to request handouts, if possible. Students are responsible for all assignments. In the case of an absence, it is the student's responsibility to seek clarification so that work is prepared for the next class meeting. Please record the names, phone numbers, and e-mails of several classmates to call for help.

All assignments should be turned in on time. If an assignment cannot be personally turned in, assignments can be e-mailed to the instructor, faxed, or delivered to the instructor's office. If an assignment is late, points will be deducted for each day past the due date.

Portfolio Maintenance:
Each student will be responsible for maintaining all materials and written assignments in an organized notebook.

Grading System:
Grades will be calculated according to the point system. The explanation of the point system describes the total number of possible points for the assignment. Grades will reflect the quality of the work, and inadequate assignments will not receive the maximum number of points.

Academic Honesty:
As members of an academic community, students are expected to be honest. Students are expected to submit their own work, to report only on what they attended, and to conduct themselves in an honest manner. Students who do not follow these honorable guidelines will be handled in a manner explained in the GSU Catalog. Please read the section on The Policy on Academic Honesty and be honest in your submissions for this course.

GSU 1010 Assignments:
Most assignments will be submitted as units, not as separate papers. Each assignment should follow the GSU 1010 guidelines for submission. Points will be deducted for variations.

- Written Personal Responsibility Assessment
  - Reason for Attending College (essay format)
  - Time Management Assessment (essay format)
  - Personal Growth Assessment (letter format)
- Career Planning Unit
  - Personality Type Inventory Print-Out
  - Academic Advisement Certification with Graduation Plan (PACE evaluation)
  - Current Résumé
  - Résumé Cover Letter
  - Interview Follow-Up Letter
- Technology Proficiency Unit
  - E-mail Assignments
  - Library Literacy Assignments

- Community Service Unit
  - Community Service Reflection
  - (3-4 hours at GSU approved site)
- Campus Exploration Unit
  - Campus Educational/Cultural Activities
  - Campus Entertainment Activity/Club Membership
  - Campus Sports Activity
  - Campus Workshop/Touch the Earth/Historic Site
  - GSU Walking Tour
- Classroom Presentation
- Midterm Exam (multiple-choice, essay, and take home items)
- Final Exam (multiple-choice, essay, and take home items)

Appendix C
Curriculum Options for GSU 1010: New Student Orientation

Self (include at least 2)
- Sexual assault
- Alcohol awareness
- Nutrition and wellness
- Stress management

Self and Others (include at least 2)
- Group dynamics
- Team building
- Personality types
- Conflict resolution
- Public speaking

Academic Environment (include at least 4)
- Library orientation/technology proficiency*
- Study strategies
- Written assessments
- Financial aid*
- Expectations in college
- Academic advisement/career planning*
- Academic integrity*
- Campus exploration

Community (include at least 2)
- Service-learning*
- Cultural diversity*
- GSU/Atlanta history
- International opportunities

*Essential topics that should be addressed in every GSU 1010

Appendix D
Funding for the Freshman Learning Community

Faculty Grants for Development of Integrated Curriculum

Year	Number of Proposals Submitted	Number of Proposals Funded	Total Funding of Summer Stipends
1999	10	8	$32,000
2000	10	8	$36,000
2001	11	9	$44,000
2002	11	9	$57,750
2003	16	12	$60,000

Note. In 1999, $20,000 was funded by the Office of the Provost with $12,000 in cost sharing by the colleges (entire amounts funded by the Provost in subsequent years).

Serving Students Through Multiple Learning Community Models

Howard N. Shapiro
Iowa State University

Chapter 7

The learning communities program at Iowa State University began in the early 1990s as a localized effort of some faculty and staff and has grown into a thriving multiple-model program that enrolls approximately half of the first-year class. Currently, students are enrolled in a wide variety of learning communities, from those designed for specific academic majors to general residential programs. In the 2002-2003 academic year, 2,139 students participated in 46 communities organized into 119 teams. Assessments indicate that learning communities at Iowa State provide students with myriad academic and social benefits. All these communities hold in common an interest in offering students an experience that integrates their academic and social lives. Many of these communities offer this integration through a variety of first-year seminars, while others embed this integration directly into pre-existing courses linked in the learning communities. How this integration occurs, either as part of a separate seminar or in other courses, is central to the discussion in this chapter.

Throughout the life of its learning communities, Iowa State has worked to institutionalize the grassroots effort without squelching the enthusiasm among early innovators. Innovations often begin with individuals and groups who invariably first work outside the existing structure of the institution. If the innovation begins to take hold, it quickly can create conflict with existing structures, and its further growth requires institutional change. How the institution responds to such change has a significant impact on the success of the innovation. Indeed, the University enhances innovation and improvement whenever it fosters such change by coordinating the formal parts of the institution with the informal networks and venues for accomplishing tasks.

Embedding Learning Communities in Wider Change

Iowa State University, established in 1868 as one of the nation's first land-grant institutions, has a traditional focus on teaching and learning. Approximately 23,000 undergraduates and 5,000 graduate students are enrolled at the institution. The University offers a wide range of programs through its nine colleges, embodying the three-part mission of learning, discovery, and engagement. Iowa State is a Carnegie Doctoral/Research Extensive institution and a member of the Association of American Colleges and Universities. The University is primarily residential, with more than 80% of new undergraduates coming directly from high school. Located in Ames, Iowa, the University admits all students who qualify, based on college entrance test scores or a minimum high school rank of 50%. Approximately 70% of the student body are from Iowa, 20% are non-Iowa U.S. students, and 10% are international. Iowa State enrolls approximately 8% underrepresented ethnic minority students. The average time to degree is about 4.5 years, and the six-year graduation rate is approximately 65%.

Learning communities at Iowa State had their origins in efforts to increase the focus on teaching and learning, particularly in undergraduate education. A small number of faculty members from across campus were aware of and involved in the national movement to become more learner-centered by delineating learning outcomes, using active learning methods, and using assessment to enhance student learning. The Center for Teaching Excellence was established in 1993 to promote learning and the scholarship of teaching and learning on campus. The provost appointed task forces in 1994 to study rewards for teaching, teaching innovation, and student services. Also in 1994, faculty in the Colleges of Education and Engineering teamed up to organize small groups of faculty to study teaching and learning principles, try new approaches in their classrooms, and support each other as they learned new ideas. That grassroots effort led to Project LEA/RN which is still active on campus (Licklider, Schnelker, & Fulton, 1997).

The provost's task force focusing on student services mirrored a parallel development in the Division of Student Affairs. The task force report called for several enhancements in student services and increased coordination between academic and student affairs units, both centrally and among the various colleges. This led the provost to increase attention on student life issues and to resource allocations that enhanced student services. These efforts reflect the decade-long movement within student affairs to recognize the crucial role residence systems and student support programs play in the academic success of students. Iowa State's residence halls established an academic unit that brought significant attention to academics and created a solid base of support for the learning communities movement. Beginning in the late 1990s, the residence system underwent a complete overhaul of its physical facilities and academic programs. Also, increased focus on academic success by the dean of students provided a strong underpinning for such activities as service-learning and leadership development that have augmented the work of learning communities.

The University program for student outcomes assessment, the development of a revised promotion and tenure policy, the creation of the position of vice provost for undergraduate programs, and the adoption of the University's strategic plans with strong goals in the area of undergraduate education are other important efforts contributing to the development of the learning communities program. Student outcomes assessment for all academic programs have been mandated by the Iowa Board of Regents since 1994. The Board also requires student outcomes assessment reports when each academic program undergoes its periodic academic review. Initially, the development and implementation of the plans were overseen by the Student Outcomes Assessment Committee, led by a faculty coordinator who reported to the provost's office. With the inception of the vice provost position in 1998, the function has moved into that office and is overseen by an assistant vice provost and a group of academic associate deans from each college.

In 1997, the University administration and the Faculty Senate began to develop in earnest a new tenure and promotion document based on Boyer's model of scholarship (Boyer, 1997). The existing document at the time called for identifying one area of scholarly excellence (i.e., research, teaching, or outreach) and tying promotion and tenure to establishing excellence in this area, while showing competence in the other two. The new policy established the principle that scholarship was expected to be balanced among disciplinary research, teaching, and outreach based on an individual position responsibility statement developed jointly between the faculty member and the academic department. Under the new policy, adopted in 1999, scholarship is expected and recognized in all areas of a person's academic assignment. This policy has paved the way for an enhanced focus on teaching and the scholarship of teaching and learning, which has helped to foster increased faculty involvement in learning communities.

The vice provosts for undergraduate programs, research, and extension, respectively, oversee the three main missions of Iowa State in learning, discovery, and engagement. The undergraduate position was created in 1998, signaling the University's commitment to enhancing teaching and learning. Successive University strategic plans covering 1995-2000 and 2000-2005 have emphasized enhanced student learning and success. Benchmarks were established and tracked, and resources were allocated to support the strategic plan goals.

Thus, the 1990s provided fertile ground in which to nurture a grassroots effort to develop learning communities. The University has faced several challenges along the way, and many continue. In particular, establishing a true culture that focuses on learning at a multifaceted university is an ongoing issue. Learning communities have contributed greatly to the development of such a culture at Iowa State, and their success has been due, in part, to a sustained effort by the University to foster such a cultural transformation.

The Development of Learning Communities

This section provides a brief summary of the key aspects of learning communities at Iowa State. Much of this information is also described in documents on the Iowa State University (2003) learning communities web site and in case studies presented by Lenning and Ebbers (1999) and Huba, Ellertson, Cook, and Epperson (2003).

Two developments in particular were responsible for the learning communities program at Iowa State. The first was a visit by Vincent Tinto in the fall of 1994, sponsored by the higher education graduate program. Tinto's seminars and meetings with key faculty and staff provided the theoretical and empirical underpinnings to the conversation that had already begun on campus. His visit set the stage for further discussions among early innovators on campus about how learning communities could enhance student learning and increase student satisfaction and retention. The initial group included education faculty, the director of the newly formed Center for Teaching Excellence, and personnel from the Registrar's Office and the Orientation and Retention Program in Student Life.

The second development was the Department of Residence Life's increased interest, beginning in the early 1990s, to support the institution's academic mission. The departmental leadership at that time became aware of residence-based academic programs, such as Freshman Interest Groups (FIGs), being developed at other universities. The department began to increase its focus on academic programming and recruited and trained staff who would expand their repertoire beyond social and personal development.

By 1994, the undergraduate colleges agreed to establish clustered course programs, many of which included residential components. By the fall of 1995, each college had established a learning community activity. Over the next two years, initial assessments on student retention and satisfaction indicated that the fledgling program was beginning to show success. However, the grassroots aspect of the effort began to encounter some difficulties as those, who had put so much personal energy into them, were starting to look for increased support and encouragement. Lenning and Ebbers (1999) list a number of challenges the program faced at that time:

- Lack of time to focus on long-term development of assessment
- Lack of knowledge and expertise in learning communities and their assessment and evaluation
- Perception that time devoted to teaching in learning communities would adversely affect promotion and tenure
- Lack of financial support and release time
- Challenges with scheduling
- Inability to orient students in how to be effective learners in the learning community setting
- Lack of planning time for faculty to collaborate on course development

In 1997-98, the provost established the Learning Communities Working Group to address these challenges and take the program to a new level. The position of vice provost for undergraduate programs was created during the spring of 1998 and was responsible for expanding learning communities and increasing coordination between academic and student affairs. Further, the University president at that time, impressed with retention data associated with learning communities, decided to fund a three-year, $1.5 million initiative to support a plan developed by the provost, vice president for student affairs, and the Learning Communities Working Group.

An administrative team was assembled and asked to expand the learning communities program based on what had been learned to that point, to carefully assess the academic impact, and to report annually for the three-year trial period. At the end of the three-year initiative, a determination would be made whether or not to formalize the budget.

Early in the implementation process, a decision was made that, for programs to qualify as learning communities, they would have to include both an integrative course-based experience and a social support component. The principal belief was that socially based learning community programs or course-based programs each have value in their own right, but programs that incorporate both and assess them as a whole would achieve a synergy that would lead to even better results for students.

The director of the Center for Teaching Excellence and the assistant director of residence were charged with providing day-to-day administrative leadership. They paid careful attention to encouraging and enhancing existing college-level efforts, expanding participation of students and faculty, and better coordinating the logistics of the multiple-model program. In addition, a comprehensive assessment effort was developed to provide the basis for continuous improvement and to document success. Several components were added, including:

- *Peer mentors.* Support was provided to hire peer mentors based on a formula of 1 peer mentor for every 16 learning community students. These peers provide direct academic and social support to the students in the learning community.
- *Grants program.* Annual grants were awarded to support social activities, field trips, assessment plans, and other program expenses. The grants did not provide salary support, as it was felt that the program could not be sustained unless departments and colleges felt the learning communities were important enough to devote their own resources to them for staffing.
- *Committee structure.* A steering committee and several standing sub-committees were established to obtain input and provide guidance. The committee structure involved more than 50 people, including faculty, staff, administrators, graduate, and undergraduate students. The assessment subcommittee was perhaps the most critical subcommittee, since the future of funding for the program depended on the results of its findings.
- *Administrative support.* About 15% of the budget provided administrative support for the wide array of activities necessary to sustain learning communities. This support went to the Registrar's office for scheduling and data gathering, the Department of Residence for assessment and programming efforts, and additional assessment support for the assessment subcommittee.
- *Faculty and staff development.* An important component of the initial program was to encourage a variety of approaches to professional development. Funding enabled groups and individuals to attend national meetings and conferences. Faculty and staff presented scholarly work related to their learning community activities and became involved in national organizations. In addition, in the spring of each year, the campus held a Learning Communities Institute. The institutes have attracted between 120 and 150 faculty and staff annually. Each year, one or more well-known keynote speakers gives a national perspective, and sessions have been devoted to highlighting successes, sharing lessons learned, and planning in individual groups.

As illustrated in Figure 1, the number of learning communities offered and student participation in them has doubled since 1998. However, the issues identified by Lenning and Ebbers (1999) are still present. Maintaining faculty and staff enthusiasm, with many other activities on their collective plates, continues to be a challenge.

Integrating Learning Through Multiple Community Approaches

The definition of learning communities used at this institution is inclusive. However, all recognized learning communities at Iowa State have some form of integrative course component, which is further supported outside class.   Academic and social issues, often central to a traditional first-year seminar, are addressed in seminars specifically designed for that purpose and attached in learning communities or, as noted earlier, embedded directly in pre-existing learning community courses. Learning communities are variously organized around specific courses, programs of study, or academic themes, and about a third have residential components. Most target first-year students, but the concept also applies to sophomore and upper-level programs.

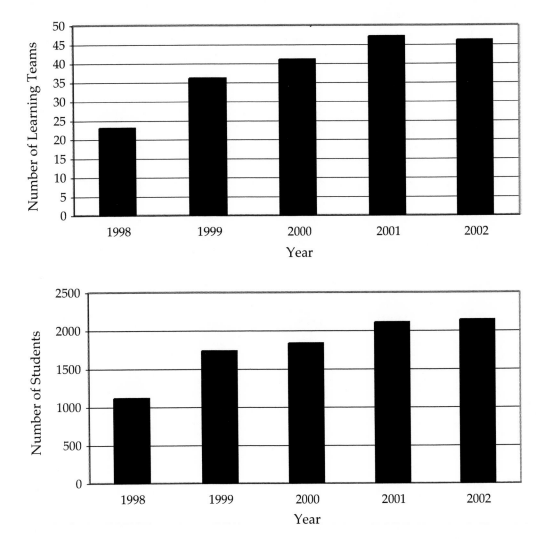

Figure 1. Learning community growth at Iowa State University, 1999-2002. From Shapiro, H. (2003). *Enhancing grassroots efforts through creation of institutional support structures.* Retrieved from: http://www.iastate.edu/~learncommunity/2003AssessmentPlenary.pdf

The multiplicity of approaches includes students co-enrolled in courses as part of larger enrollments, learning community students comprising the entire enrollment in one or more sections of a course, and students enrolling in two or more courses in different disciplines with strong integration of the course content and cooperation among the instructors.

All learning communities at Iowa State have articulated learning objectives, and they require annual assessments of how well those objectives were achieved and how assessment results are being used to improve the program. The most common objectives across learning communities include improvement of academic success skills, social adjustment, and career awareness and exploration. In addition, all learning communities must have an identified integrative concept that cuts across their component parts. Many use integrative first-year seminars to help achieve their learning objectives. Another integrative approach is the use of peer mentors. All peer mentor job descriptions include time for small-group interactions with learning community students related to achieving the particular community's learning objectives. Learning community coordinators and peer mentors organize study groups, field trips, guest speakers, social activities, and community service projects. Each learning community includes at least one instructional faculty member on its team.

The four most prevalent types of linkage between courses, as described more fully by Slagell, Faass, and LaWare (2002), are summarized below. This summary moves from the least to most integrated learning community type.

Course Clustering

In this model, students in a learning community schedule two or more classes together, but the instructors make no special effort to coordinate the curriculum or assignments and may not even be aware that learning community student cohorts are enrolled. Peer mentors and learning community coordinators work outside class to provide academic and social support. This model can lead to enhanced learning, but it has several disadvantages. Without a curricular link, the instructors do not attempt to coordinate the courses, and the opportunity for deeper, more connected learning is not seized. Also, the presence of a cohort of learning community students can create behavioral issues in the classroom.

Course Links

This model is similar to clustering, but the added feature is that the instructors are aware of the common learning community cohort in their classes, and they make some effort to communicate by sharing syllabi and being cognizant of what the students are doing in the other class. Even minimal sharing of information and acknowledgment by the instructors that the courses are linked add to the depth of learning and help students see some of the linkages among their courses. Also, sharing syllabi provides an opportunity for instructors to make sure that major assignments are not due at the same time.

Enhanced Course Link

This variation encourages even closer coordination among instructors than either of the first two. The instructors develop linked assignments and make periodic visits to each other's classes. Because of the closer connection at the course level, the out-of-class support can be better coordinated and focused on the desired learning outcomes. This concept is applicable to upper-division and first-year courses. Applying this in large section classes can be problematic if the learning community cohorts make up only a small fraction of the course enrollment.

Enhanced Course Linkages with a Seminar

In this model, student cohorts schedule two or three classes together. The discipline-based courses can be large or small section courses as long as they have enhanced links. In addition, the students all participate in a seminar/discussion session every week that is planned and facilitated by the instructors in the linked courses. This seminar/discussion section provides an environment that deepens student learning, develops integrative assignments, and encourages team teaching. Some use the seminar as a way to explore career issues or expose students to research in the field. Of course, this model requires additional resources to allow for planning time and team teaching.

Learning Community Examples

The programs described below illustrate the range of what constitute learning communities at Iowa State as well as the common academic and social features. Each of these communities includes at least one component, such as a seminar or peer mentor, that integrates elements of the entire experience.

Biology Education Success Teams (BEST). This cross-disciplinary learning community is designed for incoming students in the biological sciences. Students enroll in linked courses in English and biology as well as an orientation class. A variety of optional activities support developing their academic skills, exploring fields of study in the biological sciences, and enhancing their academic and social integration into the University. Peer and faculty mentors work with the students, and some choose to participate in service-learning activities related to environmental awareness and applying classroom learning to the natural surroundings.

Design Exchange. This is a residentially based learning community for 100 first-year students in the College of Design. Design students live on residence hall floors with approximately 50% of the students enrolled in other colleges, so they develop a variety of friendships. The design students share a common studio space and computer laboratory in the residence hall and have two upper-class design students as live-in peer mentors. They participate in a required seminar course each semester and some take a common English class. The seminar stresses portfolio development, sketchbooks, creativity, internships, study abroad, and the clarification of personal career goals.

Business Learning Teams (BLT). The Business Learning Teams are groups of business students who enroll in the same sections of three courses and reside near one another on campus. Students are placed in teams based on their residence and their course placement at orientation. Many of the courses are linked by some integrated content. One of the most common linkages is an English composition course. The students meet during the New Student Days Program before fall semester. The teams include student, faculty, and staff mentors.

WiSE Living Option. Approximately 200 women in science and engineering choose to participate in the WiSE living and learning option. Incoming women majoring in various sciences and engineering fields live together on the WiSE residence floors, attend classes together, and participate in group study sessions. Peer mentors and staff organize academic and social activities, such as seminars on interviewing and résumé writing, industry tours, tutoring, Big Sis/Little Sis mentoring, outside speakers, and faculty dinners. Assessment over many years indicates that WiSE contributes positively to the success of women in fields of engineering and science where they are underrepresented.

Assessing Multiple Learning Community Models

A number of key assessments were completed during the pilot years, leading to the eventual formalization of the learning community budget within the institution. See Huba et al. (2003) for details. Student surveys, including experimental and control groups, were instituted in 1998 and have evolved through various iterations to provide information about students' perception of their abilities in career awareness, knowledge of the discipline, teamwork, time management, critical thinking/problem solving, written and oral communication, leadership, and diversity. Other items assessed include the students' use of time, their most positive and negative experiences, and the learning community students' evaluation of their peer mentors. Key outcomes are summarized in Table 1.

Table 1
Key Outcomes of Learning Communities

Learning community students are more likely than control group students to:	• Earn higher grades • Have a professor with high expectations • Understand the nature of their anticipated major • Have experiences that helped them reach their goals • Receive prompt feedback about progress • Feel satisfied with the overall quality of their classmates • Feel satisfied with their overall experience at Iowa State • See connections among classmates • See connections between personal experiences and classroom learning
Learning community students are more satisfied with their opportunities to:	• Interact closely with faculty • Receive advice and support from faculty • Participate in clubs, organizations, and student government • Practice their skills • Apply learning to real world problems • Interact with people from different cultural backgrounds
Learning community students spend more time:	• Studying in groups • Participating in community service/volunteer work
Learning community students have significantly higher first-term grade point averages, even when controlling statistically for ACT and high school rank, than those of the control group.	

These findings support the theory that learning community participation leads to enhanced student achievement. These data are continuously collected and analyzed, and they provide a useful adjunct to other academic measures, such as data from National Survey of Student Engagement that have been collected for several years.

Retention data have been collected and analyzed on an ongoing basis. Figure 2 offers raw retention data collected after the first through fourth years for first-time, full-time, first-year students entering fall 1998. This is the first group for which four years of data have been collected. The graphs compare return percentages for learning community students and non-learning community students. Analyses of the data done by Epperson (2000) demonstrate that the learning community students are retained at significantly higher rates than the non-learning community students, even when adjustments are made for the college entrance examination scores and high school ranks of the students. The adjusted data still show a first-year retention difference between the learning community and non-learning community students of five to six percentage points, and the four-year result for the 1998 class is eight percentage points. These trends have persisted with groups entering since 1998 as well.

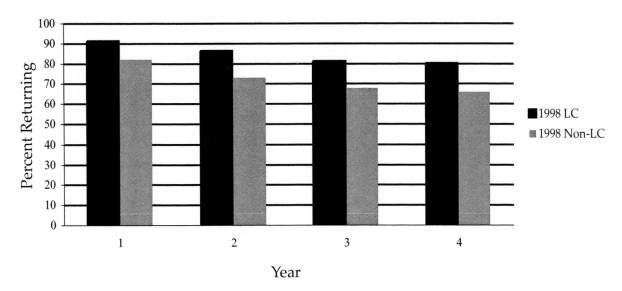

Figure 2. Retention rates for first-time, full-time freshmen entering fall, 1998.

Epperson (2000) developed a method for using adjusted retention data to make estimates of the return on investment of the $1.5 million put toward the learning communities initiative. While an argument that learning communities are solely responsible for retention increases would be specious, an assertion can be made that the program is one of many possible players in increased retention rates and an associated increase in revenues. The main factor considered by Epperson was the tuition revenue for the additional students retained, projected each year as the cohorts moved through the system. The estimates did not account for additional revenues from items such as fees, residence hall contracts, or bookstore sales. Epperson (2000) reported that from 1998-1999 through 2000-2001 increased retention resulted in $2.5 million in increased tuition revenue to the University.

Armed with the results of the student surveys and the retention analyses, the learning communities administrative group proposed formalizing the learning communities program in spring 2001. The interim president accepted the proposal, and despite difficult financial challenges, he established a permanent base budget in excess of $650,000 to support grants, peer mentors, assessment, faculty and staff development, and administration of the learning communities program. This budget is jointly administered by the vice provost for undergraduate programs and the vice president for student affairs.

Conclusion

Iowa State University has developed a wide variety of experiences for students that are classified as learning communities. The variety is characteristic of the grassroots origin of the concept on campus and the diversity of perspectives and priorities that exists across colleges at a large university. However, the commonalities among the programs—integrative learning themes and course experiences, peer mentors, a focus on academic and social development, and faculty involvement—make this complex undertaking a success. Assessment data bears out the efficacy of these traits for increased retention, student achievement, and student satisfaction.

The inclusive definition of learning communities at Iowa State allows for a wide variety of integrative academic components. Data suggest that no single first-year integrative seminar model stands out as the best. The philosophy of Iowa State's learning communities is to support multiple, department and college-based models and to provide institutional coordination that enhances, rather than overwhelms, those local efforts.

The learning communities program at Iowa State has progressed through several stages. Initially, the effort was highly localized, with individuals and small groups working together. As the program grew, it reached a critical stage where many initiatives could have failed. The enthusiasm and excitement of the initial activity could have waned if institutional barriers had become overwhelming. Because of strong presidential leadership and the broader context in which change was occurring, the program was able to withstand these challenges and become stronger. These efforts have received institutional recognition, and people have felt rewarded for their contributions.

The challenge now facing Iowa State is one of continued acceptance and integration. Some of the curricular challenges include solidifying and assessing general education learning outcomes, renewing and refreshing faculty involvement, enhancing the use of peer mentors, using instructional technology more effectively to enhance learning, developing upper-level learning communities, and increasing the use of active learning strategies by faculty. In addition, learning communities still need to be more fully integrated into the planning at the college and department levels. Finally, although the promotion and tenure policy rewards scholarly teaching, more recognition is needed for the value of high-quality scholarship of teaching and learning.

References

Boyer, E. (1997). *Scholarship reconsidered: Priorities of the professoriate.* San Francisco: Jossey-Bass.

Epperson, D. L. (2000). *Report on one-year and two-year university retention rates associated with first-year participation in a learning community at Iowa State University.* Retrieved October 7, 2003, from http://www.iastate.edu/~learncommunity/templates/retentionf00.pdf

Huba, M. E., Ellertson, S., Cook, M. D., & Epperson, D. L. (2003). Assessment's role in transforming a grass-roots initiative into an institutionalized program: Evaluating and shaping learning communities at Iowa State University. In J. McGregor (Ed.), *Learning community assessment: Four campus stories.* Washington, DC: American Association for Higher Education.

Iowa State University. (2003). *Learning communities.* Retrieved October 7, 2003, from http://www.iastate.edu/~learncommunity/

Lenning, O. T., & Ebbers, L. H. (1999). The powerful potential of learning communities. (ASHE-ERIC Higher Education Reports No. 26.6) (pp. 70-75). Washington, DC: The George Washington University, Clearinghouse on Higher Education.

Licklider, B. L., Schnelker, D. L., & Fulton, C. (1997). Revisioning faculty development for changing times: Foundation and framework. *Journal of Staff, Program, and Organizational Development, 15*(3), 121-133.

Slagell, A. R., Faass, I. P., & LaWare, M. R. (2002). *Suggestions for curricular course linkages: Report of the Iowa State University learning communities curriculum development and enhancement subcommittee.* Retrieved January 24, 2004, from http://www.iastate.edu/~learncommunity/LC%20Models%20final%20revision.pdf

Introducing the Liberal Arts Through a Multi-Layered First-Year Studies Program

Leslie Bessant, Diane Mockridge, and Deano Pape

Ripon College

Located in south-central Wisconsin, Ripon College is a selective, private liberal arts college enrolling approximately 275 to 300 new students each year and offering bachelor of arts degrees. While the college attracts students from all over the country, most students come from Wisconsin, Illinois, and Minnesota. More than 75% of the college's students live on campus.

Ripon's curriculum emphasizes an interdisciplinary approach to liberal arts education. The college's vision statement reflects this curricular emphasis:

> Ripon College enrolls, educates, and graduates women and men from diverse backgrounds who can benefit from membership in a community dedicated to the fullest development of the whole person, through a curriculum in the liberal arts and sciences integrated with extensive residential and extra-curricular programs. … The liberal arts tradition … maintains that students should be provided an understanding of the ideas, approaches, and particular skills of a variety of academic disciplines, and that they be made aware of the differences and similarities in the approaches of the disciplines to the analysis and understanding of the issues and problems of human concern. (Ripon College, 2003-2004a, p. 1)

In keeping with the college's vision, Ripon's First-Year Studies program (FYS) has been designed to introduce new students to the interdisciplinary aspects of a liberal arts education, while at the same time easing their transition from high school to college. The FYS program replaced Ripon College's initial first-year seminar, Interdisciplinary Studies 199 (IDS 199), a one-credit, half-semester course. The faculty agreed that IDS 199 seemed to help students make the transition from high school to college, but the faculty did not like the structure of IDS 199. The course was based on a common syllabus, and faculty who taught the course had to lead discussions on readings and activities that were far outside their areas of expertise. The faculty appreciated the interdisciplinary aims behind IDS 199, but they felt that teaching so far outside their fields undermined the academic rigor of the course. Student evaluations also revealed that IDS 199 lacked academic rigor. Consequently, the college administration and faculty called on the college's Educational Policy Committee to devise a program to replace IDS 199.

The Educational Policy Committee responded by proposing the current FYS program to the faculty in October 1997. In their rationale for the FYS program, the Educational Policy Committee wrote:

> Based on the experience of IDS 199, we believe that this [FYS] course will work best if the faculty teaching it are drawing on their disciplinary expertise, with the "interdisciplinarity" emerging from the interaction of faculty in different disciplines. It is necessary for the course to be graded so that students take it seriously and have the same expectations for their performance in this as in all their other classes. (Educational Policy Committee, 1997)

The Ripon College faculty approved the FYS program, and the first FYS courses and seminars were offered in the fall of 1998.

The interdisciplinarity of the current FYS program is apparent in the program description in the college catalog:

> The First-Year Studies program (FYS) has two key educational goals. First, FYS will introduce students to the teaching/learning environment at Ripon College. Second, it will prepare students to succeed and thrive at Ripon. FYS emphasizes the nature and benefits of a liberal education, and so provides a firm foundation for students as they choose their majors and build their college careers. . . . All FYS seminars will be composed of two or more courses [on a shared topic]; these courses will periodically meet together as a [combined] seminar to share their findings, discoveries, and ideas. All FYS seminars will be interdisciplinary in order to help students see how their liberal education will bring different fields of knowledge together. (Ripon College, 2003-2004b, p. 80)

The FYS program engages students in three different settings:

1. *FYS courses.* These mandatory, discipline-based courses have been carefully designed to introduce students to the course instructor's discipline, college-level academic skills, and the interdisciplinary nature of the liberal arts. Each FYS course also introduces new students to Ripon College. The First-Year Studies courses at Ripon College are analogous to first-year academic seminars with variable content on other campuses.
2. *FYS seminars.* These seminars are formed when two or three topically linked FYS courses come together periodically for interdisciplinary discussions and activities. The First-Year Studies seminar is not a course and should not be confused with a first-year seminar. Rather, it is the learning community structure at Ripon College—the vehicle for integrating the content from distinct First-Year Studies courses.
3. *Common meetings of all first-year students.* These meetings amplify the disciplinary and interdisciplinary discussions and activities of the FYS courses and seminars and reiterate the expectations of attendance at a liberal arts institution.

First-Year Studies Courses

Each FYS course introduces students to academic life at Ripon College and requires them to complete four or five formal assignments, such as essays, tests, and group presentations. The course also introduces students to college-level academic skills. The four-credit course is based in an academic discipline and taught by a full-time faculty member with expertise in that discipline. Each course addresses a specific topic, so students can observe how scholars in the instructor's discipline approach the topic.

First-Year Studies Seminars

Each FYS course shares a topic with one or two other FYS courses from other disciplines. Together, the topically linked courses form an FYS seminar. For example, the FYS seminar on "Peoples, Prairies, and Populations" links FYS courses in biology and philosophy; the FYS seminar on "War" links FYS courses in politics and government and psychology. Table 1 lists examples of recent clusters.

The FYS seminars share many of the same goals as learning communities at other institutions, but they differ from standard learning communities in one key feature: The courses do not

Table 1
Examples of Recent FYS Seminars

Topic	FYS Courses
Love	English 175: Literary Love History 175: Love in the Western World Music 175: Love and Eros in the Fine and Performing Arts
War	Psychology 175: Peace Studies Politics and Government 175: The Politics of War and Peace
Peoples, Prairies, and Populations	Philosophy 175: The Land Ethic Biology 175: The Ecology of the Tall Grass Prairie
Living in the Material World	Art 175: Art and the Earth Chemistry 175: Global Chemistry Economics 175: Environmental Economics
Music in Culture	History 175: African Songs, Oral Traditions, and History Music 175: Western Art, Music in Cultural Contexts
Impact of the Media	Exercise Science 175: Sports and the Media Communication 175: Mass-Mediated Communication Psychology 175: Do Media Make Us Who We Are?

enroll a common cohort of students. In fact, a student cannot possibly enroll in more than one FYS course because all FYS courses meet at the same time. Instead, FYS seminars physically bring together the two or three linked courses—each with its own instructor, roster of students, and disciplinary perspective—for 10 to 12 hours during the semester. The seminar meetings allow faculty members to compare and contrast the methods and perspectives of their particular discipline for the students. The seminar meetings also give students the chance to practice making interdisciplinary connections.

First-Year Studies Common Meetings

FYS common meetings bring all first-year students together. The common meetings address issues that pertain to living in a residential college, emphasizing the student's role in a community dedicated to learning and exploring new ideas, and establish the expectation that all members of the college community be treated with respect. Strategies for respecting others are conveyed through meetings focusing on harassment and diversity issues.

Common meetings are held weekly during a time reserved on the college calendar known as the Golden Hour. This hour is available for all-campus speakers, convocations, and other special events. During the first semester, many of the events are dedicated to first-year common meetings, but other students are invited and encouraged to attend in order to connect the entire community with the first-year experience.

Planning and Implementation

The first step in creating an FYS course and seminar is finding a topic that articulates connections and differences among two or three disciplines. A faculty member proposes a topic for an FYS seminar to the FYS coordinator, with some possible interdisciplinary connections. The coordinator takes the proposal to other faculty members and invites them to think about what they can bring to an interdisciplinary conversation on the topic. Interested faculty members contact the person who proposed the topic, and together they discuss how they can build an FYS seminar around the topic.

Once the seminar connections are established, faculty members begin work on their FYS course syllabi. The FYS course requires a greater amount of advance planning than most courses, because the planning occurs on three levels. First, the FYS faculty member has to plan the course content. Second, he or she has to devise and plan seminar meetings and assignments with other faculty members in the FYS seminar. Third, he or she has to incorporate the FYS common meetings between their students and students from other FYS courses, and these meetings must incorporate extended orientation activities (i.e., accessing campus resources, understanding the library).

Designing an FYS course requires the faculty member to introduce students to the discipline and to college-level academic skills at the same time. Faculty members—both inside and outside the FYS program—attend on-campus workshops designed to help them incorporate writing, oral communication, reading, and student group work into their courses and assignments.

FYS faculty members must also decide when and how they will meet as a seminar. When the faculty created the FYS program in 1997, it anticipated that FYS faculty would plan the seminar meetings during the summer, and the college offered a small stipend to acknowledge the extra time and work that would go into planning the seminar meetings. Although the stipends were discontinued in 2001 due to budget constraints, faculty members continue to meet voluntarily, albeit less frequently, with their team members.

Each FYS seminar must meet two guidelines. First, approximately 12% of an FYS course's class time—about 12 hours out of a total of 60—should be devoted to interdisciplinary activities. Secondly, the seminar's interdisciplinary activities should:

- Acquaint students with the different methodologies of the represented disciplines
- Demonstrate how the represented disciplines provide varied perspectives on a common topic
- Help students understand how the disciplines are similar to or different from one another
- Encourage students to evaluate the insights gained from the various discipline-based perspectives

Many faculty members choose to schedule their seminar meetings as two or three "mini-conferences." The mini-conference format allows the entire seminar to meet together for one or two weeks, giving the students—and the faculty—time to engage in serious interdisciplinary discussions. Each course prepares students for the mini-conference through readings, discussions, and short assignments. The mini-conference then serves as the culminating experience and assignment for that unit of the course. Each faculty member can present his or her disciplinary approach to all the students in the seminar and then discuss what he or she sees as the similarities and benefits of the different approaches. Follow-up assignments give students the chance to synthesize and contrast the different approaches of each discipline.

Other faculty members find that their topics and disciplines lend themselves to different formats for seminar meetings. For example, faculty members may exchange classes for a day or two with other FYS faculty. In other cases, faculty debates may be used to engage a particularly controversial issue.

In addition to introducing the instructor's discipline, college-level academic skills, and the interdisciplinary nature of the liberal arts, an FYS course also introduces new students to Ripon College. The FYS coordinator helps FYS faculty incorporate common meetings and orientation activities into the syllabus in ways that support the academic content of the course. Examples of FYS orientation activities for 2002 included:

- Discussion sections of Larry Watson's *Montana 1948* and other common reading experience activities
- Tour of the student services areas on campus
- Diversity workshop
- Library instructional session
- Presentation by students on succeeding at Ripon College
- Presentation on advising, course selection, and the liberal arts
- Assistance with field-trip preparation
- Student end-of-term conference/celebration day
- Common speaker/cultural event for FYS

For example, library instruction might be coupled with a short research assignment, so that the library instruction and the course assignment reinforce each other. In another instance, an introduction to the college's student support services and student life offices might be scheduled for the fifth or sixth week in the semester, so that students will know where to turn for help as they prepare for their midterm tests and papers.

Planning an FYS course syllabus is made possible by the cooperation of the Student Life staff, the librarians, and the college administration. By giving FYS faculty members the freedom to determine how orientation activities are incorporated and when seminar meetings will occur in their courses, the faculty can design courses that maintain a high degree of academic rigor while also introducing students to many aspects of Ripon College.

FYS faculty members have additional allies in outstanding upper-class students who are paid mentors for their FYS courses. Each mentor must either have taken the FYS course he or she is mentoring or be familiar with the fundamental content and perspectives of the course. The mentors receive training in tutoring skills from the director of the Communicating Plus program, a program designed to help students improve their communication and critical thinking skills. The mentors assist the FYS students in a variety of ways, including listening to student presentations, offering advice on papers and other writing assignments, and modeling participation in small-group or class discussions. The mentors attend all the class meetings of their FYS courses, including the common meetings and orientation activities. In addition, each mentor holds two office hours each week at the Communicating Plus center, where FYS students can meet their mentor on a walk-in basis.

The Student's Experience

The overarching goal of the First-Year Studies program is to create a seamless experience for the first-year student, where course, seminar, and common meetings fit together coherently. The student enrolls in a single FYS course, not an FYS seminar. Course enrollment ranges from a minimum of 12 students to a maximum of 20, and the first meeting of the course takes place during new student orientation. As the course progresses, the student learns more about the instructor's discipline and the academic skills he or she will need to succeed in college. When the FYS seminar meets for the first time, the student learns that academic disciplines have more to do with questions and approaches than discrete subject matter.

For example, students in the FYS history course, "Love in the Western World," read *The Return of Martin Guerre*, an interpretative work by the historian Natalie Zemon Davis. Students in the other two courses of the seminar, "Love and Eros in the Fine and Performing Arts" and "Literary Love," read the historical novel *The Wife of Martin Guerre* by Janet Lewis. All students in the seminar watch the film, *The Return of Martin Guerre*. The three sections then meet to discuss the material. The students divide into small groups that cross disciplinary lines, teach each other about the different texts they have read, and then discuss the similarities and differences. The next day, these interdisciplinary student groups present their ideas and conclusions to the entire seminar. The students' discussions give them the chance to see the main differences among the three academic disciplines that form their seminar.

The faculty members in the "Impact of the Media" seminar have experimented with a different version of seminar meetings. They created a triangle of courses focusing on separate but interrelated issues. The psychology and communication courses worked together on advertising and the media, the exercise science course paired with the psychology course to discuss distortions in the media, and the communication course paired with the exercise science course to look at the history of mass media and sports. The faculty members incorporated the insights that surfaced during these discussions into exam questions and essay assignments, as well as future class discussions. Students in the "Impact of the Media" seminar benefited in two ways from taking part in these meetings. First, they had a chance to compare the different disciplinary perspectives on a given issue. Second, the students compared two different interdisciplinary experiences.

Administering the FYS Program

The coordinator of the FYS program reports to the dean of faculty. There have been three coordinators to date, each a full-time Ripon College faculty member who has typically served for three years. Compensation usually takes the form of additional salary, although release time from teaching duties has also been an option.

The coordinator's first task is to recruit faculty to teach in the program. The main challenge in faculty recruitment is helping willing faculty members find and refine topics that will facilitate interdisciplinary connections and comparisons. Working a year in advance, the coordinator issues an open invitation for faculty to join the program. Following the invitation, the coordinator holds informational meetings and workshops on teaching in seminars. During faculty recruitment, the coordinator draws on faculty from across the entire college to ensure that the program has courses from all four divisions of the college—fine arts, humanities, natural sciences, and social sciences.

The coordinator plans FYS events, including the FYS Celebration (a day for presenting students' small-group projects). The coordinator also works with the library, the Center for Information Technology services, and the Student Life staff to develop orientation activities that will help students become more aware of campus resources. The coordinator also helps faculty members find ways to build the orientation activities into FYS courses. When possible, tours and other activities are customized to fit seminar themes and/or course assignments. The coordinator also assists faculty members in planning and implementing field trips, and bringing guest speakers and performers to campus. The coordinator has a modest budget for these enrichment activities.

The Faculty Perspective on FYS

Faculty members have expressed satisfaction with the FYS program in both private conversations and public meetings. They report that they believe the FYS courses and seminars convey the college's values and goals to new students. The faculty also report that they enjoy working with the other members of their seminars. Planning their seminars both before and during the term gives faculty members the chance to exchange ideas across disciplines, gain a richer understanding of a topic, and trade teaching tips. It provides opportunities for intellectual connection that are not always easy to find in small institutions like Ripon College, where teaching takes precedence over scholarly activities.

The Student Perspective on FYS

Student evaluations have shown that students understand the goals of their FYS courses and seminars and are satisfied that those goals are being met. They also show that students appreciate the opportunity to learn important skills that will help them succeed at Ripon College and in their future careers. Students report that they enjoy making connections between the disciplines and understand what a liberal arts education entails. Finally, students have expressed an appreciation for learning about resources at Ripon College and have indicated a willingness to take advantage of those resources. Table 2 offers typical responses on program evaluations to FYS goals and activities.

Refining the FYS Program

Since the late 1990s, FYS coordinators have developed a variety of program resources to help faculty create a good fit between their courses and first-year students' needs. The coordinators have learned that students get the most out of these resources if faculty control when, where, and how the resources are integrated into their courses.

For example, in the program's first year, all FYS students were required to attend meetings on issues of student success, harassment, building a college education, and course selection. The coordinator hoped the programs would give students a broader understanding of the liberal arts and life in college. However, the students perceived the meetings as having little to do with their FYS courses. In their program evaluations, students reported that they found the meetings to be pointless.

The next year, the coordinator replaced the meetings with a variety of program resources that faculty could use in their courses. FYS faculty members were free to choose which resources and orientation activities to use and when to use them. The resulting change in the students' perceptions was immediate and dramatic. In their student evaluations, they reported that they saw connections between the orientation activities and their courses. The coordinator attributed this change in student perception to the fact that the orientation activities were now more integrated into the FYS course content. Faculty members also appreciated having the autonomy to use the programs' resources at the times that worked best in their courses.

The FYS program succeeds best when faculty and students are sure that the academic integrity of their courses and seminars is sacrosanct. Students and faculty respond enthusiastically when outside programs and activities work to support their academic endeavors. By demonstrating how a variety of activities, events, and perspectives can be part of their FYS courses, the program shows students how the range of disciplines in the liberal arts can and will play an important role in their education.

Program Assessment

Student retention at Ripon College has increased over the past five years, but how much effect FYS has had on that change is not conclusive (Table 3). Because all students must take an FYS course, retention rates of students who took FYS cannot be compared with those who did not. The college has also recently introduced two other programs—the Summer Orientation program and the Communicating Plus program—and they may also have positively affected retention.

The college's Educational Policy Committee planned to conduct a formal review of the program in 2003-2004. To date, FYS program assessment has consisted of student evaluations and informal faculty comments. As noted above, both have indicated that students and faculty members are satisfied with the FYS program. The program review was predicted to provide recommendations on collection of additional data. For example, preliminary reports from the committee indicated

Table 2

Student Evaluation of Program Relative to Program Goals

Program Goals/Events	Comment
Convey the college's expectations to the students	• "I felt we addressed the issues of the college experience and talked about the transition from high school to college." • "With mandatory attendance and presentations, our work skills improved. We got a good idea of what college needs are." • "Through all the meetings, papers, and presentations, I now understand what it takes to be a good college student."
Teaching the skills students need to succeed in college	• "My FYS class helped me improve my writing skills. I know it will help in the long run." • "Allowing revisions based upon professor's suggestions helped to improve my writing and get used to college writing." • "It helped to clarify different presentation techniques (e.g., writing, presentation, reading)."
Interaction with faculty and student mentor	• "[My professor and student mentor] helped me a lot throughout the semester. They helped with study habits and just college life in general— coping with finals—coping with life." • "Every day I learned new things and skills that college professors expect from their students. FYS was a great learning experience for me as a student and a person."
Experience how a liberal arts education brings different fields of knowledge together	• "It is good to learn about different perspectives through participating in discussions with other similar classes." • "My FYS course makes me look into issues in an entirely different way. I analyze and pick apart subjects much more than I used to." • "I thought this was a good way of making us more well-rounded." • "This is very beneficial because it forces people who don't want to broaden their horizons to do so. It can help you find an interest that you didn't know you had."
Diversity workshop	• "It is important for first-year students to realize that they are now among people from many different upbringings and that they must be understanding of this."
Ripon College Reading Experience	• "I personally enjoyed the book discussions of *Montana 1948* because the book was very controversial. It brought many interesting viewpoints to life."
Successful students	• "[The best was the successful students panel] because they told you that there is help out there for you and you can succeed."
Library instruction	• "It gave me so many more sources of information that I now use all the time."
Tour of student support services and student life offices in Bartlett Hall	• "The Bartlett Hall tour was the best program because not only did we get familiar with the offices, but with the happy faces as well!"
Harassment program	• "The harassment one [was useful] because now we understand exactly what harassment is and how we can deal with the situation."
Field trips	• "The field trip was fun. We got off the campus and just saw what is happening in the environment around Ripon and the college campus."
Celebration Day	• "The FYS Celebration was enjoyable because it allowed us to benefit from learning done in our seminar as well as other seminars."
Fall Convocation	• "It really made me feel more welcome."

Table 3
Cohort Retention Rates at Ripon College

Year	Cohort Size	One Year Later		Two Years Later		Three Years Later	
			Percent (%)		Percent (%)		Percent (%)
	n	*n*		*n*		*n*	
Fall 1996	169	129	76.3	111	65.7	102	60.4
Fall 1997	135	115	85.2	99	73.3	93	68.9
Fall 1998	162	137	84.6	128	79.0	123	75.9
Fall 1999	283	241	85.2	207	73.1	200	70.7
Fall 2000	280	246	87.9	225	80.4		
Fall 2001	201	172	85.6				

Note. A cohort is established each fall and contains all first-time, full-time, degree-seeking students who begin their studies that fall. From Ripon College Office of the Registrar and Assistant Dean for Academic Affairs.

that it would recommend the FYS program survey juniors and seniors to discover how well they believe FYS prepared them for their Ripon College experience. The committee was also expected to recommend the FYS program ask participating faculty to conduct a systematic evaluation of the program.

Overall, Ripon College believes it has discovered, through the FYS program, a useful approach to meeting its mission to introduce students to disciplinary and interdisciplinary ideas, approaches, and skills. The FYS program, with its multiple layers, common goals, and flexibility, taps into the expertise of faculty members and staff throughout campus to achieve that mission.

References

Educational Policy Committee (1997, October). *Report to Ripon College faculty policy meeting*. Ripon, WI: Ripon College.

Ripon College (2003-2004a). *Ripon College catalog, 2003-2004*. Retrieved February 9, 2004, from http://www.ripon.edu/academics/catalog/03-The_College.pdf

Ripon College (2003-2004b). *Ripon College catalog, 2003-2004*. Retrieved February 9, 2004, from http://www.ripon.edu/academics/catalog/07-Courses.pdf

Reversing Attrition Rates by Integrating First-Year Academic Programs

Amanda Yale, Cathy Brinjak, and April Longwell
Slippery Rock University of Pennsylvania

Chapter 9

In the 1990s, Slippery Rock University (SRU) faced a number of enrollment-related challenges. A need existed to refocus and establish intentional, comprehensive, institution-wide, and highly coordinated recruitment and retention efforts designed to reverse a trend of declining enrollments. One of the most critical challenges that SRU confronted was improving the institution's first-year retention rates, which were reported at 69 to 71%. Since 2000, several first-year efforts have been initiated to improve student learning and success. The first-year initiative, which has had the greatest impact on students' academic and social integration as demonstrated through a series of assessment measures, is the learning community cluster. At the core of the initiative is a one-credit first-year seminar, First-Year Studies (FYRST) seminar, which is modeled on a traditional extended orientation seminar.

This chapter begins with descriptions of the institution, its students, and the issues the University faced at the time the learning community cluster and FYRST seminar (LCC/FYRST seminar) initiative was implemented. The chapter also provides a description of the initiative and its varied components including the professional development activities for faculty. The chapter offers results from several assessments used to measure the possible impact of the LCC/FYRST seminar on academic and social integration factors, student learning outcomes, academic performance, and student persistence.

The Institution and its Students

Slippery Rock University is one of the 14 State System of Higher Education institutions in the Commonwealth of Pennsylvania. Located in the rolling hills of western Pennsylvania, SRU is a public comprehensive institution with a current undergraduate and graduate enrollment of 7,530 students. The institution is composed of four academic colleges: Education; Health, Environment, and Science; Business, Information, and Social Sciences; and Humanities, Fine and Performing Arts. In a recent reorganization of the academic divisions, the University recognized the importance of integrating recruitment and retention operations by establishing a comprehensive Enrollment Services structure. The new division reports to the provost and vice president for academic affairs. The Department of Academic Services, a unit of the Enrollment Services division, coordinates orientation, first-year advisement, learning communities, the first-year seminar, tutoring, and several academic support programs and services for the institution. The LCC/FYRST seminar initiative involves faculty from each of the four colleges, the division of Enrollment Services, and many professional staff from across campus.

Between 1,350 and 1,435 first-time, full-time students enter the University each fall. Annual first-year survey results indicate that first-generation students consistently comprise 60% of the institution's new students. Additionally, records indicate that about 85% of SRU's students receive financial aid. The average combined Scholastic

Aptitude Test (SAT) score ranged from 945 to 961 between the years 2000 and 2001, with about 35% of incoming first-year students enrolling in at least one developmental course. Finally, most first-year students come from 15 counties in western Pennsylvania, many representing rural communities. These characteristics (i.e., students who are the first in their family to attend college, are in need of financial assistance, have low SAT scores, are in need of developmental coursework, and are from rural communities) are often associated with an increased risk of departing from college, especially in the first year (Tinto, 1993). In addition, SRU finds itself in a position similar to other mid-sized public universities. While the institution's fiscal resources are being stretched, demands for accountability and assessment are rising. For this reason, the institution has placed an emphasis on assessment of the LCC/FYRST seminar initiative as a first-year program and curricular experience.

The LCC/FYRST seminar program at SRU strives to help realize the Pennsylvania State System of Higher Education's vision as an accountable, collaborative, increasingly integrated network of 14 institutions focused on learning. The LCC/FYRST seminar initiative also supports the University's Performance and Outcomes Plan to enhance excellence through improved student learning and success. Further, in accordance with the Board of Governors' Goals for the State System of Higher Education, the program works toward addressing the need to improve first-year retention rates. Finally, the program supports the University's strategic plan, *Imperatives for the Future* (http://www.sshechan.edu/stplan.htm), and the updated *Imperatives Affirmed* (http://www.sru.edu/depts/provost/imperatives/impaffirm.htm) by focusing its efforts for first-year students on learning, collaboration, integration, and accountability.

The Learning Community Cluster and FYRST Seminar Program Goals

In fall 2000, SRU initiated a learning community cluster and first-year seminar as key ingredients to enhance first-year student learning and success. The goal during this first year was to determine whether a combined learning community and First-Year Studies (FYRST) seminar correlated with enhanced student success, as measured by improved retention, academic performance, and factors related to academic and social integration. The variables chosen for assessment were developed using the work of Tinto (1975, 1985, 1987, 1993), Pascarella and Terenzini (1977, 1980, 1991), and the student involvement theories of Astin (1971a, 1971b, 1993) and Pace (1984). Assessment of this initial effort sought to identify whether students who successfully completed the LCC/FYRST seminar demonstrated greater levels of integration and increased institutional commitment as measured by first- to second-year persistence, cumulative first-year grade point average, specific academic and social integration factors, and student learning outcomes.

Program Development and Design

The LCC is coordinated by the director of orientation who serves as a faculty member in the Department of Academic Services. FYRST seminar is coordinated by the director of the Academic Advisement Center. The associate provost for enrollment services coordinates assessments and data collection on student progress. Each learning community cluster co-enrolls groups of students in sections of first-year writing courses, liberal arts or major program courses, and FYRST seminars (see Figure 1). The FYRST seminar was designed as a first-semester transition course for the purpose of promoting a successful progression to college life for incoming students. Patterned after the University 101 course at the University of South Carolina, the SRU seminar introduces students to basic academic success skills and campus support services. As described in the syllabus and University catalog, the course provides students with an opportunity to become integrated into the university's community of learners by exploring the purpose and value of higher education, participating in the teaching/learning process, addressing academic and social transition issues, utilizing campus programs, services, and technology, and developing academic skills and learning strategies during the student's first semester at Slippery Rock University. (Slippery Rock University of Pennsylvania, 2003)

Students write, speak, and read about topics important to college success including time management, learning assistance applications, major and career exploration, library resources, computer use, communication skills, stress management, values assessment, social life, and relationships.

In fall 2000, the initial year of the program, the LCC/FYRST seminar consisted of 27 learning community clusters enrolling 700 (51%) first-time, full-time students. In the following two years, the program expanded to enroll 1,000 (70%) first-year students. Nearly 100 faculty, staff, and administrators from all four colleges and the academic services department have been involved as guest instructors and as financial, administrative, and moral supporters. In its fourth year, the program enrolled nearly 80% of all new first-year students.

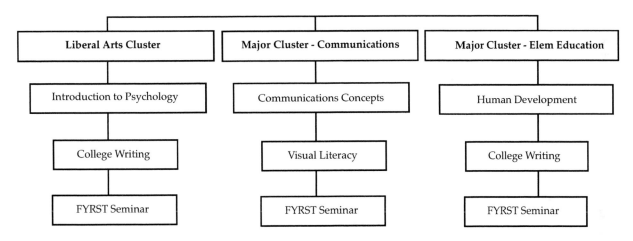

Figure 1. Learning community clusters at Slippery Rock University.

Program Structure

While different types of learning communities are identified in the literature, the most common learning clusters are linked courses (Shapiro & Levine, 1999), which describe SRU's approach. The purpose of SRU's LCC/FYRST seminar initiative is to have a single group of students share the same schedule of classes, which revolves around the liberal arts or major area. The initiative represents an intentional effort to foster more explicit connections among students, between students and faculty, and between students and various support structures. Some 60% of the clusters are organized around liberal arts courses, while 40% focus on a particular major. Whenever a major course is used in a cluster, the FYRST seminar is taught by an instructor from the students' intended major department, who often also serves as the students' academic advisor. Three types of cluster configurations have emerged from the initial LCC:

1. Model I, which is best described as a "twin cluster," is composed of one liberal arts or major program course, two college writing sections, and two FYRST seminar sections.

Students enrolled in the latter two courses comprise the entire enrollment of the liberal arts or major course.

2. Model II, which is best described as a "shared cluster," is composed of one liberal arts or major program course, one college writing section, and one FYRST seminar section. Non-LCC/FYRST seminar participants or upper-division students share the enrollment in the liberal arts or major course.

3. Model III is best described as a "pure cluster." Only students enrolled in the LCC/FYRST seminar are in each of the three courses (see Figure 2).

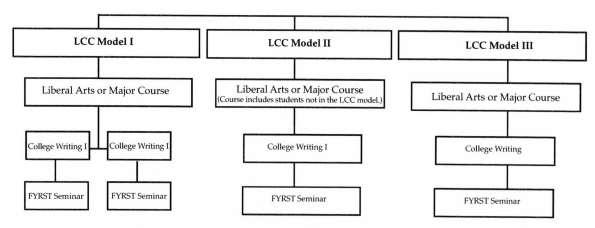

Figure 2. Models of learning community configurations at Slippery Rock University.

Initially, the first-year seminar course met for one hour per week for 15 weeks. In the second and third years of the program, about one third of the faculty chose to have the course meet more frequently at the beginning of the semester and completed the course before the end of the semester. This practice became popular among instructors as a means for developing and strengthening relationships with students earlier in the term. While each instructor is free to modify the course, common elements exist across sections, including group development, introduction to the University, introduction to learning strategies, and discussion of personal development issues. In the FYRST seminar, students complete individual projects, such as interviewing faculty and visiting different services and resources on campus. Students receive a letter grade and earn one elective credit hour at course completion. Faculty select a variety of textbooks representing traditional orientation seminar curricula. The textbook readings are intended to complement the course goals directly, but the time devoted to specific course components is determined by individual instructors.

Faculty Collaborative Initiatives

As an important component of their responsibilities, FYRST seminar instructors are encouraged to collaborate with other members of their learning community cluster instructional team. As part of the annual professional development workshop, faculty members are offered ideas for this collaboration and curricular integration. FYRST seminar faculty members report a variety of approaches to collaboration ranging from sharing syllabi and expectations to integrating writing, speaking, and other assignments on various topics. The most frequent collaborative approaches cited by FYRST seminar faculty include activities, processes, and assignments directly related to the following topics:

1. Time management as it relates to specific study applications in clustered courses
2. Learning assistance applications related to active reading, note-taking, and test preparation for clustered courses
3. Academic advisement in a specific major area
4. Major and career exploration
5. Use of library resources as it relates to researching specific course content
6. Use of the University's online course management system (Blackboard) for course communications
7. Improved writing skills related to the other courses
8. Discussions of diversity across courses
9. Improved cluster course-related communication skills

The form that integration takes generally depends on the type of cluster being offered. In interviews, FYRST seminar instructors in major clusters said they are likely to collaborate and integrate assignments. In the case of major-related clusters, the most common integrated topics relate to issues surrounding the students' intended major and specific advisement or career-focused issues. Collaborations in these courses have often included shared writing assignments and small research projects. The liberal arts cluster faculty members are more likely to share syllabi with their cluster teammates. Courses found to be highly suitable for such cross-course collaborations have included psychology, business, ethics, world history, sociology, leadership, and theater, although examples from a variety of disciplines exist. For example, one English instructor asks her writing students to compose essays related to content of the liberal arts or major courses in their cluster, while in an art history/world history link, students participate in an integrative international travel experience. Faculty members in a cluster focusing on diversity created opportunities for students to discuss values and views on diversity in courses across the cluster. Journal entries and reaction papers have also been used to integrate concepts and experiences across courses.

In addition to collaborative curricular initiatives, cluster faculty commonly discuss individual student progress, a practice that appears to occur more commonly in the major clusters than in the liberal arts clusters. As a result of faculty discussions, students having academic difficulty have been referred to University services. Faculty members engaged in this practice report that students have been responsive to the referrals and grateful for the concern about their transition needs.

Selection of FYRST Seminar Faculty and Professional Development Opportunities

Because instructors for the FYRST seminar are asked to teach a specialized course intended to help students with the transition to college and to serve as a linchpin for the entire cluster experience, selection is conducted with great care. Faculty members are recruited through campus-wide marketing efforts, and they have consistently represented each level, from instructor to full professor. Instructors receive approval to teach the course from their academic department and the Department of Academic Services. Both the academic department and Academic Services emphasize selecting faculty members who are particularly interested in and skilled at working with first-year students. Traditional teaching faculty are compensated one additional credit hour for teaching the course, while the Academic Services faculty teach the course as part of their regular work load.

Consistent with the literature on the preparation of faculty for teaching the first-year seminar course (Gardner, 1980), the instructors participate in an annual, two-day professional development experience and fall semester luncheon discussions. They also receive a variety of instructional resource materials. The professional development experience includes the following topics: (a) philosophy of the first-year seminar concept, (b) the University environment and the SRU student profile, (c) description of course content and process, (d) selection of a textbook, (e) classroom mechanics and course procedures, and (f) teaching strategies. During the workshop, participants also receive information on educational trends, student learning styles, and important changes in academic policies and procedures. The intent is to orient faculty to campus facilities, services, and personnel and to introduce them to new instructional methodologies and assessment strategies. An instructional resource handbook for each faculty member includes a course outline and sample syllabi; a description of basic elements of a first-year seminar; readings on the first-year seminar; sample classroom projects, activities, assignments, and exercises; suggested classroom assessment strategies; and grading procedures.

Luncheon discussion sessions held during the fall focus on sharing classroom activities and teaching strategies. The professional development seminar experiences include presentations and discussions among experienced first-year seminar faculty, student life personnel, and upper-division students. These experiences are designed to enhance collaboration across divisional lines as suggested by Gardner (1987) and Rice (1992).

Program Assessment Measures

Several types of data have been collected and analyzed about the LCC/FYRST program. In the initial two years of the program, data collected from the First-Year Academic and Social Experiences Survey (FASES), described below, were used to examine the possible impact on LCC/FYRST seminar participants and non-participants according to factors of academic and social integration. Each year of the program, data on first-to-second year persistence rates, academic performance, and credits earned have been obtained for LCC/FYRST seminar participants and non-participants. Data on specific student populations have also been examined to determine the impact of LCC/FYRST seminar participation on persistence. Student end-of-term course evaluations and narratives on the experience from students, FYRST seminar faculty, and LCC faculty have also been collected. In the program's third and fourth years, the First-Year Initiative (FYI) survey, administered through the Policy Center on the First Year of College and Educational Benchmarking, Inc., was given to SRU students at the end of the FYRST seminar. The survey asks students to indicate their perceptions of their first year of college in general and of gains in academic skills. Students are also asked to describe their behaviors related to FYRST seminar issues.

First-Year Academic and Social Experiences Survey (FASES)

In the first two years of the program, two groups of first-year, full-time students— FYRST seminar participants and non-FYRST seminar participants—were asked to complete the FASES at the conclusion of their first semester. The FASES includes 40 items across five academic and social integration factors. Each factor corresponds with perceived first-year student information needs and is mapped to the FYRST seminar course curriculum. Students respond to statements about their college experience using a five-point Likert scale (1 = strongly agree to 5 = strongly disagree).

The first section of the survey was composed of a multi-dimensional social and academic integration scale developed by Pascarella and Terenzini (1980) and based on Tinto's (1975) conceptual model. Tinto's model of the withdrawal-from-college process regards retention as a function of the quality of the students' interactions with the academic and social environments of the institution. Tinto's model also acknowledges that interactions with these environments are influenced by students' "background characteristics" (e.g., sex, race, academic ability, secondary school performance, family social status) and "goal commitments" (e.g., highest degree expected, importance of graduating from college) (Tinto, 1975, p. 61).

Pascarella and Terenzini (1980) identified five dimensions of institutional integration, which are represented in the FASES by five sub-scales: (a) peer group interactions, (b) interaction with faculty, (c) academic and intellectual development, (d) institutional and goal commitments, and (e) faculty concern for student development and teaching. Data on academic and social integration were collected through the survey administered before the end of the 2000 and 2001 fall semesters. Residential first-time, full-time 2000 and 2001 students received survey instruments from their residence hall coordinators and community assistants, while commuting students received a mailed survey.

In 2000, 76% ($n = 1,052$) of the surveys were returned, and 94% ($n = 987$) were usable. Thus, there was a 71% total response rate. In 2001, 66% ($n = 852$) were returned and 82% ($n = 698$) were usable, with a 54% total response rate. Results indicated that higher rates of academic and social integration are correlated with participation in the LCC/FYRST seminar.

A test of significance was run for each of the statements on the survey. In 2000, participants gave significantly lower responses (indicating greater signification) on 17 of the 29 statements than non-participants. In 2001, participants gave significantly lower responses on 23 of the 29 statements than non-participants. The survey statements, taken together, demonstrate overall perceptions of integration into the institution (see Table 1).

Table 1

Analysis of Mean Factors for Each Statement on the FASES for LCC/FYRST Seminar Participants and Non-LCC/FYRST Participants in 2000 and 2001

FASES Survey Items	2000		2001	
	LCC/ FYRST	Non- LCC/ FYRST	LCC/ FYRST	Non- LCC/ FYRST
Peer Group Interactions				
Since coming to the University, I have developed close personal relationships with other students.	1.38*	2.06	1.36*	2.01
The student friendships I have developed at the University have been personally satisfying.	1.45*	2.11	1.48*	2.17
My interpersonal relationships with other students have had a positive influence on my intellectual growth and interest in ideas.	1.65*	2.34	1.69*	2.54
It has been difficult for me to meet and make friends with other students. (Reversed)	1.82*	2.18	1.64*	2.14
Few of the students I know would be willing to listen to me and help me if I had a personal problem. (Reversed)	2.04*	2.76	2.00*	2.78
Most students at the University have values and attitudes different from my own. (Reversed)	2.61	2.61	2.32*	2.65
Faculty Interaction				
My non-classroom interactions with faculty have had a positive influence on my personal growth, values, and attitudes.	2.20*	2.42	2.28*	2.52
My non-classroom interactions with faculty have had a positive influence on my intellectual growth and interest in ideas.	2.23	2.28	2.29*	2.56
My non-classroom interactions with faculty have had a positive influence on my career goals and aspirations.	2.23*	2.56	2.24*	2.49

Table 1 continued on next page.

Table 1 continued from previous page.

FASES Survey Items	2000		2001	
	LCC/ FYRST	Non-LCC/ FYRST	LCC/ FYRST	Non-LCC/ FYRST
Since coming to the University, I have developed a close, personal relationship with at least one faculty member.	2.59*	2.78	2.52*	2.79
Most of the faculty members I have had contact with are interested in helping students grow in more than just academic areas.	2.10*	2.28	2.10*	2.43
I am satisfied with opportunities to meet and interact informally with faculty members.	2.27*	2.49	2.24*	2.58
Most faculty members I have had contact with are genuinely interested in teaching.	1.96*	2.29	1.62*	2.34
Academic and Intellectual Development				
I am satisfied with the extent of my intellectual development since enrolling in the University.	1.99	2.10	1.91*	2.09
My academic experience has had a positive influence on my intellectual growth and interest in ideas.	1.91	1.99	1.92*	1.99
I am satisfied with my academic experience at the University.	1.92*	2.13	1.90*	2.27
My interest in ideas and intellectual matters has increased since coming to the University.	2.12	2.21	2.10*	2.25
I have no idea at all what I want to major in.	3.24*	3.86	3.26*	3.90
I am more likely to attend a cultural event (for example, a concert, lecture, or art show) now than I was before coming to the University.	2.60*	2.87	2.54*	2.90
I have performed academically as well as I anticipated I would.	2.53*	2.73	2.51*	2.74
Institutional and Goal Commitment				
It is important for me to graduate from college.	1.16	1.16	1.14*	1.35
I am confident that I made the right decision in choosing to attend the University.	1.73*	2.03	1.60*	2.20
It is important to me to graduate from the University.	1.49*	1.78	1.30*	1.92
Getting good grades is not important to me. (Reversed)	1.74	1.76	1.76	1.77
It is likely that I will return to the University next fall.	1.49	1.60	1.26	1.28
Faculty Concern for Student Development				
Few of the faculty members I have had contact with are generally outstanding or superior teachers. (Reversed)	2.65	2.60	2.40	2.36
Few of the faculty members I have had contact with are generally interested in students. (Reversed)	2.60	2.56	2.22	2.14
Few of the faculty members I have had contact with are willing to spend time outside class to discuss issues of interest and importance to me. (Reversed)	2.75	2.70	2.95	2.90
Few of my courses this year have been intellectually stimulating. (Reversed)	2.76	2.75	2.95	2.87

$^*p < .05$

Note. Lower numbers indicate higher satisfaction.

For each of the two years, students enrolled in the cluster had significantly greater results on four of five integration scales: (a) peer group interactions, (b) interactions with faculty outside of the classroom, (c) academic and intellectual development, and (d) institutional and goal commitment. Only the scale of faculty concern for student development was not statistically significant, where perceived levels of concern were similar for participants and non-participants. A lower number indicates greater satisfaction (see Table 2).

Table 2

Analysis of Means for the Five Dimensions of Academic and Social Integration of LCC/FYRST Seminar Participants and Non-LCC/FYRST Seminar Participants in 2000 and 2001

Academic and Social Integration Dimension	2000		2001	
	LCC/FYRST	Non-LCC/FYRST	LCC/FYRST	Non-LCC/FYRST
Peer Group Interactions	10.95*	14.06	10.49*	14.29
Faculty Interactions	15.58*	16.42	15.29*	17.71
Academic and Intellectual Development	16.31*	17.89	16.14*	18.14
Institutional and Goal Commitment	7.61*	8.33	7.06*	8.33
Faculty Concern for Student Development	10.76	10.61	10.52	10.27

*$p < .05$

Note. Lower number indicates higher satisfaction.

In 2000 and 2001, program participants who responded to the FASES were found to be significantly more likely to access student services than non-participants. For these items, students were asked to indicate the number of times they visited a service per academic term. Two services, the writing center and student health, were not accessed by program participants at higher rates in 2000, while all others were (see Table 3).

Survey administrators did not control for the fact that students volunteered for the program, a possible confounding variable, in either year of survey administration. It is believed that student motivation to participate derives from both internal and external forces. At SRU, nearly half of first-year students participated in the seminars in 2000, and nearly 70% of the students participated in the program during 2001. The belief is that many students volunteer to participate while others are advised to do so by their FYRST orientation advisor, and others are strongly encouraged to enroll by their parents, student orientation leaders, and peers. Regardless of the student's motivation, findings indicate some positive institutional integration among those who participate.

Student Persistence and Measures of Academic Performance

Data on cumulative first-year grade point average and credits earned were collected at the end of the 2000 and 2001 spring semesters, while data for first- to second-year persistence rates for these years were collected in the 2001 and 2002 fall semesters on the 15th day of the term, the official date for collection of retention statistics. These data indicate that students who participate in the LCC/FYRST seminar are retained to their second year at higher rates than non-participants. Credit hours earned and cumulative GPA are slightly, but not significantly, higher for students who participated in the LCC/FYRST seminar (see Table 4).

Table 3

Comparison of Mean Scores on the Use of Student Services for LCC/FYRST Seminar Participants and Non-LCC/FYRST Seminar Participants in Fall 2000 and Fall 2001

Student Service	2000		2001	
	LCC/FYRST	Non-LCC/FYRST	LCC/FYRST	Non-LCC/FYRST
Total Use of Services	19.35*	11.20	18.50*	10.15
Academic advisement assistance from a faculty advisor	3.15*	1.14	3.84*	1.59
Assistance from a faculty member outside of class	3.11*	1.08	3.42*	1.42
Assistance from student life personnel	.44*	.32	.56*	.33
Career Services	1.14*	.35	1.32*	.45
College skills workshops	.36	.30	1.98*	.63
Counseling Center	.21*	.14	.18*	.11
Financial Aid	1.51*	.66	1.62*	.51
Housing	.41*	.32	.58*	.39
Library services on the Internet	2.01*	1.39	2.59*	1.68
Library services at the library	2.19*	1.63	2.22*	1.46
Resident coordinator	.68*	.50	.79*	.52
Social Equity Office	.22	.15	.25	.18
Student Health Center	1.39	1.44	1.40	1.38
Tutoring services	2.07*	.71	2.11*	.67
Writing Center	.57*	1.00	.35	.32

*$p < .05$

Note. Higher numbers indicate higher number of visits to student services.

Table 4

Analysis of Mean Scores on Credits Earned, Academic Performance, and Second-Year Return Rates of LCC/FYRST Seminar Participants and Non-LCC/FYRST Seminar Participants

	2000 Cohort		2001 Cohort		2002 Cohort	
	LCC/ FYRST	Non-LCC/ FYRST	LCC/ FYRST	Non-LCC/ FYRST	LCC/ FYRST	Non-LCC/ FYRST
Credits earned	27.43	26.57	27.46	26.71	28.12	27.31
First-year cumulative GPA	2.60	2.58	2.73	2.71	2.75	2.74
Second-year return	70.7%*	67.3%	74.7%*	71.2%	79.5%*	74.6%

*$p < .05$

The LCC/FYRST seminar program was examined to determine its impact on special populations of students, especially those who might be at greater risk for attrition. These data suggest that academically at-risk students (i.e., special admissions students) in the program are retained at a significantly higher rate than similarly prepared students who do not participate. Additionally, students of color in the cluster program were retained at a significantly higher rate than non-participating students of color (see Table 5).

Table 5

Analysis of Mean Scores on Second-Year Return Rates for Special Admits, Students of Color, and Major Program Clusters of LCC/FYRST Seminar Participants and Non-LCC/FYRST Seminar Participants

Student Group	2000 Cohort		2001 Cohort		2002 Cohort	
	LCC/ FYRST	Non-LCC/ FYRST	LCC/ FYRST	Non-LCC/FYRST	LCC/ FYRST	Non-LCC/ FYRST
Special Admits	60.2%*	57.7%	54.2%*	44.4%	69.3%*	54.2%
Students of Color	78.1%*	54.1%	62.5%*	53.67%	57.17%*	50.0%

*$p < .05$

First-Year Initiative (FYI) Project

During the fall 2002 semester, 72% of students enrolled in a FYRST seminar completed the FYI survey at the end of the course, representing 53% of first-time, full-time 2002 students. Survey results indicate that program participants are significantly more likely than comparison groups of students enrolled in similar seminars at like institutions to say that the course improved study strategies, critical thinking, connections with faculty and peers, knowledge of campus policies, knowledge of academic services, managing time/priorities, knowledge of wellness, a sense of belonging/acceptance, and satisfaction with college/university (See Table 6 for a detailed description of one year of the FYI project results).

Course Evaluations

A standard evaluation of teaching effectiveness was administered to LCC/FYRST students at the end of the 2002 fall term. The survey asked students to respond to a number of items related to effectiveness of FYRST seminar teaching as listed in Table 7. For each of these statements, the mean factors for the FYRST seminar were higher than the mean factors for the overall institutional

Table 6

Analysis of Mean Factors of Student Learning Outcome Factors for Slippery Rock University FYRST Seminar Participants, the 'Select 6' Benchmarking Institutions, Carnegie Class Institutions, and Total Institutional Data for the Fall 2002 First Year Initiative Project

Factor Descriptor	SRU FYRST Seminar	'Select 6' Institutions	Carnegie Class Institutions	Total Institutional Data
Course improved study strategies	4.58	4.23***	4.24***	4.25***
Course improved academic/cognitive skills	3.97	3.69***	3.99	3.98
Course improved critical thinking	4.51	4.13***	4.39*	4.35**
Course improved connections with faculty	4.71	4.50***	4.60*	4.55**
Course improved connections with peers	5.26	4.61***	4.82***	4.69***
Course increased out-of-class engagement	3.73	3.75	3.79	3.79
Course improved knowledge of campus policies	5.06	4.93*	4.74***	4.78***
Course improved knowledge of academic services	5.38	5.12***	4.98***	4.97***
Course improved managing time/priorities	4.76	4.36***	4.47***	4.45***
Course improved knowledge of wellness	4.35	4.06***	4.08***	4.11***
Sense of belonging/acceptance	5.69	5.38***	5.46***	5.43***
Usefulness of course readings	4.43	3.98***	4.40	4.34
Satisfaction with college/university	5.62	5.40***	5.48**	5.40***
Course included engaging pedagogy	4.76	4.51***	4.72	4.67
Overall course effectiveness	4.75	4.44***	4.66	4.57***

$^*p < .05$
$^{**}p < .01$
$^{***}p < .001$

undergraduate course totals. Numbers in the table are percentages of students who indicated a high level of satisfaction on each item. Because these percentages are aggregated, a test of statistical significance was not possible. However, the trends suggest overall higher levels of satisfaction on measures of teaching effectiveness in the FYRST seminar.

Faculty and Student Open-ended Qualitative Commentary

Narratives collected from LCC/FYRST seminar faculty and students at the end of the first semester of the program provided faculty and students opportunities to respond to a series of open-ended questions. According to faculty respondents, the most valuable aspects of the program included student development of supportive peer relationships, student willingness to interact/respond more often in class, and their apparent ability to develop relationships with faculty more easily. Regarding the least valuable aspects of the program, faculty respondents were most likely to leave this section blank or to indicate that students were too interactive in class. Faculty members who were asked to comment on the aspects of the LCC/FYRST seminar initiative they enjoyed most indicated their appreciation for high levels of student interaction, the opportunity to assist first-year students with their transition, and the opportunity to work with other colleagues interested in student transition.

Table 7

Comparisons of Percentages on the Student Survey of Course Effectiveness for the FYRST Seminar Participants and the University Total (All Courses) for Fall 2002

Response Items	Fall 2002	
	FYRST Seminar (%)	University total (all courses)(%)
Course objectives/goals were clear throughout the semester.	95.8	92.0
Course addressed course objectives/goals.	95.0	93.5
I received clear instructions for completing assignments.	94.2	86.9
I received feedback helping to improve my understanding/performance.	94.3	83.4
I received graded/non-graded responses on coursework in reasonable time.	95.2	90.0
My learning was evaluated in a variety of ways.	90.5	79.6
Criteria (standards) on which my work was evaluated were clear to me.	94.5	84.3
Course provided opportunities for me to use critical thinking.	83.6	87.4
Course provided opportunities for me to seek more knowledge on subject.	81.5	89.3
Class sessions had a clear purpose.	87.3	86.5
Instructor created an atmosphere encouraging expression of ideas.	96.8	89.3
Instructor was available to meet with students during office hrs/appt.	97.9	91.0
I felt comfortable asking the instructor for help if I needed it.	96.0	89.6
Instructor attempted to involve all students in classroom activities.	97.0	88.8
The teaching in this course was effective.	90.7	86.0
I learned a lot in this course that was valuable to me.	92.7	83.0

Students indicated that the most valuable characteristics of the program for them were the opportunities to make friends, get to know other students, and study with other students. Students most frequently left blank the section on the program's least valuable characteristics or indicated that their cluster courses were not interrelated. Students who were asked to comment on which aspects of the LCC/FYRST seminar initiative they enjoyed most noted their appreciation for meeting other students, learning about institutional services and resources, and building relationships with the faculty.

Using Assessment Data to Celebrate Successes and Enhance Program Improvement

Program administrators consider the assessment project on the effectiveness of the LCC/FYRST seminar to be in its infancy. Studies are planned to refine the understanding of program impact based on participant gender, major, and academic preparation. Collection of longitudinal data is planned that would further compare earned credit hours, year-to-year retention, cumulative academic performance, and graduation rates. Although positive results have been realized in the past from clusters that loosely couple course content and processes, program administrators and faculty members intend to continue the recent trend of more closely integrating linked courses.

In sum, using multiple measures, results confirm the existence of a meaningful relationship between successful completion of LCC/FYRST and higher levels of academic and social integration, participant use of student services, first- to second-year student persistence, and self-reported student learning outcomes. Even when results were not found to be significant, the observable means for many of the variables was greater for the LCC/FYRST seminar participant group than for the non-participant group. The direction of the relationship is indicative of a positive association of the LCC/FYRST seminar initiative with these variables.

As a result of the assessment findings, several modifications have been made to improve the program. The fact that academically at-risk students and students of color who participate in the program experience greater levels of persistence than similar non-participants has led to more concerted efforts to encourage their participation. Given that assessments indicate that students who participate in major clusters persist at a higher rate than liberal arts cluster participants and non-participants, efforts have been made to increase the number of major-specific clusters.

Program administrators are also considering the most effective ways to apply research on institutional integration to the specific needs of the student body at SRU. For example, administrators are examining how to highlight those aspects of a seminar that correspond to the socialization components of Tinto's model. That is, social integration for SRU students may be a necessary precursor to academic integration, regardless of academic preparation. Especially for first-year students, a level of social comfort in and out of the classroom may be needed before students are able to take risks in the more formalized learning environment. Further, peer group influences may have a considerable impact on SRU students' willingness to participate in class and to make a commitment to course requirements. The social aspects of the clustered courses, in particular, may serve as the institution's key to easing the transition of students into the campus environment.

One research domain not yet explored extensively is the impact of teaching a FYRST seminar on faculty development and teaching practice. Possible factors for future study may include whether and how teaching practice in other courses is modified, how student advising practices change, and whether the character and amount of out-of-class interactions with students changes.

One recent addition to instructional practice that may have implications beyond the LCC/FYRST program is the institution's online course management system, Blackboard. During the fall semester of 2003, FYRST seminar faculty, who now represent 13% of the institution's instructional staff, were introduced to Blackboard as a tool available for use in the seminars and other courses. Two levels of functionality have been designed to allow ongoing online faculty discussions during semesters when FYRST seminars are offered and to allow faculty joining the learning community cluster to access information about the FYRST seminar. The Seminar's Blackboard site also includes information on general student transition issues for use by faculty members and campus support services staff. The site includes information on library resources, discussion topics, and instructional ideas from faculty across a variety of disciplines.

All resources related to the LCC/FYRST seminar program are now hosted electronically where they can be downloaded and customized. Faculty members may also now request a course site for their FYRST seminar section that allows them to post course materials, announcements, and reading assignments and communicate with students on assignments, readings, institutional services, programs, and processes. Faculty members also use the tool to facilitate online discussions among students or to facilitate collaboration with other LCC faculty and post materials for use across clustered courses.

In the inaugural semester, more than 40 FYRST seminar faculty members chose to develop and customize their own course environments. The faculty said they viewed the online environment as a means of enriching and supplementing their class sessions and discussions, as well as developing collaborative efforts with the cluster faculty. They also believed Blackboard increased student opportunities for interaction with faculty and other students beyond the weekly class meeting.

Conclusion

Creation of the LCC/FYRST seminar program is one of several initiatives across campus believed to have had bearing on an 8% increase in first- to second-year student retention from fall 2000 to fall 2002 (70.1% to 78%). The program has also helped to focus the attention of upper administration on retention issues. The evidence suggests that SRU's Learning Community Cluster initiative and First-Year Studies seminar offer considerable benefits to students. In the future, program administrators intend to create a residential component for some of the clusters, to increase major program clusters, build additional collaborative efforts among all faculty members who teach in a cluster, increase participation of non-faculty as FYRST instructors, increase the presence of additional campus professionals in the program as guest instructors, and enhance electronic resources for FYRST seminar faculty. Current and future improvement efforts will all continue to focus on both the academic and social integration of first-time students at SRU.

References

Astin, A. W. (1971a). The methodology of research on college impact, Part I. *Sociology of Education, 43*, 223-254.

Astin, A. W. (1971b). Two approaches to measuring students' perceptions of their college environment. *Journal of College Student Personnel, 12*(2), 169-172.

Astin, A. W. (1993). *What matters in college? Four critical years revisited.* San Francisco: Jossey-Bass.

Gardner, J. N. (1980). *University 101: A concept for improving university teaching and learning.* Columbia, SC: University of South Carolina, University 101. (ERIC Document Reproduction Service No. ED192706)

Gardner, J. N. (1987). The freshman year experience. *College and University, 61*, 261-274.

Pace, C. R. (1984). *Measuring the quality of college student experiences.* Los Angeles: University of California, Higher Education Research Institute.

Pascarella, E. T., & Terenzini, P. T. (1977). Patterns of student-faculty informal interaction beyond the classroom and voluntary student attrition. *Journal of Higher Education, 48*, 540-552.

Pascarella, E. T., & Terenzini, P. T. (1980). Predicting freshman persistence and voluntary dropout decisions from a theoretical model. *Journal of Higher Education, 51,* 60-75.

Pascarella, E. T., & Terenzini, P. T. (1991). *How college affects students.* San Francisco: Jossey-Bass.

Rice, R. (1992). Reactions of participants to either one-week pre-college orientation or to freshman seminar courses. *Journal of The Freshman Year Experience, 4*(2), 85-100.

Shapiro, N. S., & Levine, J. H. (1999). *Creating learning communities.* San Francisco: Jossey-Bass.

Slippery Rock University of Pennsylvania. (2003). *2003-2004 Undergraduate Catalog.* Retrieved from http://www.sru.edu/catalog/courses_1.asp

Tinto, V. (1975). Dropouts from higher education: A theoretical synthesis of recent research. *Review of Educational Recreation, 45,* 89-125.

Tinto, V. (1985). Dropping out and other forms of withdrawal from college. In L. Noel, R. Levitz, & D. Saluri (Eds.), *Increasing student retention: Effective programs and practices for reducing the dropout rate* (pp. 145-147). San Francisco: Jossey-Bass.

Tinto, V. (1987). *Leaving college: Rethinking the causes and cures of student attrition.* Chicago: University of Chicago Press.

Tinto, V. (1993). *Leaving college: Rethinking the causes and cures of student attrition* (2nd ed.). Chicago: University of Chicago Press.

Learning In and About Community in a "World Class" City

Jodi Levine Laufgraben

Temple University

Temple University, a state-related institution in the Pennsylvania Commonwealth System of Higher Education[1], is a public, comprehensive research university serving more than 30,000 students, including 20,000 undergraduates. Just over 40% of Temple's undergraduate population is ethnic minority, half of those African American. Of the entire undergraduate population, about 6,300 are incoming students, including transfer students, with 3,700 first-time, first-year students. In addition to the main campus in Philadelphia, Temple has four regional campuses as well as international centers in Tokyo and Rome. Temple has 17 schools and colleges, offering degrees in 133 bachelor's areas, 125 master's areas, 58 doctoral areas, and 6 professional areas. Undergraduate admissions and recruitment literature promote the range and quality of academic programs offered at a large university along with the benefits of attending college in a "world-class" city. In recognition that its size might be overwhelming for first-time college students, Temple began offering learning communities in 1993 to "create a small college atmosphere at a large university." A first-year seminar was added in 1995 with the purposes of (a) helping students learn about learning, (b) promoting learning in and about community, and (c) creating a place for students to process content from other courses.

This chapter begins with a brief overview of Temple University's Learning Community Program and first-year seminar offerings. It continues with a focus on Learning for the New Century, the one-credit version of the seminar open to any first-year student, and a discussion of how the seminar is integrated in several learning communities. Administration of the seminar, including teacher selection and training, is described. The seminar's philosophy and goals, connections to learning communities, and curricular and pedagogical approaches are then discussed. The chapter includes results from two administrations of a national benchmarking survey and faculty focus groups.

Learning Communities at Temple University

Temple University undertook a major general education reform initiative in the 1980s and sought to create learning communities with the goal to improve teaching and curricular cohesiveness in this new general education (core) curriculum program. A shrinking applicant pool and declining enrollments also precipitated the need to attract and retain good students. Temple offered its first learning communities in fall 1993. The Learning Community Program was implemented to address two growing concerns: (a) creating community at a predominantly commuter campus and (b) improving teaching and learning at the first-year student level.

Linked-Course Learning Communities at Temple University

The majority of learning communities are linked-course structures that satisfy core, college, or major requirements. Most often, a pairing includes one of two first-year writing courses: Introduction to Academic Discourse (English 0040) or College Composition (English C050). Other communities feature a first-year math course such as college mathematics, pre-calculus, or calculus. Courses in the communities may also come from schools/colleges and departments across the University, including chemistry, women's studies, African American studies, criminal justice, psychology, sociology, journalism, theater, film and media arts, and engineering. Many learning communities include a section of the freshman seminar, Learning for the New Century, as a third course.

Students enroll in communities as cohorts of 15 to 25 students. Faculty work together and with the students to integrate course material and promote collaborative learning. The Learning Communities Program now enrolls more than 1,100 students each fall; most are traditional-aged, first-semester college students and more than half live on campus.

Emergence of the Freshman Seminar

The freshman seminar was created and piloted after faculty in learning communities voiced concerns about the challenges of teaching classes of entirely first-year students. Teachers were particularly concerned about students' academic preparedness and their lack of academic skills suitable for the college classroom. The seminar program expanded steadily, and Temple now offers four versions of a first-year seminar. Learning for the New Century is a one-credit course available to any Temple student but primarily designed for the student undecided about his or her major. The other three seminars are college-based and focus on transition to college as well as introduction to disciplines and careers: (a) The School of Communications and Theater's Freshman Seminar, (b) The Fox School of Business and Management's Introduction to Business, and (c) The College of Science and Technology's Introduction to Academics in the Sciences.

Two of the seminars—Learning for the New Century and Introduction to Business—are linked to learning communities. These seminars serve more than 1,000 students each fall. The Fox School of Business and Management Learning Clusters bring students together in four classes: (a) a large, 350-400 person business law class; (b) a computer applications course with lecture, recitation, and lab; (c) a small, first-year writing course; and (d) the Introduction to Business freshman seminar. In each cluster, the students are typically enrolled in at least two or three of the courses: the law lecture and the seminar, and/or the smaller writing class or computer recitation.

This chapter, however, focuses primarily on Learning for the New Century (referred to throughout as "the seminar"), the seminar with the largest total enrollments (more than 600 students for fall 2003) and the version serving students across Temple's undergraduate schools and colleges. Learning for the New Century is a one-credit course that meets two hours per week for 11 weeks of the fall semester. Students receive a letter grade, and the credit applies toward graduation. The course description that appears in the online and paper versions of the *Undergraduate Course Descriptions Guide* reads as follows:

"Learning for the New Century" introduces first-year students to the purposes of higher education and to the skills needed to use information technology and academic resources successfully in college and also in preparation for the workplace of the 21st century. The seminar also focuses on topics useful to college students, including time management, teamwork, study skills, and academic and career planning. (Temple University, 2003-2004)

Learning Community and Freshman Seminar Goals

As the 10th anniversary of learning communities at Temple University approached, program leadership decided in 2002 that it was time to revisit program goals. Undergraduate retention rates had improved significantly and with more and more students residing on campus, University officials believed that the institution had made significant progress in building a sense of community and increasing student satisfaction with the Temple experience. New priorities included the ongoing improvement of teaching and promoting deeper and more meaningful learning. In addition, the results of several learning communities assessment activities (e.g., faculty interviews, student surveys) revealed a need to clarify the program's goals. In spring 2002, a team consisting of program leadership, faculty, and a former learning community student attended a regional learning communities retreat with the task of establishing new goals for the program. After two days of discussion about the academic and social aims of learning communities and the freshman seminar, three clear goals emerged: (a) to promote the integration of knowledge across disciplines, (b) to support students' transition to college-level learning, and (c) to enhance connections between and among students and teachers.

The freshman seminar is the primary site for accomplishing that second, important goal of learning communities: to support students' transition to college-level learning. Each "Learning for the New Century" section, whether linked to a learning community or offered as a stand-alone course, is designed to assess students' levels of self-awareness and study skills and help students discover and apply the knowledge and tools necessary to grow academically and socially. Seminar goals are to:

1. Enhance students' intellectual and social development
2. Promote collaborative learning and group work
3. Practice technology applications and retrieval of information

When the seminar is linked to a learning community, there is an additional goal of helping students process what they are learning in their discipline-based courses. Seminar instructors are part of the learning community teaching team and are encouraged to work with team members to integrate curriculum across all courses in the community. The seminar is the ideal setting for students to model and practice good study skills and to discuss what they are learning in their other courses.

Seminar Course Administration

Each fall, 25 to 28 sections of Learning for the New Century are offered. Close to half are linked to learning communities. The remaining sections are free standing but are often selected by students enrolled in a community that does not include a linked seminar. Students register for the seminar during the summer when they attend New Student Orientation. Academic advisors are the primary recruiters for the course.

The course is housed within the Division of University Studies, the academic home for students who have not chosen a major and students preparing for allied health programs. The assistant vice provost for University Studies has primary responsibility for the Learning Communities and Freshman Seminar programs. There is no separate course budget. Funds for the seminar are included in the resources for the Learning Communities program. Budget items include: stipends for peer teachers, funds for an annual summer teacher training workshop and an end-of-semester teacher luncheon, and resources for duplicating course materials and the Instructor's Guide.

Teacher Selection and Training

The lead instructor for the seminar is a faculty member, academic administrator, academic advisor, or student affairs professional. Instructors are traditionally recruited from the Colleges of Liberal Arts and Allied Health Professions, the Office of the Vice Provost for Undergraduate Studies, the Division of Enrollment Management, and several student affairs offices including the Student Assistance Center, Career Development Services, Student Activities, and the Counseling Center. Each lead instructor partners with an undergraduate peer teacher. Instructors are not paid for teaching the seminar. Faculty teach the seminar on a volunteer basis, whereas administrators and staff teach the seminar as part of their job functions.

Peer teachers are upper-class students (at least sophomores) with cumulative grade point averages of 3.0 or higher. Peer teacher selection is a competitive process that includes an application, short essays, a group interview, and a mock lesson demonstration. Peer teachers represent majors from across the University. The majority of applicants are students nominated by freshman seminar instructors. Each peer teacher receives a one-time payment of $250 for co-teaching a section. After the selection process is complete, the new peer teachers participate in a two- to three-hour information session where the role of the peer teacher is discussed in greater detail. An academic advisor in the Division of University Studies assists with the coordination of the peer teacher program.

Each summer, all instructors and peer teachers participate in a one-day teacher training workshop. Appendix A is a sample workshop agenda. The workshop focuses on the goals of the course and effective teaching approaches. Returning seminar instructors share their best practices and offer advice to new teachers. Occasionally, an outside speaker, typically a trainer provided by the publisher of the course textbook, facilitates a session on teaching practices. At the workshop, instructors and peer teachers are introduced and have at least an hour to begin discussing ideas for their individual sections. Planning then continues in person or via e-mail during the summer. Seminar instructors whose sections are linked to learning communities are also invited to attend the one-day learning communities faculty development workshop.

While there is no standard or required syllabus, instructors receive course guidelines that recommend components for the course. The guidelines and a sample syllabus are included in the Instructor Guidebook which is distributed at the summer workshop and can also be found online (www.temple.edu/lc/faculty_resources.html).

A listserv, FSTEACH, is used to communicate with teachers throughout the summer and academic year. It is primarily used to share suggestions for assignments or class activities, send reminders about upcoming events, and make general announcements.

About six weeks into the fall semester, seminar instructors and peer teachers are invited to a number of "how's it going" sessions. These meetings are facilitated by the assistant vice provost for University Studies and the academic advisor who assists with the peer teacher program. This is a chance for teachers to share what is and is not working in their classes. Instructors typically come away from these sessions with good ideas for assignments or class activities. Teachers can also get advice on better ways to support students who are disruptive and/or in danger of failing the course.

At the end of the semester, all instructors are invited to an appreciation lunch and course debriefing. While the primary purpose of this event is to express gratitude for the teachers' commitment to the course, it is also a valuable opportunity for program leadership to learn about teachers' experiences, collect feedback on the course text, and invite suggestions for improvement.

Curricular Design and Pedagogical Strategies: The Link to Learning Communities

Two years of data from the First-Year Initiative Survey revealed that course instruction (i.e., engaging pedagogy) has the greatest impact on student satisfaction with the course. The seminar guidelines emphasize the importance of using active teaching techniques that fully engage and involve students in the learning process. When planning and teaching the course, seminar teachers are encouraged to include:

- A variety of teaching methods
- Meaningful class discussions
- Interesting subject matter
- Challenging assignments
- Productive use of classroom time
- Encouragement to speak in class
- Opportunities for students to work together
- Meaningful homework

The Role of the Seminar in Learning Communities

When a seminar is linked to a learning community, the discipline-based courses in the community influence both the content and pedagogy of the seminar. As noted above, the seminar instructors are part of the learning community teaching team. Each teaching team meets prior to the start of the fall semester to develop a community plan. The community plan worksheet (Appendix B) asks each team to outline a curricular theme for their community. A separate item on the worksheet asks the team to outline the role for the freshman seminar.

In the African-American Experience in Philadelphia learning community, a combination of college composition, African American history, and the freshman seminar, students explore Philadelphia's rich African American history in all three courses. In the seminar, students study the city's history through class discussions, journal assignments, and projects. They are encouraged to reflect on their own experiences of race both on and off the Temple campus. When a theme is threaded across the courses in a learning community, deeper learning of both skills and content occurs. In this community, students not only learn about Philadelphia but also have the opportunity to relate lessons of race relations to their own lives. An important outcome is that students learn and understand the importance of respecting diverse experiences. In the seminar, students practice important habits of discussion and debate, skills they then apply to other courses.

In one of the School of Business Learning Clusters, various components of a freshman seminar (Introduction to Business) research project are discussed or completed in the computer science and English courses. Students in the seminar are required to subscribe to the *Wall Street Journal* in both paper and electronic form. The Computer Information Systems faculty assist the students with the electronic subscription process and then in locating material for their seminar research project. The English teachers provide students with general information about writing research papers, including how to properly document sources, especially media and electronic resources.

Modes of Teaching and Learning

Lecture is probably the least used mode of teaching in the seminar. Creating community requires regular use of discussion, in-class group work, team projects/assignments, and out-of-class activities. In the seminar, and across learning communities, students are not passive learners. They share responsibility for learning with their teachers and peers. The seminar is the ideal setting or lab for learning "community." In learning communities, "learning" and "community" are both means and ends: community as a strategy to strengthen learning and learning to work and understand more deeply the value and challenges of community (MacGregor, 1996). The skills and behaviors of learning and community can be taught, discussed, practiced, and assessed in seminars linked with other courses.

The seminars support the academic and social goals of learning communities in several ways: (a) group work, (b) study skills practice, (c) discussion of topics related to the learning community theme, (d) assignments related to the learning community theme, and (e) conversations about student success.

Group work. Group activities are commonly used to introduce students to campus resources, particularly the academic support centers (i.e., Writing Center, Math and Sciences Resource Center, Disability Resources and Services) that can aid student learning in discipline-based courses. Group activities are also used to help students get to know each other and to practice collaborative learning. Students might be divided into groups to embark on a scavenger hunt, collecting brochures from various offices that they bring back and share with their peers. In a variation of the scavenger hunt, students are divided into groups and assigned a particular office or program to research. Groups then present the information to their classmates.

Many seminar instructors use group activities to familiarize students with each other and their new roles as college students and partners in the learning process. For a lesson on substance abuse and wellness, students in one class were divided into groups and each group acted out a scenario of a peer who drank too much. The other groups offered intervention strategies and reactions. In another seminar, students used role-playing to develop realistic financial plans and budgets. Group activities are also commonly used to practice study skills and reinforce learning in the discipline-based courses in the learning community.

Study skills practice. When a seminar is linked to a learning community, it becomes a learning lab to reinforce the learning and skills necessary to succeed in other courses. Time management discussions highlight the amount of time and out-of-class preparation required to succeed in other learning communities courses. A unit on note-taking will typically use course notes from one or both of the courses in the community. Reading strategies are practiced using course textbooks. In the Thinking Beyond the Self learning community—a larger sociology class linked with smaller sections of first-year writing courses and freshman seminars—the seminar instructors schedule times to attend the sociology lecture with their students. The instructors take notes and then, during their regular seminar meetings, the students and their teachers discuss the differences in the style and content of their notes.

Units on test-taking strategies are usually scheduled around one of the course exams. In one seminar, students practice writing essay exam questions in preparation for their history midterm. Students are divided into groups and asked to re-read a chapter in their history textbook. Each group then develops two to three potential essay questions the history teacher might ask about the assigned materials. Groups exchange questions and take turns answering each other's essay exams. A prize is awarded to the group that comes closest to accurately predicting a question that appeared on the history test. After the exam, the class debriefs their study strategies to determine what did or did not work in terms of their test preparation plans.

In another seminar, paired with a math and psychology course, the instructors have students download a practice midterm, posted for the psychology course a week or two before the test. The students work through it in class, discussing the questions and how to study.

Students comment that "learning to learn better" and practicing new and different ways to prepare for tests and assignments are the benefits of the seminar. This strategy, described by Jean Henscheid as "mixing Supplemental Instruction approaches with metacognition and thinking across disciplines" (personal communication, September 2003), is encouraged in freshman seminars and discussed with teachers at the annual summer workshop.

Discussion of topics related to learning community theme. Many seminar classes open with a discussion of what is being discussed in the other courses in the community: "What did you do in history today?" or "What is your current topic for composition?" The seminar becomes a site for brainstorming course content or requirements. One seminar instructor regularly asks her students to discuss what they are learning in the other courses in the community. When one student raises a concept that he or she is having difficulty understanding, a fellow student typically offers a helpful explanation.

Current events related to the learning community theme are also popular discussion topics. In one seminar linked to a math class, students discussed recent economic trends. During the presidential election year, students in another seminar—linked with a sociology class—discussed the candidates' views on issues impacting societal values and norms.

The Freshman Summer Reading selection provides another common discussion topic across the courses in the community (For more on Temple's summer reading program, go to www.temple.edu/summerreading). Each teacher might discuss the text from a different perspective, helping students recognize and value disciplinary difference. *Fast Food Nation* (Schlosser, 2001) was Temple's first summer reading selection. Students in the history class of the education learning community discussed the historical impact of the meat-packing industry on the current fast food market. Meanwhile, in seminar, students talked about the financial and public health implications of serving fast food in public schools.

Assignments related to the learning communities theme. Freshman seminar assignments often require students to draw on content or skills being learned in the other courses in the community. For example, seminars linked with math courses might ask students to apply basic mathematical concepts, like calculating interest, when talking about financial responsibility and budgeting. Students in seminars linked with psychology might take a personality inventory like the Myers-Briggs and then apply their knowledge of personality and individual behavior to discussions of their own personality traits.

In the Thinking Beyond the Self seminar, which is linked with sociology, students work in teams to compile ethnographies of college student behavior. Students discuss concepts such as culture, norms, and group dynamics in the sociology course. In the seminar, each group prepares a written paper and oral presentation on a particular aspect of college student culture: entertainment, health and wellness, fashion, sports and recreation, and technology. In addition to reinforcing basic sociological concepts, the assignment is an important exercise in team building and collaborative learning. Before starting their study, each group creates a team name and logo and a charter governing the expectations for group members.

Seminar assignments are typically graded exclusively by the seminar teachers, but in some learning communities different components of an assignment may be graded by other teachers in the community. For example, in the education learning community, students are asked to prepare a group research paper for their history course, but the oral presentation piece of the project takes place and is graded in the seminar. In seminar, students learn the basics of preparing oral presentations, including an introduction to PowerPoint. Both the history teacher and the seminar instructors provide students with feedback on their outlines and early drafts. Students present their papers about two weeks before the final project is due and are able to incorporate teacher and peer feedback into their finished work.

Conversations about student success. Linking the seminar to a learning community provides opportunities for teachers to discuss how students are doing. Typically, a student who does not regularly attend one course in the community also has attendance problems in at least one other course in the community. A student falling behind in seminar assignments may be struggling to keep up with other assignments in the community.

In a cluster of introduction to psychology, developmental English, and freshman seminar course, the teachers meet regularly to discuss student attendance and academic progress. In class, they reinforce the importance of regularly attending all class meetings and staying on schedule with readings and assignments. The teachers across the learning community help students understand how to apply study skills such as reading strategies, time management, and test preparation to the disciplinary expectations of each of their courses.

In the sociology learning community, teachers also meet regularly to discuss student progress and performance. In this community, the freshman seminar sections become a site for reflection, where students are regularly asked how things are going in the other courses in the community. One seminar teacher helps his students evaluate and prioritize their concerns. For example, a small group of students were complaining about another teacher in the community. When the seminar instructors raised this issue with the whole class, it became apparent that the small group of students did not represent the majority of the students' feelings. When the seminar instructors asked the whole class what intervention, if any, was necessary, the group offered constructive feedback on how the unhappy students could improve their experiences in the other course.

Assessment and Evaluation

The primary mode of assessment for the seminar (Learning for the New Century) has been end-of-course evaluations. In fall 2001 and fall 2002, the course was assessed using the First-Year Initiative Survey (FYI), a survey developed by The Policy Center on the First Year of College and Educational Benchmarking, Inc. (EBI). Informal assessment activities include reflective interviews with course instructors and peer teachers. In addition, some seminar teachers use Student Management Teams (SMT) to collect feedback on student experiences in their particular sections.

First-Year Initiative Survey (FYI)

The FYI report provided useful information on the factors influencing student satisfaction in the seminar. Students reported a strong sense of belonging and acceptance and overall satisfaction with Temple. They indicated their intent to return to the University for the next fall term and also that they would recommend Temple to a friend.

In terms of creating a community for students, on both the 2001 and 2002 administrations of the FYI Survey, students reported that the seminar encouraged them to work collaboratively with their peers. The course helped them identify peers with similar interests and helped them form new friendships. They got to know their classmates and felt encouraged to speak in class. The course also helped students form more meaningful connections with their teachers.

While perceptions of course effectiveness improved from the 2001 to 2002 administration of the survey on several critical factors, data indicated a need for additional improvement in the areas of engaging pedagogy and usefulness of course readings. Additional assessment was conducted to learn more about what "successful" seminar instructors were doing in terms of engaging pedagogy. For two consecutive years, seminar instructors from the sections with the highest factor means were invited to reflective interview sessions to share what did and did not work in their classes. The interviews were facilitated by the assistant vice provost for University Studies.

Reflective Interviews

Since the FYI factor analysis indicated that engaging pedagogy is the top predictor of student satisfaction with the freshman seminar, participants were asked to describe some of the teaching strategies and activities they used to engage students. A summary was compiled and printed in the Freshman Seminar Instructor's Guide. Tips for engaging pedagogy included:

- Varying the modes of instruction (e.g., lecture, discussion, group work)
- Inviting a variety of speakers to the class
- Using small group work
- Planning activities that keep students focused on the learning task
- Promoting discussion at the beginning of class
- Using ice breakers earlier in the semester to get students familiar with each other so they will feel comfortable participating in discussions
- Allowing flexibility in the syllabus for students to suggest topics and issues they want to address in the course
- Focusing on skills that students do well instead of giving the impression that the course is about their deficiencies
- Advocating small changes in behaviors and encouraging students to set goals for their participation in the course

This group of teachers also shared examples of specific assignments they used to promote group work, class discussion, and time management. Many of these teachers relied on skits/role-playing activities, educational games, and innovative homework assignments. Ideas were shared at the summer training workshop and were also printed in the Instructor's Guide.

Student Management Teams

Some seminar instructors rely on student management teams (SMT) to collect ongoing information on students' experiences in their sections. An SMT consists of the professor(s) and three to four students from the class. The student members of the team collect feedback from their classmates, maintain a log of suggestions, and regularly meet with the seminar instructors to share information and offer suggestions for improvement (Revak & Nuhfer, 2001).

One seminar instructor relied on her SMT to collect information on students' perceptions of the course text, assignments, and their overall learning communities experiences. The SMT reported that the class found it helpful that the seminar was linked to their sociology and writing classes. The students felt very comfortable with each other and formed study groups. They also liked that all three courses met in back-to-back class periods on Monday, Wednesday, and Friday mornings. In terms of suggestions for improvement, the SMT requested more information on student organizations and activities. They also wanted to spend more time discussing various Temple policies and procedures and the role of different offices. Another student request was to devote more class time to academic planning and career exploration.

Another seminar instructor reported that her SMT also provided useful feedback on students' overall learning community experience and their progress in the other courses. At one meeting, her SMT reported that the class was anxious about an upcoming math exam. The next class the seminar instructor talked about the exam, reviewed study skills, and discussed test preparation strategies. The teacher also offered advice for reducing test anxiety.

At present, assessment of the seminar primarily focuses on student and instructor experiences in the course. Approaches for measuring integration of knowledge across the courses in the communities are being considered. In 2002, Temple began using a standardized course and teaching evaluation. The instrument does, however, allow for supplemental questions. Items related to deeper learning of course concepts and students' perceptions of their intellectual development were added to the survey for fall 2003 and administered in seminar sections linked to learning communities as well as in free-standing sections.

Conclusion: Looking Ahead and Planning for Growth

Planning for the seminar includes both short-term and long-term objectives. The immediate focus is on regular improvements to the course for the upcoming academic year. Long-term discussions focus on the role of the seminar in potential new models for Temple's general education (core) curriculum.

Short-Term Planning

Assessment information continues to direct course improvements. The Instructor's Guide was developed to provide instructors with practical advice on teaching techniques. In the summer training workshops, teachers work in groups to develop innovative assignments that make meaningful use of the seminar text. Freshman seminar instructors continue to meet with other members of the learning community teaching team to discuss curricular connections and the role of the seminar.

New modes of delivering the seminar are being piloted. Philly 101 is a version of Learning for the New Century that introduces students to Temple as well as historical landmarks and neighborhoods in and around the city. Students learn facts about the city, use the public transportation system, and sample many famous Philadelphia foods. This notion of "regional study" is being applied to other seminars in learning communities as well. In the African-American Experience learning community, the teaching team, which includes the seminar instructor, chooses the history of race relations in Philadelphia as the curricular theme across the courses. In the history/ education learning community, students prepare group projects researching aspects of Philadelphia history or culture. The idea of topical seminars that explore regions and cultures outside Philadelphia is now being considered, based on the positive student feedback collected in a focus group with Philly 101 students.

In fall 2003, a lecture and recitation format of the seminar was offered. Students attended a 100-person lecture one day a week and smaller, 20-person recitations later in the week. Peer teachers led the recitations. This model explored a low-cost alternative to increasing course enrollments, since one challenge of offering smaller 20 to 25 student sections is finding enough faculty or staff volunteers to teach the course. While the experimental section was not linked in learning communities, this model may be used within learning communities in the future. A 50-to-100-person seminar could be linked to communities that already feature a larger course (i.e., 50 or more students) linked with smaller writing sections. The lecture portion of the seminar would be the site for introducing concepts and themes across the community, and the peer-led recitations would focus on discussing these themes and practicing study skills.

Long-Term Planning

Seminar offerings have expanded annually, and several other Temple undergraduate schools and colleges are now considering developing discipline-based seminars. The role of the freshman seminar has also been discussed as part of the University's ongoing general education review and reform process. There is growing faculty and administrative support for making seminars available to all or specific groups of entering students or in developing new communication (e.g., first-year writing) courses that would include University 101-type seminar topics (e.g., study skills, time management, campus resources) while continuing to be linked to learning communities to allow for integration of curriculum.

Increasing the credit value of the course is another goal. The seminar continues to be a one-credit course, something students often complain about on course evaluations or in discussions with their teachers. Many students feel the course requires too much work for a one-credit experience. One reason for the increasing workload in the seminar is that the course is often seen as the appropriate site for remedying students' skill deficiencies. When students needed e-mail training, it was built into the seminar syllabus. When other concerns are raised—academic honesty, substance abuse, chronic absenteeism, student debt—it is inevitable that someone will suggest this topic be addressed in the freshman seminar. The danger is that the seminar will suffer from "mission creep," that in trying to do so much for all, the seminar will fail to provide a positive and useful course experience for many.

If Temple is to expand its seminar offerings or require all first-year students to take a seminar, then staffing will be a problem, even if the schools and colleges retain their college-based versions. Recognizing and rewarding faculty who teach the course will be another major challenge. With first-year enrollments at their highest ever levels, finding classroom space might also be an issue.

The general education reform process also provides an exciting opportunity to expand linked-course learning communities around new core (general education) courses. Additionally, some of the new requirements being considered may be ideally suited to the team-taught learning communities model or to the formation of communities for upper-division students. Some possibilities include service or experiential learning in junior-level communities and capstone experiences for graduating seniors.

The good news is that the conversations about expanding first-year seminars come from a general belief—supported in part by assessment results, student feedback, and faculty perceptions of the value of the course—that first-year seminars and learning communities create a supportive learning environment for entering students.

Notes

[1] Pennsylvania has four state-related universities and a 14-institution state university system. According to the Pennsylvania Department of Education, state-related status is one that has been conferred upon four institutions of higher education through their initial charter or subsequent legislation. Such status defined these schools as "instrumentalities of the Commonwealth" in the Commonwealth System of Higher Education (http://www.pdehighered.state.pa.us/higher/cwp/view.asp?A=6&Q=41016).

References

MacGregor, J. (1996). *Goals and practices associated with learning community programs.* Retrieved March 29, 2004, from http://learningcommons.evergreen.edu/docs/Good_practices_in_LCs.doc

Revak, M., & Nuhfer, E. (2001). *Student management teams as assessment tools.* Retrieved March 29, 2004, from http://www.brevard.edu/fyc/listserv/remarks/revakandnuhfer.htm

Schlosser, E. (2001). *Fast food nation: The dark side of the all-American meal.* New York: Harper-Collins.

Temple University (2003-2004). *Undergraduate course descriptions guide.* Retrieved February 9, 2004, from http://www.temple.edu/bulletin/ugradbulletin/ucd/ucd_freshseminar.html

Appendix A
Freshman Seminar Instructor Workshop Agenda

9:00 – 9:45	Welcome and ice breaker
9:45 – 10:00	Assessment update: How are we doing?
10:00 – 10:45	Advice from experienced seminar teachers
10:45 – 11:00	Break
11:00 – 12:15	Teaching with *Elements of Learning* Incorporating *Lies My Teacher Told Me*
12:15 – 1:00	Lunch and getting to know your teaching partner
1:00 – 2:15	Discussion circles

- *Teaching time management*
- *Making students aware of new policies*
- *Promoting student involvement and planning out-of-class activities*

2:15 – 3:00	Extra planning time for teaching teams

Appendix B
The Learning Communities at Temple University
Community Plan Worksheet

Semester: Fall 2003

Teacher	Department	Course	Campus Phone	E-mail

Learning Community Title: Provide a title denoting the curricular theme for your learning community. The descriptive title should be no longer than five to seven words and should appear on the syllabus for each individual course in the community. [Example: *Hyperlink to History* might be the title for a learning community pairing American History Since 1877 with Introduction to Internet.]

Curricular Plan

1. What central questions or themes will your learning community explore?

2. How will the individual courses integrate the theme for this learning community?

3. What pedagogical strategies (e.g., collaborative learning, group projects, journal writing) will be implemented to promote the integration of knowledge?

4. In what ways will this learning community support students' transition to college-level learning?

5. In what ways will this learning community experience enhance connections between and among students and teachers?

6. If your learning community includes a section of the freshman seminar (Learning for the New Century), how do you plan to incorporate the seminar in terms of advancing the curricular theme?

7. What skills or knowledge should students acquire as a result of their participation in this learning community?

8. How will you assess student progress in terms of the outcomes described above?

Welcoming the First Class of First-Year Students with an Integrated Experience

Glenn Blalock, Sandra S. Harper, and Andrew Piker

Texas A & M University – Corpus Christi

In 1994, Texas A&M University-Corpus Christi welcomed its inaugural class of first-year students. Planning for their admission offered faculty, staff, and administrators of the University a unique opportunity to review the literature on effective student learning and craft the first-year experience accordingly. The A&M-Corpus Christi faculty recognized the challenge they were facing. Prior to 1994, the student body consisted of upper-level undergraduate students and master's students, and the faculty had not had to develop a core curriculum or general education requirements. With the prospect of educating first-year students for the first time, the faculty at A&M-Corpus Christi made a commitment to a particular vision of student learning that was both deep and personal, valued integration and application, and resulted from active engagement with course content and with other learners. Further, these faculty members were committed to the ideal that their vision of student learning would serve the numbers and kinds of students likely to attend a public university in a state with a rapidly increasing population.

Out of this commitment emerged the key characteristic of the Texas A&M University-Corpus Christi first-year experience—its requirement that all first-year, full-time students participate in an interdisciplinary learning community during both semesters of their first college year. Making this commitment especially challenging to meet was the complex learning community structure envisioned by the faculty. The learning community would link two large lecture courses (approximately 200 students), English composition courses (25 students per section), and first-year seminars (25 students per section) with the seminar serving as the integrative engine for the learning community. Despite the challenge of scaling the effort to involve every student, the institution continues to be committed to the mandatory participation of all first-time, full-time students in learning communities. Sustaining this institutional commitment has been a major undertaking as the size of the first-year class has grown from approximately 400 students in 1994 to more than 1,200 in 2003.

This chapter begins with a description of the institution and its learning communities configurations: tetrads (i.e., four courses linked together) and triads (i.e., three courses linked together). That is followed by a description of the seminars—their evolving focus and content—and the ways this evolution has occurred in response to the needs of a burgeoning A&M-Corpus Christi student body with diverse academic backgrounds. Finally, assessment data, changes in the program resulting from analyses of these data, and anticipated emphases as the program continues to mature are described.

Institutional Background

Texas A&M University-Corpus Christi is a Hispanic-serving institution that enrolls 6,500 undergraduate students and 1,500 graduate students. It is a moderately selective Master's I comprehensive university that is moving toward doctoral-intensive status with the expectation that it will be attained by 2010. Located on the Texas gulf coast in the city of Corpus Christi, the institution is composed of four colleges: Arts and Humanities, Business, Education, and Science and Technology. Texas A&M University-Corpus Christi is

> devoted to discovering, communicating, and applying knowledge in a complex and changing world. The University identifies, attracts, and graduates students of high potential, especially those from groups who have been historically under-represented in Texas higher education. Through a commitment to excellence in teaching, research, and service, Texas A&M University-Corpus Christi prepares students for lifelong learning and for responsible participation in the global community. (Texas A&M University-Corpus Christi, 2003a, p. 8)

To highlight its emphasis on the learning community concept, the University faculty established a goal of attaining a statewide reputation for an exemplary undergraduate education, anchored by an integrated core curriculum and learning communities (Texas A&M University-Corpus Christi, 2003b). The reputation of the learning communities has grown significantly over the last several years. In 2001, the governor honored the Texas A&M University-Corpus Christi First-Year Learning Communities Program with the Texas Star Award for its exceptional contributions to the state's *Closing the Gaps* higher education plan. The Policy Center on the First Year of College recognized and commended A&M-Corpus Christi in 2002 as 1 of 13 Institutions of Excellence in the First College Year. In 2003, the American Association of State Colleges and Universities (AASCU), in conjunction with the Policy Center, named A&M-Corpus Christi as 1 of 12 Founding Institutions in the national Foundations of Excellence in the First College Year project.

First-Year Learning Communities and the First-Year Seminar

Developing the first-year seminars and integrating them effectively into the learning communities program has been a long and difficult process at A&M-Corpus Christi. As Henscheid notes in chapter 1 of this monograph, first-year seminars tend to stress either *learning* or *community*. First-year seminar faculty members at A&M-Corpus Christi have struggled to find an appropriate way to balance these two emphases and to fulfill the seminar's integrative function within the learning communities. Finding this balance has been especially challenging because the idea of "learning communities" has been evolving and expanding.

The work of Ernest Boyer was central to the initial design of the first-year experience at A&M-Corpus Christi. Faculty were especially influenced by Boyer's (1987) concern about the loss of community in higher education and his vision of community that encompassed both social and classroom activities. This interest in community led faculty to the National Learning Communities Project in Washington state and to the significant work being done on the first college year at the National Resource Center for The First-Year Experience and Students in Transition at the University of South Carolina. Equally important to the initial design was the growing body of work on writing across the curriculum and on collaborative learning, two powerful initiatives in higher education that promoted the kinds of transformation called for by Boyer. As A&M-Corpus Christi faculty were developing their first-year program, they found further support for their efforts in the Texas Higher Education Coordinating Board's guidelines for and assumptions about core curriculum competencies, goals, objectives, and perspectives. For example, the guidelines stress critical thinking, writing, and understanding contrasting views. In the first-year learning communities, the faculty wanted to emphasize academics, interdisciplinary activities, critical thinking, information literacy, writing, and discussion (Meyer, 2002).

From this matrix of educational influences, the A&M-Corpus Christi faculty designed learning communities that linked large lecture environments with the small-class environments of English composition and the newly created first-year seminar. The same 25 students enrolled in the seminar and composition courses, and they joined similarly linked cohorts in the large lecture classes. The lecture courses and the composition course provided the disciplinary knowledge, and the seminar served as the conceptual linchpin holding the community together and integrating learning across the disciplinary courses within the community.

Students in the seminar and the composition course worked individually and collaboratively, using discussion and write-to-learn activities to engage concepts and material from the linked lecture and English composition classes. Ideally, senior professors facilitated the seminars, serving as master learners (i.e., learning role models) and assisting students with their individual needs.

To emphasize connections among the disciplinary courses within the learning communities, all involved faculty developed overarching themes or questions to guide the course content, or they developed lists of keywords or key concepts that all instructors in the learning community would use throughout the semester. Arranging for assignments and activities that emphasized interdisciplinary connections also helped ensure that the seminars would serve as more than study halls or lecture discussion sections. Initially, the learning communities comprised two large lecture sections, English composition, and first-year seminar. The first tetrads offered students the following combinations:

- environmental science/sociology/first-year seminar/English composition
- history/political science/first-year seminar/English composition
- psychology/music/first-year seminar/English composition

As the institution doubled its size during the 1990s, the college deans and faculty realized that the goal of using full-time faculty members as seminar leaders was impractical. Tenured and tenure-track faculty were still integral to the first-year learning communities, but their roles were as large lecture instructors or composition instructors. Thus, graduate students or adjunct instructors who received summer training prior to their teaching assignment became seminar leaders.

During this embryonic stage of the program, the first-year seminars focused primarily on *community*—following a curriculum that emphasized the general skills students need for the transition to college and attempting to orient and acclimate students to campus resources and activities as a way to help them "survive" the first college year. The focus on *learning,* which became a separate concern, took the form of weekly reviews of lecture material and of introducing students to generic study skills. The implementation of these two functions in the seminar gave it, in effect, a split personality. The misalignment between the initial vision and the actual implementation prevented the seminar from fulfilling its integrative role in the learning communities.

At this stage of development, the learning communities were not functioning as they were originally intended. Instead, they were merely courses linked together, with minimal integration of content or learning. Student evaluations and faculty involved in the program indicated that the learning communities were not working as planned, and the first-year seminar was identified as one of the primary problems. The seminar was especially prominent in student complaints because it was required of all students, it had no specific disciplinary status, and the learning community requirement was unique among state schools.

After a comprehensive administrative review of the program at its five-year mark, faculty members came together in a provost-sponsored retreat in May 2000 to refocus the learning communities—and more specifically the first-year seminar—on *learning* explicitly linked to the content of the large lecture courses and composition courses. Faculty also agreed to focus on active learning, emphasize higher order thinking skills, and act more purposefully in forging connections among the courses in the learning community.

Several major developments occurred as a result of this retreat. Faculty members revised the mission statement of the seminar as follows: "The First-Year Seminar at Texas A&M University-Corpus Christi immerses students in an active learning environment which provides an integrated curricular context in which to develop skills and a sense of academic community" (Pamela Meyer, personal communication, May 2000). The consensus of the retreat group was that the A&M-Corpus Christi faculty needed to put the *seminar* back into first-year seminar. Specifically, an integrated discussion of ideas and issues needed to be the backbone of the first-year experience. To achieve that vision, faculty needed to be willing to communicate with and support one another at all levels. Retreat participants came to the following conclusion: "Since integration is the key, all participants must unlock their disciplines and walk into each other's academic lives. The ideal is that each team member spends time planning and developing integrated exercises" (Pamela Meyer, personal communication, May 2000).

The vision of the first-year seminar and learning communities articulated at the retreat, with its emphases on an academically focused first-year seminar and on seminar-centered integration of the learning communities, redirected the First-Year Learning Communities Program. Some of the key elements of that development are described below.

Intersections

The most significant outcome of the retreat was a radical revision of the first-year seminar—its curriculum and its role in the learning community (LC). In particular, the seminar was reconstructed as the site for "situated learning" (Lave & Wenger, 1991). That is, students would learn the skills needed for success in college in the context of academic content they would find important and relevant to their lives. To focus the seminar on *learning*, five broad intellectual activities are used to guide the work done in the seminar: (a) using discussion as a way of teaching and learning, (b) developing critical thinking skills, (c) developing information literacy skills, (d) using writing to learn (especially reflective writing), and (e) developing metacognitive skills. In 2003, two additional overarching intellectual activities were added: (a) civic engagement, as our campus began its active participation in the American Democracy Project, and (b) a strengths-based approach to learning and success, with all first-year students, seminar leaders, composition faculty, and student service professionals engaging and implementing the StrengthsQuest™ program (Clifton & Anderson, 2002). In addition to these emphases, the necessity for connections among the courses in the learning communities has been highlighted. The seminar is the site where students engage in assignments planned by the LC team, using content, concepts, and material from the lecture course(s) and the composition course. Extensive planning and the strategic use of interactive web-based discussion tools enable these connections. To model integration and reflective learning, student performances in seminar and composition were evaluated through a portfolio system, with students submitting one portfolio to both the seminar leader and the composition teacher several times during the semester. The implementation of electronic portfolios is in the near future.

The seminar classes now challenge students to use higher order intellectual skills to grapple with course content from multiple perspectives, to engage in research, and to participate actively in class and small-group discussions in the classroom and in online discussion forums.

A typical activity sequence for students requires them to read for their lecture (and/or composition course); respond to those readings in an online discussion forum, using prompts developed by LC teachers; respond to their classmates' entries; engage in class and small-group discussions; and reflect on their learning performances. Much of this activity sequence takes place in the seminar, which becomes the place where students most fully engage the intellectual work expected of them in the lectures. Students are writing regularly, learning how to use critical thinking and critical reading skills, and practicing their information literacy skills. Through the process of ongoing reflection, they are learning how to learn. A representative writing assignment sequence for students asks them to choose a topic of interest, develop a research question, conduct research, and compose several pieces of formal writing related to the topic. They will engage these activities in the composition course and the seminar. Using lecture course content and concepts as they conduct the research and write, students share their writing with each other, in composition class and the seminar, use online forums for exchange and response, and earn grades in all three (or four) courses for their work.

Several times during the semester, students submit portfolios for evaluation. Though teachers often stipulate one or two specific pieces of work to include, students must make most choices as they attempt to provide evidence of their learning for the portfolio period. Students select from the wide range of work they have done, include it in the portfolio, and compose an extensive reflective overview for the portfolio to help instructors understand what is included in the portfolio, why it is included, and how it serves as evidence.

The emphasis on learning and on academic content does not mean that seminars (and other LC courses) are not also providing students with assistance in developing success skills to help them with their transition to college. Students have access to such assistance as needed on an individual or small-group basis. Because learning is situated and context-specific, that understanding is applied to student success skills, as well. No whole-class sessions focus on study skills, note taking, or time management, for instance. Not all students need or are ready for that kind of information at the same time. Instead, seminar leaders (and other LC teachers) monitor student performance regularly, and when students appear to need assistance, seminar leaders intervene and help. Because of the seminar's small size and the personal relationships that develop through conferences and in-class discussions, seminar leaders can help individual students develop the success skills that they need, in a meaningful context, when they need it. Prior to their enrollment, students learn about the rigorous intellectual nature of the seminar as described above and also indicate that the experience "will focus on other aspects of [their] successful transition to college life" (Texas A&M University-Corpus Christi, 2003c).

The current approach to the seminar is the right one for Texas A&M-Corpus Christi. Students recognize that *learning* and *community* are complex concepts, that students are members of many communities simultaneously, and that the ideal outcome of their education is not isolated learning within individual classes, but rather learning in, for, and with a community.

Before taking on their instructional roles in the learning communities, new seminar leaders complete a semester-long course during the summer. During the course, they learn theories of active learning, the concept of the learning paradigm (Barr & Tagg, 1995; Tagg, 2003), the idea of a learning community, and practical methods for engaging students in active learning. The core texts for this course are *Discussion as a Way of Teaching* (Brookfield & Presskill, 1999) and *Engaging Ideas* (Bean, 1996). Faculty teaching in the lecture courses and in composition receive these same texts. Before each semester begins, LC faculty meet several times to plan their connections; and they gather one time before each semester in Teaching Institutes, a professional development opportunity for all LC teachers. LC faculty members meet with their colleagues regularly during the semester and attend professional development workshops focusing on issues related to working in the LC environment.

Another positive result of focusing on *learning* in first-year seminars and learning communities has been reconceiving the structures of learning communities. Because the students have increasingly diverse backgrounds (especially in terms of the college credit they bring to their first year), a single LC configuration is too rigid and restrictive. As a result, new configurations for LCs have been introduced and the ways students are enrolled in existing LCs have become more flexible. A primary principle guides the LCs: Students should experience authentic connections among courses. So students are enrolled in at least a seminar and one connected course, because the seminar provides the energy and the space for integration.

Table 1 lists the LC variations that might be offered. Some of the configurations are semester-dependent (i.e., fall or spring); others are sensitive to faculty rotations (i.e., who teaches what and when). Within many of the configurations, the number of students who have placed out of one or both semesters of required composition is accounted for.

Currently, three configurations for LCs exist: (a) tetrads, which connect two lectures, a seminar, and composition; (b) triads, which connect one lecture, a seminar, and composition; and (c) developmental LCs, which connect several developmental courses (e.g., math, composition, reading) with a seminar. The first two configurations provide links for students who do not need composition. In the developmental configuration, students may be enrolled in one, two, or three developmental courses as part of the LC.

The different configurations create different expectations for seminars, beyond their primary roles. In the non-composition links, for instance, the seminars provide students with more explicit guidance in college-level writing expectations. However, even though seminar roles may differ in some ways from one LC configuration to another, the first-year seminar fulfills its primary objective in all of the learning communities—emphasizing *learning* in the context of community(ies).

Administrative Oversight

As the content of the first-year seminars has evolved, so has the administrative structure of the University Core Curriculum Program (UCCP). Initially a full-time administrator (the director of the UCCP) administered the core curriculum, which included the first-year seminar program. As the institution became more aware of the needs of first-year students, the UCCP became the administrative home for developmental education, academic advising, orientation, the Texas Academic Skills Program, and a host of other academic support activities. The curricular focus of the UCCP became lost amidst a number of competing obligations.

At the same time that the content of the first-year seminars needed reconsideration, the administrative structure also needed to be transformed to reflect the academic nature of seminar, the First-Year Learning Communities Program, and the UCCP as a whole. The support functions were removed from the UCCP, and it was placed under the direction of two core curriculum co-directors. These co-directors are faculty members actively involved in core curriculum instruction who serve three-year terms. The revolving nature of the leadership is intended to inject new ideas into the program, while maintaining a faculty focus on seminar and core activities. The new structure also merged the first-year seminar direction with that of the first-year writing program. The meshing of the two programs extends to the assignment of office space, as the first-year seminar leaders share newly renovated office space with the first-year composition instructors. The core co-directors report directly to the provost/vice president for academic affairs and are administratively responsible for overseeing the development, maintenance, and assessment of the general education program and the First-Year Learning Communities Program. These co-directors have assumed a 50% administrative role to carry out those responsibilities.

The current administrative structure is intended to ensure that the program is "faculty-owned" and that it will work to be responsive and sensitive to faculty input. However, without the support of the University administration and a dedicated budget, the administrative structure would be much less successful, and the kinds of changes described above would not have been possible. Because the faculty-as-administrators report to the provost, they have access to information and to support that is not constrained by exigencies of a particular college or other administrative unit.

Table 1
Learning Community Configurations at Texas A &M-Corpus Christi

Lecture	Lecture	Lab	Seminar	Composition
Environmental Science	Sociology	Environmental Science	Yes	Yes
Environmental Science	Sociology	Environmental Science	Yes	No
Sociology			Yes	Yes
Sociology			Yes	No
Environmental Science		Environmental Science	Yes	Yes
Environmental Science		Environmental Science	Yes	No
U.S. History to 1865		Political Science: U.S. Government	Yes	Yes
U.S. History to 1865		Political Science: U.S. Government	Yes	No
U.S. History to 1865			Yes	Yes
U.S. History to 1865			Yes	No
Political Science: U.S. Government			Yes	Yes
Political Science: U.S. Government			Yes	No
U.S. History, 1865 to present		Political Science: State and Local Government	Yes	No
U.S. History, 1865 to present		Political Science: State and Local Government	Yes	No
U.S History, 1865 to present			Yes	Yes
U.S. History, 1865 to present			Yes	No
Political Science: State and Local Government			Yes	Yes
Political Science: State and Local Government			Yes	No
Psychology		Music	Yes	Yes
Psychology		Music	Yes	No
Psychology			Yes	Yes
Psychology			Yes	No
Music			Yes	Yes
Music			Yes	No

Table 1 continued on next page.

Table 1 continued from previous page.

Lecture	Lecture	Lab	Seminar	Composition
Biology I	Chemistry I	BIOL	Yes	Yes
Biology I	Chemistry I	BIOL	Yes	No
Biology II	Chemistry II	BIOL	Yes	Yes
Biology II	Chemistry II	BIOL	Yes	No
Developmental Reading	Developmental Math	MATH	Yes	Yes
Developmental Reading	Developmental Math	MATH	Yes	No
Developmental Reading			Yes	Yes
Developmental Reading			Yes	No
Developmental Math		MATH	Yes	Yes
Developmental Math		MATH	Yes	No
Communication: Speech	Developmental Reading		Yes	Yes
Communication: Speech	Developmental Reading		Yes	No

Equally important to the effectiveness of the administrative structure has been the program's stable budget, most of which is invested in first-year seminar leader salary and professional development (e.g., sponsoring workshops and colloquia, purchasing books, and supporting limited travel). Since the material support of the learning communities program and seminar is stable and not dependent on soft money, program administrators have had enough latitude and independence to support the changes made in the program.

Assessment

First-year seminar students evaluate both the seminar itself and the learning communities program as a whole. Seminar evaluations were a major factor in the decision to increase the emphasis on academic learning of the first-year seminar. The Office of Planning and Institutional Effectiveness, under the direction of the associate vice president for planning and institutional effectiveness, systematically administers the National Survey of Student Engagement (NSSE) and the Noel-Levitz Student Satisfaction Inventory (SSI) to first-year students. Texas A&M University-Corpus Christi students score above the national mean on these surveys with respect to a variety of items concerning, for example, feeling a sense of belonging on campus, being made to feel welcome, feeling that the institution shows concern for the students as individuals, and having an enjoyable experience on campus. These data suggest that the first-year program is helping students to develop a sense of community and to smooth social transitions to college life.

Because the shift to a more academic focus for the seminar is a relatively recent phenomenon, assessment data regarding the learning focus is sparse, although preliminary indications are favorable. Comparisons of first-year students' responses on the spring 2001 NSSE to the national mean found that A&M-Corpus Christi students reported engaging in the following activities at rates higher than the national sample: (a) working on a paper requiring integration of ideas from various sources, (b) preparing multiple drafts for an assignment, (c) making presentations, (d) using an electronic medium in an assignment, and (e) having serious conversations with students of a race or ethnicity different from their own. A&M-Corpus Christi students were also more likely than the national sample to report feeling they had learned to write more clearly and effectively (Piker, 2002).

First-year students were surveyed twice during the fall semester (at the beginning and at the end) in 2000, 2001, and 2002 to examine outcomes related to participation in the first-year seminar. Students believed they had improved in a number of areas and reported statistically significant improvement in lecture note-taking skills, reading retention, time management, participation in class discussions, critical thinking, the ability to make connections among course content, writing ability, study skills for major test, and the amount of time spent studying for major tests. No statistically significant gain was reported (although students did report some improvement) on two items: (a) listening during class and (b) working with others in groups (Texas A&M University-Corpus Christi, 2002).

The learning community lecture courses are also offered as free-standing courses outside the learning community structure. For example, students might enroll in the core psychology course as a free-standing course rather than a linked one, while meeting their learning community requirement by enrolling in learning communities that include other lecture courses. The presence of both free-standing and linked versions of various core lecture courses made a statistical analysis possible to compare the performance of first-year students enrolled in courses that were part of the required learning communities to that of students who were enrolled in the same courses outside of the learning community structure. The analysis showed a significantly higher course withdrawal rate and lower course grades among those students who were not in a learning community. The positive results associated with learning community participation were slightly stronger among women and Hispanics (Sterba-Boatwright, 2000). These results mirror results from studies of the Chapman Community and Honors Program at Bowling Green State University, which found these programs to be particularly advantageous to women and students of color (Knight, 2003).

A more recent Texas A&M University-Corpus Christi study suggests that positive aspects of learning communities may vary depending on the type of learning community configuration. Group learning and student learning results in the triad of political science/first-year seminar/composition were compared to results in the tetrad of political science/history/first-year seminar/composition and in stand-alone political science sections. The learning community with one large lecture course (the triad) created a group of students who worked together, increased intellectual interaction, and enhanced student learning. Yet the tetrad configuration did not yield these same results (Huerta, in press). The difference between the triad and tetrad results may indicate that learning community instructors and students have been better able to make connections among classes and effectively engage and analyze course material in clusters with fewer courses. The difference in results may also suggest that graduate students as seminar leaders have been better able to integrate the materials from one lecture course (as opposed to two lecture courses) with the content of the composition course.

Next Steps for the Program

The Texas A&M University-Corpus Christi First-Year Learning Communities Program continues to evolve. A coordinated approach to training and the development of a common syllabus for first-year seminar leaders will provide students with a more consistent experience across sections. Without a common syllabus for the first-year seminar classes, students could have radically different requirements, even within the same learning community, for completing the course. Given the scope of the program—with all first-year students enrolled in learning communities and with each learning community including between six and eight linked sections of seminar and composition—a common syllabus seemed appropriate. The common syllabus establishes the number of portfolios that students will assemble, a consistent approach to attendance and participation, and a common statement about expectations. Also, because some seminars are taught by new instructors every year, the syllabus includes an explanation of the kind of learning environment the seminar is meant to promote. This helps instructors across the program to address new students' resistance to active learning. It also reminds the instructors that they are expected to develop and maintain an active learning environment in their classes. The syllabus materials do not restrict seminar leaders' ability to make creative use of the unique interactions within their learning community or within their individual seminars. However, it is clear that one of the important characteristics of a community is the common core experience shared by community members.

The extensive assessment of the entire core curriculum mandated for all Texas universities by 2004 is predicted to provide comprehensive data for additional program improvement. Assessment of the program will focus on replicating the results and extending the research questions emerging from the Sterba-Boatwright (2000) and Huerta (in press) studies. In particular, future assessments will examine academic outcomes as measured by methods other than student self-reports. This is especially important since recent research indicates a significant variance between student self-report data and actual learning outcomes in some academic disciplines (Clark, 2002).

Two major initiatives embraced by the institution in 2003, the Policy Center on the First Year of College's Foundations of Excellence initiative and the AASCU/*New York Times* American Democracy Project, will enhance the A&M-Corpus Christi learning communities program. The Foundations initiative emphasizes the need for University commitment to the first-year college experience by intentionally linking academic and student affairs efforts. As 1 of 12 founding public institutions in the Foundations initiative, A&M-Corpus Christi plans to devote a year to reconsidering the ways that the first-year learning communities program can continue its emphasis on learning while integrating more fully and effectively the resources and activities available through student affairs. The forging of new relationships between learning communities and student affairs will achieve a synthesis of *learning* and *community* that does not sacrifice the focus on academics or the goal of assisting students with their transition to college. It will encourage students to make connections with student affairs as part of their academic pursuits and develop and use assignments and activities that challenge students to integrate their academic *learning* with their learning about the University *community* represented by student affairs. Newly developed academic assignments and activities will invite students to locate, evaluate, use, and reflect on the wide range of resources available through student affairs. Just as students develop habits of mind that lead to deeper learning in their academic pursuits, they will develop an awareness of the resources available to them that will enrich them as active citizens, both on and off campus. In addition, the emphasis on success in the first-year program will be enhanced by participation in the Foundations initiative through the succeeding college years to result not only in degree completion but also the habit of lifelong learning.

Activities associated with the American Democracy Project will be threaded through assignment sequences in the first-year seminar and the first-year composition classes in an effort to increase the number of undergraduate students who are committed to engaging in meaningful civic actions.

Conclusion

The first-year seminar was initially envisioned as a site for learning about learning. However, it quickly became an orientation-focused survival skills course. With the revisions of the seminar and the reconsideration of its role in the learning communities, the seminar is accomplishing its mission of emphasizing academic learning within the context of a supportive community and fulfilling the promise inherent in *learning communities*. The introduction and initiation of the American Democracy Project to the learning communities program and the seminar expands the sense of *learning community* to a concept called *community learning*. By integrating the concept of civic engagement into the learning communities, and specifically the seminar and composition courses, students and faculty will be challenged to engage in learning that recognizes the value of linking the academic community to the communities beyond the campus. As learning communities and seminars emphasize *community learning*, they will be inviting students and faculty to do more than "learn about" the communities in which they are situated. Eventually, the ideal metamorphosis of the first-year learning community program at Texas A&M University-Corpus Christi would be to develop learning communities engaged in community learning that inextricably links the academic community to the communities in which students will continue to participate when they graduate. The first-year seminar is central to this civic engagement effort, as a site where students not only learn to learn, but also begin to use their learning for the benefit of others.

References

Barr, R. B., & Tagg, J. (1995). From teaching to learning: A new paradigm for undergraduate education. *Change, 27,* 12-25.

Bean, J. (1996). *Engaging ideas: The professor's guide to integrating writing, critical thinking, and active learning in the classroom.* San Francisco: Jossey-Bass.

Boyer, E. (1987). *College: The undergraduate experience in America.* Hoboken, NJ: Wiley.

Brookfield, S. D., & Presskill, S. (1999). *Discussion as a way of teaching: Tools and techniques for democratic classrooms.* San Francisco: Jossey-Bass.

Clark, R. A. (2002). Learning outcomes: The bottom line. *Communication Education, 51*(4), 396-405.

Clifton, D. O., & Anderson, E. (2002). *StrengthsQuest: Discover and develop your strengths in academics, career, and beyond.* Washington, DC: Gallup.

Huerta, J. C. (in press). Do learning communities make a difference? *PS: Political Science and Politics.*

Knight, W. E. (2003). Learning communities and first-year programs: Lessons for planners. *Planning for Higher Education, 31*(4), 5-12.

Lave, J., & Wenger, E. (1991). *Situated learning: Legitimate peripheral participation.* Cambridge, UK: Cambridge University Press.

Meyer, P. (2002, October). *First-year learning communities overview.* Presented at the Institutions of Excellence Site Review Symposium, Corpus Christi, TX.

Piker, A. (2002, October). *First-year learning communities assessment.* Presented at the Institutions of Excellence Site Review Symposium, Corpus Christi, TX.

Sterba-Boatwright, B. (2000). The effects of mandatory freshman learning communities: A statistical report. *Assessment Update, 12*(2), 4-5.

Tagg, J. (2003). *The learning paradigm college.* Bolton, MA: Anker Publishing.

Texas A&M University-Corpus Christi (2002). *First-year seminar fall 2000, fall 2001, and spring 2002 pre- and post-test results status report.* Corpus Christi, TX: Author.

Texas A&M University-Corpus Christi (2003a). *Undergraduate catalog 2003-2004.* Corpus Christi, TX: Author.

Texas A&M University-Corpus Christi (2003b). *Faculty handbook.* Corpus Christi, TX: Author.

Texas A&M University-Corpus Christi (2003c). *UCCP1101/course description.* Retrieved March 29, 2004, from http://firstyear.tamucc.edu/wiki/UCCP1101/CourseDescription

Using Learning Communities to Meet Diverse Student Needs at a Research University

Joel Nossoff and Dan Young

University of New Mexico

Chapter 12

The University of New Mexico has adopted multiple models of seminar-embedded learning communities to serve the wide range of needs of its growing and diverse first-year student population. This chapter contains descriptions of these models, paying special attention to their differences and similarities.

Institution Description

The Carnegie Foundation classifies the University of New Mexico Main Campus (UNM) as 1 of 151 Doctoral/Research Universities–Extensive (Carnegie Foundation for the Advancement of Teaching, 2000). With a total enrollment of about 25,000 students, the UNM first-year class in fall 2003 was 3,004, almost double the 1996 first-year class (University of New Mexico, 2003a). In addition to Schools of Medicine and Law, UNM is composed of eight undergraduate colleges and schools: Arts & Sciences, Fine Arts, Engineering, Education, Nursing, Architecture and Planning, Anderson School of Management, and University College. Virtually all first-year students are admitted first to University College. From there, they transfer to one of the other colleges. University College advises all first-year students and administers most of the Freshman Academic Choices, including the learning community programs described in this chapter.

New Mexico is a large state with a small, mostly rural population. The average family income is lower than the national median (U.S. Census Bureau, 2003), but New Mexico is rich in population diversity, history, culture, and physical attributes. With relatively low selectivity in admissions, UNM is the four-year, public school of choice for most New Mexico students who choose to stay in state. As the flagship university, UNM draws its first-year students largely from among the Anglo, Hispanic, and Native families of the state. In 1999, UNM initiated several strategies to improve the lower-division education of undergraduates. The first-year population was marked by large annual increases, caused primarily by the initiation of the New Mexico Lottery Scholarship in 1996. Yet UNM continued a 20-year history of low graduation rates and low retention of first-year students. In fact, the rates were among the lowest of all Carnegie Doctoral/Research Universities–Extensive institutions (America's Best Colleges, 1999).

Description of Seminars

Freshman Seminar

One of the first strategies to address these low retention rates was the creation of a first-year seminar. At the initiative of the president, a campus-wide subcommittee developed the course "Arts & Sciences 198 – Introduction to Undergraduate Education" with the following catalog description:

3 Credit Hours. Variable content in an academic discipline. Develops academic skills through study of the content areas, including scholarship, research, comprehension, analysis, synthesis, evaluation, application, critical thinking, and communication of ideas. Through study of the content areas, strengthens connections to campus, faculty, other students, fields of study, and cultures of research, scholarship, and higher learning. Through study of the content areas, facilitates transition and adjustment to University environments. Prerequisites: open to new freshmen in their first year only. Co-requisites: some sections may require co-registration in another specified course. [Traditional Grading]. (University of New Mexico, 2003b, p. 143)

The course fits in the typology of the first-year seminars as academic with variable content (National Resource Center for The First-Year Experience and Students in Transition, 2002). During the course development process, Vincent Tinto of Syracuse University visited UNM and suggested the concept of learning communities. The subcommittee quickly decided to link A&S 198 with first-year English (ENGL 101) to form Freshman Learning Communities (FLCs). "Freshman Seminar" refers to the academic with variable content course in each FLC. The first-year English, public speaking, or other course linked with the Freshman Seminar is referred to as a "linked course." Two courses in each FLC are referred to as being linked. When there are more than two courses in a Freshman Interest Group (FIG) or Living and Learning Community (described below), they are referred to as being blocked. The FLC program, with its linked courses, grew rapidly from four pairs of courses enrolling 76 students in fall 2000 to 24 pairs of courses enrolling 493 students in fall 2003.

The first-year seminar concept has evolved since its initial implementation. Increasingly, UNM is offering traditional first-year courses in a freshman seminar/freshman learning community option. For example, Introduction to Anthropology (Anthropology 101) is typically offered as a large (200-300 students) lecture section, with first-year through senior-year students. For the FLC, it is offered as a small, thematically based freshman seminar, with 22 first-year students co-enrolled in ENGL 101. The courses are scheduled back-to-back, in the same room, and the two instructors closely integrate the course content. The topics for writing in the FLC first-year English sections are the topics of study in the linked freshman seminars. One quarter of FLCs are linked or blocked with A&S 198 in place of another course from the first-year curriculum.

The FLCs have broadened the linkages now to include either first-year English or public speaking (Communication & Journalism 130), where the topics of student presentations are drawn from the freshman seminar and other course combinations. The FLCs that first-year students choose most frequently, and that academic advisors recommend most often, are those based on UNM Core Curriculum courses taught as freshman seminars. Other popular combinations include courses that introduce students to professions or fields of study (e.g., Introduction to Management, Medicine and Disease, Introduction to Education in New Mexico, Working with Children, Youth and Families).[1] Typically, students would not be exposed to such topics until they reached upper-division courses or graduate or professional school.

Freshman Interest Groups (FIGs) and Living & Learning Communities (LLCs)

In 2001, UNM initiated additional learning community options that put more emphasis on the social and less emphasis on the academic aspect of community than the FLC model. The purpose in designing the FIGs and LLCs was to provide a broader range of opportunities for the diverse student population. The organizational and conceptual center of the FIG and LLC programs is a one-credit seminar—the Freshman Interest Group Seminar (USP 101) and the Living & Learning Community Seminar (USP 102)—that is blocked with one or two other courses. The Faculty Senate approved these seminars as one-credit, graded courses, but they are now offered as variable (one to three) credit courses. The seminars were conceived as credit-bearing, graded courses in order for first-year students to consider the seminars an important component of their course load.

According to the typology of first-year seminars (National Resource Center, 2002), the FIG and LLC Seminars could be categorized as extended orientation hybrids—i.e., the seminars are intended to go well beyond introducing the students to the social and organizational structure of the University because the seminars also reveal the academic life. Furthermore, from the outset it was intended that the seminars not have a rigid, common curriculum. According to the UNM *Catalog*, USP 101 is:

> Designed to accelerate successful transition to university life. Enrollment limited to 25 incoming freshmen. Co-requisites: most sections will require co-registration in another specified course or courses. USP 102 is designed to accelerate successful transition to university life. Enrollment limited to 18 incoming freshmen with specific academic interests. Students live in the same dormitory. Co-requisites: most sections will require co-registration in another specified course or courses. (University of New Mexico, 2003b, p. 556)

As prospective FIG and LLC seminar leaders are told, success can be measured in many ways, including retention in the second semester and beyond, and achievement of Lottery scholarships (described in greater detail below). Success can also be measured more personally through gaining greater knowledge of one's self, developing friendships, gaining increased confidence in navigating the UNM system, and developing relationships with UNM faculty and staff. The FIG and LLC seminar leaders are told that their primary responsibility is to create an open, communicative, collaborative, trusting, and supportive environment within the seminar. Seminar leaders are encouraged to apply their unique strengths, interests, and backgrounds to the design of their courses, and a wide range of seminar designs has emerged. All FIG seminars and two of the LLC seminars are blocked with one or two other courses (i.e., "Students are co-enrolled in courses as part of the larger enrollment in at least one other course" Henscheid, Chapter 1). Syllabi of the courses in which the students are co-enrolled are not tailored for the FIG and LLC students, except for those of the seminars, and they are typically large lecture classes.

There are three reasons for this arrangement. First, large lecture classes are typical in large institutions that emphasize research and graduate education. Creating a community within a subsection of such classes mitigates some of the disadvantages of their large size. Second, the blocked courses provide common academic experiences that can serve as a focus for development of study skills. Third, the small scale of the FIG or LLC seminar allows discussion of the central concepts and applications of the blocked courses, which is not possible in the large lecture sections.

The two seminar structures and three learning community models constitute the range of Freshman Academic Choices available to first-year students at the University of New Mexico. These programs have been designed to facilitate successful transitions to the university.

Roles of the Seminar in the Learning Community

UNM seeks variety and encourages creative responses from the instructors who teach the freshman seminars in the FLCs and the FIG and LLC seminars. In Chapter 1, Henscheid identifies 12 approaches first-year seminar instructors take in linking the seminar, in content or process, with other courses in the learning community. All of those approaches can be found somewhere within the UNM system, although some approaches are more commonly addressed than others (see Table 1).

Table 1

Approaches for Linking First-Year Seminars to Other Courses in the UNM Learning Communities

Approaches to linking	Freshman Seminar in the FLC	USP 101 FIG Seminar	USP 102 LLC Seminar
The seminar serves as a "learning lab" for students to practice skills from other courses.	Some	Some	—
The seminar shares common readings, assignments, and projects with linked courses.	All	—	—
The seminar pulls together concepts from other courses.	—	All	Few
The seminar serves as a place to process concepts and draw larger meanings for meta-cognition and learning about learning itself.	—	All	All
The seminar serves as a place for faculty members from other courses in the link to visit and discuss connections.	All	All	All
The seminar instructor and instructor(s) from other linked courses assign one grade for individual or multiple assignments or for the entire term.	Some	—	—
The seminar serves as a place to review linked syllabi to keep students "on track."	—	All	Few
Seminar discussions explicitly link personal and/or social concepts with concepts learned in the other course(s).	—	All	Few
The seminar serves as a place to discuss process skills important to achievement in the linked courses.	—	All	Few
The seminar serves as a site for community building.	All	All	All
The seminar serves as a site for career exploration related to learning community themes and topics.	Some	Some	All
The seminar serves as a site for service-learning connected to learning community themes and topics.	Some	Some	Some

Note. Adapted from Henscheid, 2000 and Jean MacGregor (personal communication, February 14, 2003)

Rationale for Models

Variety of Models

Over the past four years, a wide variety of models have been developed to achieve the goal of increased student retention. These models seek to involve a wide range of university personnel

—tenured, tenure-track, and non-tenured faculty; staff members from student and academic affairs; and graduate students. Although a few freshman seminar instructors employ undergraduates to assist in their FLC, none of these models have systematically involved students as peer instructors. UNM presents a wide variety of courses that appeal to a broad range of students and are accessible to students with varying degrees of academic preparation. Courses that have stringent prerequisites, such as calculus, are neither linked nor blocked because such courses are accessible to a narrow range of students. Employing a variety of models also supports the university's strong commitment to encouraging interaction among students of diverse perspectives and backgrounds. As discussed below, the models derive their funding from many sources and require the cooperation of many different units on campus. They serve as an organizational nexus for the entire university and a point of origin for new modes of interaction and collaboration across campus.

Freedom of Choice

It was determined early in the planning process that first-year students would not be required to participate in an FLC, FIG, or LLC. They could choose, instead, to register for a traditional pattern of unrelated and unlinked first-year courses. This approach was adopted for several reasons.

- When students enroll voluntarily in one of these options, they are more committed to (and less resentful of) the learning community courses they select.
- In the early stages, there were insufficient resources to offer sections for required enrollment for all or selected groups within the first-year class.
- When a sub-group of first-year students is given requirements that other students are not, that group of students is typically labeled at risk, and the requirement is labeled remedial. As a result, faculty and students resist participation.
- UNM seeks the challenge of designing programs that would attract student and faculty participants without coercion.

Intersections/Integration of the Seminars in Each Learning Community Type

Freshman Learning Communities

In most FLCs, the discussions, readings, problems, and presentations of the freshman seminar and the linked course are integrated. In first-year English, the topics of the expository compositions are usually drawn from the freshman seminar and might be submitted for both classes. In public speaking, students develop and give presentations on topics from the freshman seminar, with skill-building and coaching from the public speaking instructor, and coaching on content from the freshman seminar instructor.

In a few instances, two instructors link two freshman seminars to form an FLC. In fall 2003, a music appreciation course was linked with "Cultures of the World" (anthropology). The instructors integrated their courses by introducing music across cultures and by studying cultures through their music. Another FLC linked a course in interpersonal communication to "Introduction to the Study of Language" (linguistics).

Freshman Interest Groups and Living and Learning Communities

The one-credit seminars of the FIGs and LLCs are intended to serve a number of integrative roles. They help integrate students socially by creating smaller scale classes that intentionally promote community building. They work to integrate the students into the University as an organization by helping students become more familiar with services, organizations, and opportunities. They work to integrate academic knowledge across disciplines and into the students' experiences. The blocked courses attempt to demonstrate how abstract academic content can be integrated into students' personal experiences and how disciplines relate to each other and the world.

Pedagogical Approaches

Multi-contextuality

The fundamental pedagogical approach of the Freshman Academic Choices is captured in Ibarra's (2001) conceptual framework of multi-contextuality, which draws on Hall's (1959) seminal works. The central assumption of this conceptual framework is that individuals develop their sense of reality and normality within specific cultural frameworks that influence how they learn and express themselves. The basic polarity of this framework is low context versus high context. Low-context learning environments are synonymous with the typical arrangement of universities where objectivity, univocality (i.e., one voice predominates), abstraction, and noncontextualized knowledge received from authorities are emphasized. High-context environments, on the other hand, emphasize community, collaboration, multivocality, and contextualized knowledge built through an interactive process.

One of the differences within the diverse student body is its position on the high/low context continuum: Many Native and Hispanic students generally come from high-context backgrounds, as do many other students. The interdisciplinary, community-oriented, collaborative approaches of Freshman Academic Choices address the strengths of high-context students and help them to understand and enable them to succeed within the low-context world of academia. Low-context students gain as well. They benefit from the increased opportunities to process actively and reflect on their learning while also absorbing how to make sense of diverse perspectives.

Inquiry-Based Learning

In the FLCs, the emphasis is on active, inquiry-based learning; on developing communication skills in the context of disciplinary knowledge; and on teamwork in faculty-student and student-student relationships. As noted above, freshman seminar instructors work closely with linked-course instructors to coordinate and integrate the two courses.

The Interdisciplinary Nature of Knowledge

Instructors in the FLCs highlight the interdisciplinary nature of knowledge, learning, and the world. They do this first through the integration of the freshman seminar and the linked course. Then the freshman seminars approach their themes from many disciplinary perspectives.

Class Size

The FLCs provide first-year students with balance to large sections and to lecture-format classes that are typical of the lower division. They give first-year students a taste of the teaching and learning found in upper-division courses and graduate school. The FIG and LLC seminars augment and complement the large lectures' content.

Building Community

The small size and intentionally engaging nature of the FLC, FIG, and LLC seminars will hopefully help build community among the students. The two courses in each FLC are scheduled back-to-back in the same classroom, which provides a consistent time and place in which to develop community. In the FLCs students are frequently engaged in short-term and long-term small-group projects, both in and out of class. These small-group projects help students develop the academic, social, and personal relationships that typify an academic community. The amount of time students spend together in and out of class by participating in the FIGs and LLCs helps them build academic and social support networks.

Details of Administration

Seminar Instructors

FLC instructors. Instructors of freshman seminars in the FLCs are typically tenured or tenure-track faculty or full-time lecturers. A few are part-time adjunct instructors. Most teach the freshman seminar as an overload to their regular teaching load, with extra compensation. Linked course instructors (e.g., first-year English, public speaking) are typically graduate teaching assistants or full- or part-time lecturers; a few are tenured or tenure-track faculty. They also normally teach such courses as stand-alones. Class size ranges from 20 to 25.

FIG and LLC instructors. In 2001, two LLCs focused on fine arts and engineering. The seminar leader for the engineering LLC was an experienced advisor in the School of Engineering. The freshman seminar worked with the dean and associate dean of the College of Fine Arts to identify a graduate student with the requisite knowledge and skills in that college. After interviewing applicants, one was selected. During that first year, an undergraduate fine arts major was also hired to help lead the Fine Arts Seminar.

In the second year (2002), the program expanded to four LLCs, adding a Management LLC and an Architecture and Planning LLC. The Engineering Seminar leader continued, an academic advisor was selected to lead the Fine Arts LLC, and graduate students were selected for the two new LLCs. This arrangement continued in the 2003 LLCs. In fall 2002, 20 FIGs were scheduled: 10 of the FIG seminars were led by graduate students, and 10 were led by student affairs staff. In fall 2003, 18 of the 22 FIG seminars were led by student affairs staff, and four were led by graduate students.

Instructor Selection and Professional Development

Freshman Seminar. For the FLCs, faculty members submit freshman seminar proposals that are reviewed and selected by the FLC Advisory Committee, and their participation is endorsed in writing by their chairs and deans. English or public speaking instructors for linked courses are selected in a collaborative process involving the course department, the freshman seminar instructor, and the FLC director. FLC instructors participate in a two-day faculty institute each May, a one-day meeting in August, and an evening meeting at about mid-term.

FIGs and LLCs. The selection process is different for graduate students and student affairs staff who lead the FIG and LLC seminars. In late fall semester, a call for proposals circulates among staff members. This call describes the nature of the one-credit seminar, its connection with the blocked course(s), and the process for selecting proposals. A committee representing both academic and non-academic units reviews the proposals. Among the criteria for selection are experience of the applicants, clarity of the description of the seminar, range of suggested blocked courses, and likelihood of attracting students to the option.

After the staff positions are filled, gaps in the blocked course offerings are located. Student affairs staff members tend to block their seminars with courses from the social and behavioral sciences, so those offerings are balanced with courses selected from other areas, such as physical and natural sciences and humanities. After identifying a full range of courses, FIG seminars are blocked with courses with permission from each department. Once permission is granted (no department has turned down a request), graduate students who are pursuing degrees in the additional areas are recruited. The graduate students' application materials are screened, and two or three members of the selection committee interview the most promising students.

FIG and LLC seminar instructors participate in three days of orientation: two in mid-May and one in mid-August. The word "orientation" was chosen purposefully to suggest that finding a common direction between their seminars is an important task for the leaders. Because there is no common syllabus for the seminars, it is essential that all seminar leaders be united in their understanding of the program's purpose.

Funding Sources

Funding sources form a virtual mosaic, representing the breadth and depth of campus involvement and commitment to these learning communities. Starting in 1999, then President Bill Gordon directed private funds from the UNM President's Club to a UNM Endowment for Academic Excellence. The Endowment provides the president with discretionary start-up funds for new initiatives to improve UNM. The first project he selected was the Freshman Seminar Program. The Endowment continues to fund most of the FLCs, FIGs, and LLCs.

When the vice president for student affairs provided additional funding for the FIGs, teaching positions in FIG and LLC seminars were opened to student affairs staff. This allowed a rapid expansion of the FIGs and LLCs. In 2002, the provost provided funding for additional FLCs, FIGs, and LLCs in the regular instructional budget of the university. A major source of support comes from costs that are shared with academic departments. In the FLCs, the two primary linked course departments, English (for first-year English) and Communication and Journalism (for public speaking), pay normal compensation to instructors of first-year English and public speaking, and the FLC adds a training and preparation stipend. The University College is also a funding source for these Freshman Academic Choices.

Allocation of Funding

FLC. The base-added cost to offer one FLC in 2003 was $6,000. Four thousand dollars of that is extra compensation to the freshman seminar instructor to teach the class as an overload. The freshman seminar instructor and linked English or public speaking instructor are each paid $1,000 for preparation and participation in the summer faculty institute. Because linked instructors are paid normal on-load compensation by their departments, their compensation is not an added program expense. Cost for training, supplies, equipment, and program support is between $5,000 and $10,000 annually. The dean of University College pays the full-time director.

FIGs and LLCs. The FIG and LLC seminars are a less costly approach to promoting student success because the administrative work is less intensive than with the FLCs. Since the FIG and LLC seminars are simply blocked with one or two other courses, no extensive collaboration is needed to align course content as there is with the freshman seminars and linked courses in the FLC model. Furthermore, the FIG and LLC seminars only carry one credit and meet only once a week. FIG and LLC seminar leaders receive $1,500 to teach their one-credit seminars and an additional $100 for participation in the three-day orientation. In a few cases, two instructors will co-teach a seminar, in which case the $1,500 is split between them, but each receives $100 for attending the orientation. Cost for training, supplies, equipment, and program support is between $5,000 and $10,000 annually. The dean of University College pays the full-time director of these programs.

Coordination

The dean of University College administers all FLCs, FIGs, and LLCs, and there is a high level of coordination among and within the programs. Administrators of the three models work to make the programs complementary rather than competitive. Among the programs, there is full collaboration in development of a unified web site and annual catalog of Freshman Academic Choices. Selection of themes and courses for FLCs, LLCs, and FIGs is coordinated to assure diversity of offerings and reduce duplication. Recruitment of students to the range of Freshman Academic Choices is unified in all promotions, publications, and presentations. They share a separate section in the UNM *Schedule of Classes* and a separate and unique section number in the course numbering system. The automated registration system is programmed so students must enroll in the complete set of linked or blocked classes. A formal advisory committee with 35 members works with the directors to provide additional guidance and support across programs. An advisory group also helps with FIG and LLC proposal review, interviewing prospective seminar leaders, program review, and other advisement functions. This group is smaller and less formal than the FLC advisory group, because the FIGs and LLCs are more autonomous than the FLCs and require less coordination with academic departments.

The residential character of the LLCs greatly increases the logistical complexity and need for close coordination among multiple academic and administrative units. Most incoming first-year students register for their classes during mandatory orientation. These two-day orientation sessions run all summer, but the housing office finalizes its residence assignments by mid-July. This means that LLC students must be identified and confirmed well before the final orientation in late August. This requires an intensive mail, e-mail, and telephone campaign, which is followed by numerous personal contacts with students and their parents.

Curriculum Design

FLC. Faculty members from all colleges are invited to submit proposals for freshman seminars to link with English composition, public speaking, or a similar course. Proposals for seminar sections are drawn from general education courses or for courses that help students explore careers in medicine, nursing, and health-related fields; teaching; law; engineering; and management. For fall 2003, 47 FLC seminar proposals were submitted, and 25 were selected.

FIGs and LLCs. Graduate student-taught seminars generally focus more on the content and academic skill development connections with the blocked courses, while staff-taught seminars are more focused on themes (i.e., career exploration, common first-year experiences). The staff-taught seminars also tend to be more humanistic than academic, although the differences represent points on a continuum rather than a strict dichotomy. Staff and graduate students are invited to serve as instructors based on their expertise and experience.

A major portion of the three-day FIG/LLC instructor orientation is the development of the curriculum and instruction of the seminars. Instructionally, the orientation emphasizes inductive methods that build on students' previous knowledge and on their new experiences at the university. In terms of content, it emphasizes the knowledge, skills, and attitudes that lead to success as a student. Faculty in the FLCs are free to participate in instructional development opportunities offered through this program and other units on campus.

Student Recruitment

Efforts to recruit students are greatly facilitated by two-day summer orientation sessions that are required for every first-year student. The orientation includes academic advising and registration. A highly developed marketing effort begins each March when the fall *Schedule of Classes* is finalized. The booklet *Freshman Academic Choices* and its companion web site are revised in early May each year. The booklet is mailed to every first-year student and their parents before orientation. Students receive it in the information packet at orientation and parents receive it in the parent information packet for the Family Connection (parents' orientation).

Advisors and orientation leaders are critical to the recruitment efforts. Every May, a series of meetings is held with academic advisors and orientation student/peer leaders to brief them on the FLCs, FIGs, and LLCs. Some FLC and FIG seminar instructors come to these meetings to talk about their classes. Because of the special residential component of the LLCs, targeted mailings are sent to first-year students interested in the theme (usually an academic major). Most LLC students, who are committed to an LLC, are guaranteed a room with other LLC students before they arrive for orientation, advising, and registration.

Throughout the summer, the enrollments in each FLC, FIG, and LLC are monitored, and advisors and student orientation leaders receive regular updates. The update lets them know which learning communities have been filled and which are still open. In some cases, key advisors help with filling underenrolled courses. In those instances, instructors are sometimes brought in to meet the advisors. The result of these recruitment efforts is that typically the FLCs and FIGs have 85% to 95% of total seats filled, with most sections completely filled. The LLCs are typically 100% filled.

Assessment

From the beginning, assessment has been designed into the Freshman Academic Choices. Because the programs were initiated to address certain institutional problems, the goals and objectives of the programs are measurable and show progress toward desired outcomes.

Academic Performance Measures

The performance of learning community participants and non-participants are compared on several academic factors, including grade point average and persistence rates. While some institutions seek to improve first-year student performance and retention by raising their admission requirements, UNM has not adopted that strategy. Instead, UNM focused on fulfilling the promise of access, especially to underserved and underrepresented populations, by improving the academic performance of the students. Table 2 shows that the average incoming academic preparation of first-year students has varied little over time. Most measures have dropped since 1997. Only a few measures show slightly higher values.

It is often difficult, if not impossible, to attribute differences in performance to the programs themselves. There are many other intervening variables that may affect outcomes. Still, the upward trends in the data for overall first-year performance are gratifying. Figure 1 shows a steady increase in the grade point averages of first-year students even though the student preparation levels remained constant or dropped.

Table 3 shows that first-year student retention to the third term began to rise in 2000, when UNM initiated several improvements in the first-year experience, with the highest rate in fall 2002. Table 4 compares retention to the third term for fall 2002 program participants and non-participants. Statistical tests of significance have not been conducted. Fall 2002 was the first year all programs were in place. Therefore, results for this one cohort allow comparison across the programs.

Table 2
Academic Preparation of Entering Fall Cohorts of First-Year Students at UNM

	1997	1998	1999	2000	2001	2002
High School Grade Point Averages	3.28	3.25	3.27	3.29	3.31	3.31
High School Rank (%)	69.0	68.0	68.0	69.0	69.0	68.0
Average ACT/SAT[a]	22.73	22.25	22.03	22.07	21.86	22.11
Average ACT score	22.6	22.1	21.9	21.9	21.7	21.6
Average SAT score	1077	1077	1068	1082	1060	1112
Average Number of College Prep Units[b]						
Total	15.18	15.15	14.64	14.80	14.36	14.09
English	4.01	4.03	3.92	3.95	3.91	3.88
Math	3.45	3.31	3.18	3.31	3.26	3.20
Social Science	2.74	2.95	2.70	2.57	2.41	2.32
Science	2.68	2.57	2.60	2.62	2.53	2.50
Foreign Language	2.30	2.28	2.24	2.34	2.25	2.20
College Prep Grade Point Average	3.05	3.04	3.06	3.05	3.07	3.07

Note. All values are means for the indicated measure. Source of data is UNM Office of Institutional Research. Tests for statistical significance have not been applied.
[a] Includes converted SAT scores.
[b] 1 college prep unit = 2 semesters or 1 year of subject.

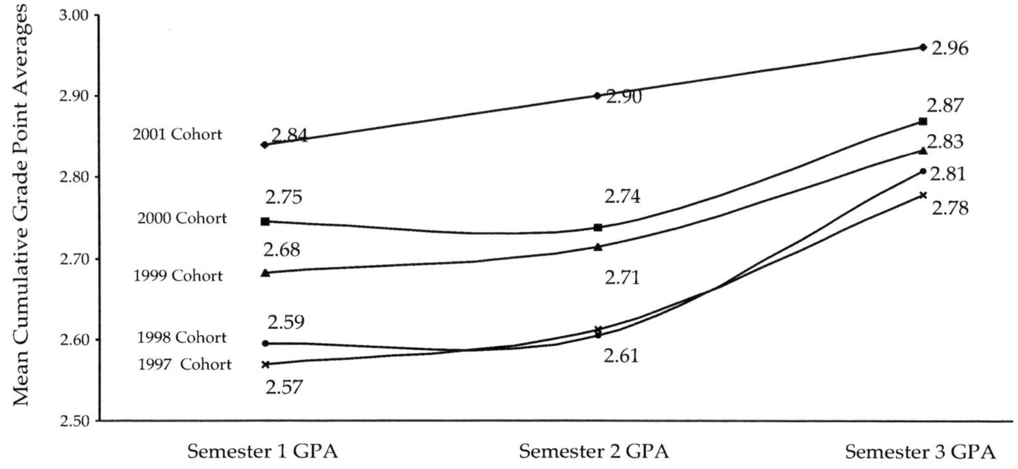

Figure 1. Mean grade point averages of successive first-year student fall semester cohorts at UNM. GPA calculation only includes students who complete a particular semester. A student is considered "full-time" if he or she was enrolled full-time during their first semester. Data from UNM Office of Institutional Research. No test of statistical significance was applied.

Table 3

Third Semester Retention of First-Year Student Cohorts

	Entering Fall Cohorts					
	1997	1998	1999	2000	2001	2002
Percent retained to third semester (%)	71.5	69.9	71.6	73.4	76.3	76.2

Note. Source of data is UNM Office of Institutional Research. Tests for statistical significance have not been applied.

Table 4

Third Semester Retention of First-Year Program Participants and Non-Participants Fall 2002 Cohort

	All first-year students ($n = 2,821$)	FLC students ($n = 394$)	LLC students ($n = 43$)	FIG students ($n = 377$)	Non-participants ($n = 2,007$)
Number retained	2,140	309	39	275	1,517
Percent retained (%)	75.9	78.4	90.7	72.9	75.6

Note. Source of data is UNM Office of Institutional Research. Tests for statistical significance have not been applied.

Lottery scholarship attainment is a critical indicator of success, because that scholarship requires first-year students to earn a 2.5 GPA on a minimum of 12 credit hours in their first semester. If they attain that, any New Mexico high school graduate may receive a tuition scholarship for up to eight semesters. If they do not earn the minimum GPA in their first semester, they never receive the scholarship. As a consequence, the first semester is critical to the ability of many students to pay for their college education. Table 5 presents results on attainment of lottery scholarships.

In addition to the academic performance factors, information and data for formative assessment help to improve the programs.

Table 5

First-Time UNM First-Year Students Achieving New Mexico Lottery Scholarship

Fall semester	1997	1998	1999	2000	2001	2002	2003
Eligible first-year students (%)	53.1	56.2	60.8	63.6	67.5	68.8	69.8
Number of first-year students achieving lottery scholarship	855	1,230	1,364	1,417	1,367	1,606	1,769

Note. Source of data is UNM Office of Institutional Research.

Evaluations by Students

FLC. For the FLCs, each student completes two web-based surveys at the end of the semester: (a) an FLC end-of-semester feedback form (narrative responses to six open-ended questions) and (b) a freshman seminar course evaluation (forced choice responses indicating degree of satisfaction with 22 variables).

These provide program directors and instructors class-by-class information about the classes, with the ability to determine which FLCs were more successful in meeting program goals. The information helps to decide whether or not to bring back an instructor and to repeat a Freshman Seminar/FLC.

FIGs and LLCs. During the final week of classes, FIG and LLC students are asked to respond to an eight-item, open-ended questionnaire. The responses are ranked on a one-to-five scale. The most telling responses are to question 8: "If you knew someone who was coming to UNM next year, would you recommend the FIGs (or LLCs) to him/her?" More than 85% of FIG and LLC students would either "recommend" or "strongly recommend" joining a FIG or LLC.

Focus Groups

In the first and second years (2000 and 2001), FLC faculty and students were engaged in focus groups that helped identify strengths and weaknesses in the program. Students praised the opportunity to make friends and find academic support, while faculty members voiced concern about time for necessary collaboration. This and other information collected through the focus groups are used to improve the recruitment, selection, and training of faculty. They also are used in faculty training to help faculty understand student perceptions about their FLC experiences (Lichtenstein & Dennison, 2002; Dennison, 2002).

National Survey of Student Engagement (NSSE)

Each year since 2000, UNM has administered the College Student Report of the National Survey of Student Engagement (NSSE) to a random sample of first-year students and seniors, and a targeted sample of FLC participants. The aim is to determine if the FLCs have any effect on the engagement of students as measured by NSSE. These data have been collected, but not yet fully analyzed. Again, the intent is to find improvements in the entering class as a whole, which would reflect FLC's impact.

Future of the Freshman Academic Choices

Continuation and Expansion

In fall 2003, 42% of first-year students voluntarily registered for an FLC, FIG, LLC, or the University Honors program, another opportunity for students to enter low enrollment courses. The strategic goal of UNM is for all first-year students to be registered in one of these programs in their first semester. An increase in the number of FLCs, FIGs, LLCs, and the capacity of the University Honors Program is planned. More of the FLCs and FIGs will be designed to include and integrate Introductory Studies courses (i.e., developmental courses in math, writing, and college reading).

Freshman Introductory Studies Cohort

In fall 2003, the Freshman Introductory Studies Cohort (FISC) began. This option is designed for students whose placement test scores require them to take Reading and Critical Thinking (Introductory Studies Reading, IS-R), a college preparatory course. Typically, IS-R students have the smallest range of course options since most university courses are reading intensive. FISC combines IS-R, a course in macroeconomics (Economics 105), and a one-credit FIG-type seminar. The FISC reading instructor modifies her instruction by using economics texts as the focus of skill building; the instructor of the FISC seminar reinforces the reading skills and helps the students with the economics content. Enrollment for both the IS-R and FISC seminar is capped at 25 and comprises the same set of students; the economics course is a typically large lecture course of more than 250 students. The economics course is not adapted to the skill level of the IS-R students (i.e., the point is to help students with reading difficulties succeed in a regular reading-intensive academic course). The close collaboration that has developed thus far among the instructors bodes well for the success of this pilot effort.

All students who enter the University of New Mexico are offered an opportunity to choose the learning community best suited to their needs. They base their selection on a topic that interests them, a desire to make friends quickly and increase connections with faculty members, and the necessity of learning important academic skills. Through the FLCs, FIGs, and LLCs, the institution makes every attempt to help students learn through community.

Notes

[1] Due to space limitations here, the number of examples from each learning community model has been minimized. Readers are invited to access several at www.unm.edu/freshman. A version of the booklet *Freshman Academic Choices* may also be downloaded at that web site.

References

America's best colleges. (1999, August). *U.S. News and World Report.*

Carnegie Foundation for the Advancement of Teaching (2000). *The Carnegie classification of U.S. institutions of higher education.* Retrieved September 29, 2003, from http://www.carnegie foundation.org/Classification/CIHE2000/PartIIfiles/u.htm

Dennison, C. (2002). *Freshman learning communities and student engagement.* Unpublished master's thesis, University of New Mexico, Albuquerque.

Hall, E. T. (1959). *The silent language.* Greenwich, CT: Fawcett.

Henscheid, J. M. (2000). [Responses to 1997 National Survey of First-Year Seminar Programs]. Unpublished raw data.

Ibarra, R. A. (2001). *Beyond affirmative action: Reframing the context of higher education.* Madison, WI: University of Wisconsin Press.

Lichtenstein, M., & Dennison, C. (2002, May). *Satisfaction with freshman learning communities and program impact: All learning communities are not created equal.* Paper presented at the Association for Institutional Research Forum, Tampa, FL.

National Resource Center for The First-Year Experience and Students in Transition. (2002). *The 2000 national survey of first-year seminar programs: Continuing innovations in the collegiate curriculum* (Monograph No. 35). Columbia, SC: University of South Carolina, Author.

U.S. Census Bureau. (2003). *State rankings - Statistical abstract of the United States: Resident population; median household income; American Indian, Alaska Native resident population.* Retrieved August 9, 2003, from www.census.gov/statab/ranks/rank07.html, www.census.gov/statab/ranks/rank01.html, www.census.gov/statab/ranks/rank33.html.

University of New Mexico. (2003a). *Freshman cohort tracking reports.* Albuquerque, NM: Author, Office of Institutional Research.

University of New Mexico. (2003b). *The University of New Mexico catalog, 2003-2005.* Albuquerque, NM: Author.

The Flexible First-Year Seminar as the Centerpiece of Five Learning Community Programs

Phyllis Endicott, Diana Suhr, Sharon McMorrow, and Pat Doherty

University of Northern Colorado

Chapter 13

Since 1991, faculty and staff at the University of Northern Colorado (UNC) have created several types of learning community programs to serve entering students. The centerpiece of these varied programs is a flexibly designed first-year seminar, Undergraduate Studies and Liberal Arts (ID 108), which encourages students to connect to faculty, fellow students, course concepts, and academic or pre-professional interests (see Appendix A for a general syllabus).

This chapter begins with descriptions of the institution and ID 108 and illustrates the role this course plays in five learning community programs offered to subgroups of the student population. The chapter also offers results from four types of assessments used in UNC's learning communities, including longitudinal studies of retention and graduation rates and results from open-ended surveys of students and faculty, interviews, focus groups, and student surveys administered within and outside the learning communities. These assessment results have been instrumental in improving program design and services. Despite funding constraints, program coordinators believe the learning communities and the ID 108 class, which gives them coherence, have been securely institutionalized.

Institutional Background

The vision statement of the University of Northern Colorado (UNC) describes the institution as "a leading student-centered university that promotes effective teaching, life-long learning, the advancement of knowledge, research, and a commitment to service" (University of Northern Colorado, 2003, p. iv). Enrolling more than 10,000 undergraduate and 1,250 graduate students, UNC is a moderately selective, multipurpose public institution. Located in Greeley, a traditionally agricultural, but increasingly suburban, area 60 miles north of Denver, Colorado, the institution is composed of five colleges: Arts and Sciences (A&S), Education, the Monfort College of Business, Health and Human Sciences, and Performing and Visual Arts. A&S administers learning community programs appropriate for most majors in the five colleges and for all undeclared students. Flexibility is the philosophy that underpins UNC's learning communities. As described in this chapter, students who are decided about their majors early in their academic career, including students interested in education or pre-health professions, will find learning community offerings that are specifically tailored to their academic choices. Other students who have interdisciplinary interests or those who are provisionally admitted to the university will find learning communities appropriate to their needs.

The First-Year Seminar: Learning Community Centerpiece

As UNC has developed its learning community programs, the first-year seminar, ID 108, has been a constant. Although many students report they select a learning community because they want to enroll in the courses offered in the package, assessments indicate that many of the social, academic, and pre-professional benefits of learning community participation are attained through this one-credit course at the heart of each community. To provide structural coherence, the ID 108 instructor also teaches another linked course. The seminar helps students adjust to the new campus environment, and many sections incorporate thematic or pre-professional assignments, activities, and assessments germane to the linked classes.

Typical of first-year seminars at other institutions, every section of ID 108 is expected to address extended orientation topics designed to help students with the transition to college. These include an introduction to the liberal arts tradition; UNC's general education program; and campus resources, such as the tutoring and career centers, computer labs, and the library. Often students begin a library or computer-based assignment during their ID class and submit their work for grading in a linked class. They also become familiar with computerized career-exploration software and UNC's online registration and information system. To support the statewide emphasis on timely graduation, ID 108 includes an examination of personal and academic goals, career exploration, major selection, and the creation of a four-year graduation plan. The class uses the UNC-specific booklet *Staying on Track: The Four-Year Graduation Guide* to explain many University policies and requirements, and all participating students are required to obtain academic advising while completing their four-year plans. Instructors use common grading criteria to evaluate the four-year graduation plans.

In this course, students write journals or reports reflecting on various aspects of their academic and co-curricular experiences. Most students also complete small group projects and presentations. Some ID 108 sections require participation in service-learning activities, such as working with children in the larger community. Individuals and groups of students in many classes attend events relevant to the learning activities taking place in their communities. Students earn letter grades for ID 108, a one-credit elective class.

Creating Programs to Meet Varied Student Needs

Across all five learning community programs, ID 108 serves as the center, holding elements of the student experience together. Likewise, the link with other courses offers the seminar a multi-course context in which to introduce students to cross-disciplinary concepts and college success topics. Past attempts to offer the first-year seminar as a stand-alone course and to separate learning communities from the seminar have proven much less successful than the integrated model. For example, in its beginning, the Cluster Learning Community (described below) was offered without ID 108, but the seminar was soon linked in the program primarily for the convenience it offers in scheduling interdisciplinary meetings and the time it allows to address topics important to first-year student success. Isolated first-year seminars have also been attempted at the institution and largely abandoned. At one point, UNC's stand-alone ID classes were offered as a selection of seminars called Major Connections taught by outstanding senior faculty. Despite the expertise of these instructors, they found it difficult to build connections with students in a class that met only once a week over a 15-week semester. Many of these faculty members have now become part of the institution's learning community programs.

The Freshman Challenge – Learning Communities for Conditionally Admitted Students

ID 108 was first embedded in Freshman Challenge, UNC's first learning community, which is designed for the institution's 200 to 300 conditionally admitted students. Beginning in 1991, one faculty member taught both the first-year seminar and a section of English composition to the same cohort of 25 students and replaced trained undergraduates as the primary academic advisors for Challenge students. Each ID 108/English instructor's contract included three hours of tutoring and advising per week for each composition class taught, with this extra support focused on each instructor's own cohort of composition/ID students. The paired learning community offered in Challenge (see Figure 1) has since expanded to become a multi-course, general education-based learning community.

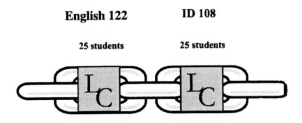

Figure 1. The Challenge learning community at University of Northern Colorado.

Courses in the Challenge learning community are chosen primarily from among traditional first-year offerings. The primary goal of this simple learning community is to help students with their transition into the university community, quickly and effectively connecting them "to the people and resources they need to succeed in college" (Shapiro & Levine, 1999, p. 23). Many of these connections are encouraged in ID 108, which introduces campus resources and provides a place to discuss general education, major selection, and the four-year planning process. The seminar and expanded conference hours also give instructors an opportunity to address typical adjustment issues and individual concerns. Responses to student surveys have indicated a degree of stigma related to enrollment in the Challenge learning community, a sentiment that has diminished as additional learning community programs have been developed.

The Cluster Program – Interdisciplinarity Emphasized in the First-Year Seminar

Interdisciplinarity is the focus of ID 108 linked to courses through the Cluster Program, which was launched for fully admitted first-year students in 1992. In these clusters, cohorts of 20 to 25 students co-enroll in two or three large lecture classes, where they form a subset of the total course enrollment. Each cohort of Cluster students also comprises the entire enrollment of an English composition class and the ID 108, taught by the English faculty member (see Figure 2).

In this learning community, ID 108 is a vehicle for intellectual exploration, where students are asked to bring together concepts and themes from the other linked classes. In the Cluster seminar, all students and faculty members meet monthly to discuss interdisciplinary themes created by the faculty in consultation with the learning community program coordinator. These themes are reinforced by integrative end-of-the-semester assignments, often collaboratively graded by all instructors in the cluster. For example, students in an American Studies cluster (i.e., American history, U.S. geography, and English composition) discussed historical and geographical concepts of "community" as evidenced by the Puritans and by contemporary ethnic groups in their ID 108 class.

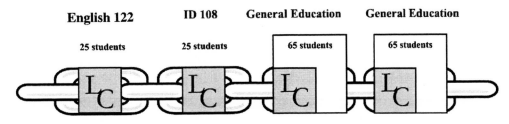

Figure 2. The Cluster learning community at University of Northern Colorado emphasizes interdisciplinarity.

Another year, this cluster took a field trip to Dearfield, the first Black settlement in Colorado; to Five Points, an historic Black community in Denver; and to a Black western history museum, also in Denver. Upon their return, each student wrote a paper reflecting on their experiences for collaborative review by their cluster instructors.

Each of the learning communities, including Cluster, has evolved to better meet student needs. For example, when the program was launched, the Cluster coordinator predicted that its interdisciplinarity would appeal primarily to well-prepared students and, therefore, the program includes some of UNC's most difficult general education classes in clusters. Also, as noted above, the original program did not offer ID 108 or the tutoring and advising support included in Challenge. Given the demanding nature of the linked classes and the lack of extra support, Cluster began as an honors-type program that appealed to high-achieving students. Assessments suggested that, as a consequence, strong students thrived in the program while weaker students fared less well. And even the strongest students, it was discovered, would have benefited from added academic advising and personal support. Once learning community staff perceived these limitations, Cluster added ID 108, taught by the English instructors, and extra conferencing hours with these faculty members.

Academic Advantage – A Flexible Learning Community Open to All

The content of ID 108 is more loosely coupled with courses in Academic Advantage than in other learning community configurations. Academic Advantage, a learning community program created in 1993, co-enrolls each cohort of students in a core class (e.g., English composition, speech, or lower-division math) and the first-year seminar and provides students extra conference hours with the core class instructor. The program also co-enrolls each cohort of students in a larger general education class such as psychology, sociology, anthropology, or history. While the structure offers the potential for cross-disciplinary assignments and other content connections, these features are not always present and themes are not pre-planned. Advantage ID 108 is focused on extended orientation in student success topics and generally serves as a venue for creating connections between students and faculty, not necessarily content or concepts across courses. A typical Advantage design is illustrated in Figure 3.

The chief advantage of the program is its flexibility for students and instructors. Because connections among Advantage classes remain largely structural, new links are relatively easy to add to the schedule during summer registration when student demand for course links often exceeds supply. Also, because each link is small in terms of credits (7 or 8 credits in each link as opposed to 10 to 12 credits in the Cluster program), Advantage can easily form the foundation for degree programs by meeting specific first-year requirements. Advantage offers course links to all first-year students during both fall and spring semesters (with spring continuation optional) and works to fulfill the institutional goal of providing a learning community experience for all students who desire it.

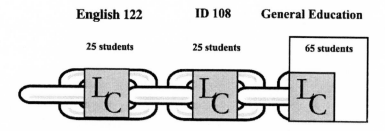

Figure 3. Academic Advantage learning community at University of Northern Colorado.

Ascent –A Learning Community for Pre-Professional Health Students

The Ascent learning community offers participating students opportunities to share readings and complete other assignments related to pre-professional health programs in the ID 108 course. Each year since its inception in 1994, Ascent has attracted some 75 students and guarantees enrollment in the introductory chemistry and biology courses required for admission to graduate pre-medical and allied health sciences programs. Ascent students co-enroll in the courses listed above, English composition, and ID 108 during both fall and spring semesters of their first year (see Figure 4 below).

While Ascent does not feature intentional opportunities for collaboration among its science faculty, the English instructor and program coordinator build appropriate content links in ID 108. The seminar has been customized to address issues relevant to the medical profession, and faculty members have used texts related to health professions for both the English composition classes and the seminar. In addition, Ascent incorporates community building features and events into the program, such as a Mad Scientists' Party at Halloween and field trips to nearby medical schools.

Intensive advising and careful course planning, a primary focus of Ascent's ID 108, are essential elements of this learning community program. Ascent advisors monitor test scores earned throughout fall and spring classes, urging students to seek assistance with or withdraw from courses they are not passing. The advising component of this program sometimes involves carefully moving students out of these highly competitive majors and toward more appropriate ones, as warranted. Additional academic and community-building support is provided for the Ascent science classes through a Supplemental Instruction (SI) tutorial program.

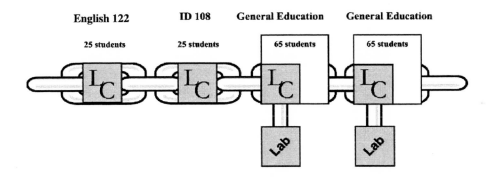

Figure 4. The Ascent learning community at University of Northern Colorado is designed for students majoring in pre-professional health.

Class Act – A Learning Community for Future Teachers

Pre-professional issues for future elementary teachers are the focus of Class Act ID 108, the seminar linked to the learning community program created in 1998. With the help of their instructors, Class Act students in ID 108 identify how state standards for entrance into the teaching field are addressed in the classes they are currently taking and discuss how teachers might apply those standards in an elementary classroom. Students also receive a list of volunteer opportunities that allow them to work with children before they begin their teacher preparation program. Class Act enrolls more than 200 students per year and is intended for students in the strictly structured Interdisciplinary Studies Liberal Arts major (IDLA), the only UNC major leading to elementary licensure. As is the case for Ascent, Class Act students are guaranteed enrollment in the classes necessary to fulfill major requirements.

Together, all Class Act instructors focus on the state content standards and on the qualities that make an outstanding teacher in disciplines represented by the linked courses. Class Act follows the Ascent structure, with a typical Class Act link including English composition or speech communication, ID 108, and two other courses (with or without labs) such as American history and introduction to literature, world geography and earth sciences, or American government and introduction to cultural anthropology.

Learning Community Administration and Faculty Development

The A&S Dean's Office serves as the administrative home to the five learning community programs, which serve more than 800 students. These programs are overseen by three coordinators, one of whom is also a general coordinator. The general coordinator serves as year-round director, managing administrative issues, supervising staff training, and overseeing budgets, recruitment, and marketing efforts. An organizational chart for academic year 2001-2002 appears in Appendix B. The dean and staff have assisted in assigning faculty, gaining support of chairs and other administrators, and seeking approval of the ID 108 curriculum. Working with the provost, the dean built a stable annual budget for the learning communities. While the cost of delivering linked classes is part of the regular A&S instructional budget, extra funding for learning community staff was obtained from the Challenge budget and from state funds. Participating faculty from English, math, and speech are paid for teaching the ID classes and for providing extra support to students. Tenured and tenure-track faculty sometimes have this work computed in their teaching loads, but more often the work counts as departmental service. A few faculty members have even volunteered to teach ID 108 as an overload, because they view this connection with first-year students as a way to recruit majors and assimilate students into their disciplines. Many faculty members report learning community involvement on annual evaluations and on applications for tenure, promotion, and teaching or advising excellence awards.

In-service training for learning community faculty members on the content and instructional strategies of ID 108 has expanded over the years to include both large and small formal sessions and ongoing conversations about broad pedagogical topics. The in-service training has become an opportunity for learning community instructors to share ideas on building rich and frequent opportunities for assessment, creating varied assignments, employing strategies for collaborating with other linked course faculty, implementing ideas for engaging students in the UNC community, and employing strategies for establishing connections with and among students. Although faculty members do not receive a stipend for attending in-service meetings, attendance is excellent because, as participants report, they enjoy the collegial atmosphere and value the chance to learn ways to improve their teaching and their relationships with first-year students.

Assessment

Over the years, UNC's learning community coordinators have employed a variety of assessment strategies to gauge program success and make necessary adjustments. The learning communities couple standard UNC course/instructor evaluations with tailored assessments that include open-ended surveys of students and faculty, interviews and focus groups, surveys administered to participants and non-participants, and analyses of longitudinal retention and graduation rates. As the centerpiece of all five learning community programs, ID 108 features strongly in both qualitative and quantitative assessments. In addition, because academic advising is central to the ID 108 class, administrators are highly confident that assessment results for these areas are directly related to the seminar experience.

Levels of Persistence

Since 1992, second-year return rates for students in all learning communities administered by A&S have been compared to return rates of those students who elected not to participate in a learning community. The entering index number is used to determine admissions eligibility and derived from combining the cumulative high school grade point average and the score on the American College Testing (ACT) assessment. The highest possible index number is 154. From 1992 to 2001, learning community participants returned at higher rates than non-participants for all years but one, 1994. The higher return rates continued even though the entering mean academic index numbers of the learning community students were lower than those of the comparison group. The only exception, the 1994 cohort, had a lower return rate and considerably lower mean index number (i.e., a return rate of 63.7% and a mean index number of 95.9) compared to the percentage return rate and aggregate mean of non-participating students (i.e., a return rate of 69.7% and a mean index number of 103.6). Learning community participation may also have an impact on persistence to graduation, as positive relationships have been seen in four-, five-, and six-year graduation rates for 1992 to 1998 learning community cohorts.

Subgroups of learning community students vary in their academic preparation. Regardless of index number, Cluster students graduated at higher rates than non-participating students, except in 1997. Advantage graduation rates generally lag behind those of other groups. This is not unexpected, given their measurably lower preparation for college compared with other students. Ascent students, in a challenging pre-health curriculum, graduate at solid rates, and data from Class Act students were strong in 1998, the first year of analysis. The strong performance of these students may correlate with their clear professional aspirations and high level of fit with a primary institutional mission. Throughout all five learning community programs, a volunteer effect (i.e., students may fare better because they are motivated to seek the additional academic enrichment and support of a learning community) may also contribute to stronger performance. The aggregate comparative impact, however, may be ameliorated by several factors. For example, a small number of students cannot enroll in their first choice learning community and, therefore, do not enroll at all. Other students who may have volunteered do not because their required classes conflict with learning community options, and some out-of-state students might have volunteered but did not hear about learning community and, thus, did not join. The impact of the volunteer effect across learning communities at UNC is still in need of further examination.

Short-Answer Surveys of Students and Faculty

Surveys administered to learning community students in the ID 108 classes every fall ask open-ended questions regarding general program goals (e.g., connections with faculty, peers, academic programs, and university resources) and specific activities, many linked directly to the ID 108 experience (e.g., four-year planning, social events, or speakers). Overall, students report that UNC's learning communities help them adjust to college, learn what services are available, and connect to faculty members. Across all programs, students generally note the benefits of their involvement (Table 1).

Responses on faculty surveys have reinforced these themes. Faculty members indicate they appreciate the closer relationships formed among students, between professors and students, and among professors through ID 108 and the learning community. Respondents have noted they enjoy planning the interdisciplinary or pre-professional course activities offered in ID 108, a task they indicate provides both an intellectual challenge and a chance to work with colleagues from other disciplines on substantive academic content. As one person indicated, "The only time you usually work with faculty from other departments is on committees. This [learning community work] is a chance to work together on your discipline."

Table 1

Perceived Benefits of Learning Community Participation

Benefits	Student Comments
Making friends and adjusting to college	"I liked the idea of being in classes with the same people."
	"I met new people quickly, formed study groups, and made friends because we had all our classes together."
Getting needed classes and good schedules	"They promised classes that would otherwise be hard to get into."
	"I understand what elective courses as well as major courses are necessary to obtain a degree in my field of study: Political Science."
Getting to know professors, friends, and study partners	"I know all about my professor's research and her family. My roommate barely knew her teachers' last names."
	"I enjoyed Class Act because you gain a personal relationship with your professors and peers, which increases your chances of success."
Understanding interdisciplinary connections	"Having the professors put all the information together made me see how history, politics, and culture are related. I could see the big picture."
Receiving help with major, career, and scheduling	"The four-year planning was important. I had some idea where I was going with my major [and] right now, I know I'll be able to get two courses I need … Lots of my friends will have to take classes they don't want just because they're freshmen. They don't even realize that yet."

Negative comments from faculty are rare and minor. While they often note that learning community students are more active in class discussions and more likely to make use of office hours than non-learning community students in the same sections, a student who inadvertently registers for a learning community outside his or her area of interest occasionally causes a faculty member extra effort. Because learning community students often earn higher grades than their classmates and can even drive up the class curve, the occasional underachieving learning community student comes as a disappointment.

Interviews and Focus Groups

Along with data collected through surveys and informally, the programs have conducted two formal evaluations, primarily gathering focus group data. In 1997, an evaluator from outside the University found that administrators were highly supportive of "undergraduate programs that assist learning and promote retention" (Tompkins, 1997, p. 8). He also discovered participating faculty were enthusiastic about learning community work, with one commenting, "This is my most enjoyable service" (p. 3). The faculty members reported that they believed working with new students immediately upon their entrance to the University is important; as one said, "Every freshman should be involved [in a learning community]" (p. 3). One instructor mentioned that learning communities can provide important support for minority students, while another noted that the opportunity "to work productively with colleagues ... is less an obligation than a reward" (p. 4).

Students interviewed praised the quality of teaching in their classes and the willingness of their faculty to help them learn. Many singled out their ID 108/English teachers, who selected reading and writing assignments connected to other learning community classes. Ascent students appreciated the ID 108/English instructor's "genuine concern" for student learning (p.3). One student cautioned that if a cluster theme was not a good fit for the student, he or she might "lose interest in all of the courses" (p. 3). Several Ascent students reported they had selected UNC because it was the only institution in the state with a pre-health learning community.

A later evaluation conducted by UNC doctoral students (Guido-DiBrito, 2001) revealed that, with the occasional exception of perceived quality of instruction, students felt positively about their experience. The themes from that study are listed in Table 2.

Table 2

Perceived Benefits of Enrollment in ID 108

Benefits	Student Comments
Priority course registration	"You were guaranteed a seat in the class, you didn't have to fight, you didn't have to green card, you didn't have to wait and see because upper classmen get first pick ... And that's what I really, really liked about this community" (p.9).
Support and care	"I learned a lot. We had a lot more study groups and stuff in the [ID 108] class. I felt that I was connected with not only the director who formed them but also because I knew everyone in the class ... If a big test was coming up, we would all get together and we'd crash together" (p.10).
Value of ID 108	"I thought that the ID class was going to be a blow off class, but I found out there was much more work than I expected. It was good; [and] it helped me a lot ... I like the four-year plan we had to fill out. I'd say a lot of people are still using it. It helped me with the classes I still need to take because I planned ... what I needed to take to graduate in four years" (p.10).
Social opportunities	"I liked meeting with the same group of people. To me, it made that transition from high school so much easier because I didn't have [just other students who] I didn't know in every single class. [In the four Cluster classes], I knew the same 25 people" (p.11).
Academic support	"I felt more comfortable calling people and asking for help because I knew that they were having the same problems. . . I didn't go through the whole semester without understanding something. There was always someone there to call to help me" (p.12).
Instruction	"I think teachers should be, like, reaching out and trying to help you. I think that is what the [ID 108] small class environment is made for, it's for the teacher to be able to reach out and help people, and I don't feel like I got that at all in my history class, and that was my biggest class."

Program Evaluation of the First-Semester Experience

Beginning in fall 1999, data from self-report questionnaires, gauging levels of student satisfaction with components of the first semester of their UNC experience, have been added to focus group data described above. Questionnaire data are drawn from learning community participants and from comparable non-participating students and elicit perceptions on academic advising, campus services, goal setting, academic confidence, and engagement with the institution.

Results from the fall 2001 cohort are displayed below as typical of those seen from all cohorts. While satisfaction levels varied across learning communities, in general, data gathered from participating students in this cohort indicated these students were more satisfied with their first-semester experiences at the University than non-participating students (Tables 3 and 4). Questions were based on goals of the ID 108 course and the learning community experience in general.

Table 3
Fall 2001 Program Evaluation Mean Comparisons on First-Semester Experience

My first semester experience at UNC encouraged me to:	All learning community students	Students not in LCs
understand and use campus services	4.25	3.82
explore or confirm my choice of a major	4.24	3.65
understand general education requirements	4.42	4.00
develop a four-year graduation plan	4.54	3.22
connect with peers (i.e., friends, study partners)	4.31	3.93
become better acquainted with one or more of my professors	4.12	3.56
feel more confident about my goals (i.e., academic, personal, career)	4.10	3.61
feel I made a good choice in selecting UNC for my education	4.14	3.74

$p < 0.05$
Note. 1 = strongly disagree, 2 = agree, 3 = neither agree or disagree, 4 = agree, 5 = strongly agree. From UNC Office of Institutional Research and Planning (9/11/2002).

Comparisons between participating and non-participating student academic achievement, as measured by probationary status and grade point average, have also been made. Results for the fall 2001 cohort were typical of other cohorts of learning community students. Academically at-risk students (i.e., the lowest 20% of regularly admitted students in terms of high school GPAs and standardized test scores) participating in learning communities earned slightly higher GPAs (2.56 cumulative GPA in the first year versus 2.49) and were less likely to be placed on academic probation at the end of the first year (10.8% versus 12.5%) than at-risk students not in learning communities. At-risk learning community participants also returned at a higher rate than comparable non-participating students in spring 2002 (91.6% versus 86.7%) and the subsequent fall (68.5% for learning community students versus 61.1% for non-participating students).

Table 4

Fall 2001 Program Evaluation Mean Comparisons on Meeting with Advisor

When I met my academic advisor,	All learning community students	Students not in LCs
I received helpful information about my plan of study.	4.29	3.97
I felt my questions were taken seriously.	4.45	4.24
I was treated in a friendly, professional manner.	4.56	4.41
I felt I could get help with personal concerns if needed.	4.21	3.99

p < 0.05

Note. 1 = strongly disagree, 2 = agree, 3 = neither agree or disagree, 4 = agree, 5 = strongly agree. Academic advising is a key component of the ID 108 course across programs. From UNC Office of Institutional Research and Planning (9/11/2002).

Course evaluations for the fall 2001 first-year seminars are also typical of those seen throughout the life of the program (see Table 5). Of the 584 students enrolled during that term, 463 (79%) completed a standard Student Course Instructor Survey. Results from this cohort show the degree to which students felt the instructor was approachable was rated highest (mean rating of 4.6 on a 5-point scale) followed by the degree to which the instructor was perceived as treating students fairly (mean rating of 4.5). Of the 11 questions on the survey, the lowest rated items pertained to the course itself. For example, "I learned a lot in this course" had a mean rating of 3.5. "I would recommend this course to other students" had a mean rating of 3.6. The other nine survey items rated at 4.1 or higher.

Table 5

Fall 2001 First-Year Seminar: Student Course Instructor Survey Mean Item Responses (N = 463)

I felt free to approach the instructor.	4.6
Instructor treated all students fairly.	4.4
Instructor treated all students with respect.	4.5
Instructor explained subject matter clearly.	4.1
Instructor provided helpful feedback on assignments/exams.	4.1
Instructor explained assignments clearly.	4.1
Instructor graded my work fairly.	4.3
Instructor is an excellent teacher.	4.2
I learned a lot in this course.	3.5
I would recommend this course to other students.	3.6
I would recommend this instructor to other students.	4.1

Note. 1 = strongly disagree, 2 = disagree, 3 = neither agree or disagree, 4 = agree, 5 = strongly agree.

Estimating the Financial Impact of Learning Community Participation

Even for students with lower entering index numbers, second-year return rates for UNC's learning community students have been consistently higher than those of non-participating students. Increased retention of learning community students could translate into important financial gains for the institution. If, for example, non-participating students from the fall 2001 cohort had returned for a second year at the same rate as community students, a total of $537,150 in tuition, fees, and state appropriations may have been realized. This estimate is rough for a variety of reasons. It does not take into account the higher tuition rates typically paid by out-of-state students, nor does it predict the revenue gains in subsequent years from additional students being retained until graduation.

Using Data for Program Improvement

Data from assessments and evaluations have been used in a variety of ways to improve UNC's learning communities. Following the external program review, the learning communities gained office space, staff, and funding. A learning community director, who now serves at a high administrative level at the institution, was also appointed as a result of the review. While many changes affected larger program design elements, some targeted the ID 108 classes specifically. For example, when surveys revealed that Cluster students were not receiving sufficient academic and career advising or completing four-year plans, ID 108 was added to this program. Some Cluster students also complained that planned interdisciplinary themes were not being realized. Having the ID 108 instructor take the lead in coordinating the integrative assignments and having thematic discussions held during the seminar with all faculty present has helped Cluster live up to its potential. In the Ascent ID 108 course, surveys had consistently indicated that students became less certain of their career goals as the semester progressed, often because of the rigor of the pre-med curriculum. In response, the ID 108 instructional staff added a class session and individual advising addressing alternate career options, especially in the allied health sciences.

Looking Ahead to a Sustainable Future

Despite generally positive assessment results and increasing recognition within the institution, managing and sustaining UNC's learning communities remains a challenging task. At the time this chapter was being written, funding was a major concern. During academic year 2002-2003, Colorado cut $90 million from its higher education budget, with a loss to UNC of 11.2% of its state allocation. Administrators predicted that UNC could lose $11 million or 25% of its state funding during 2003-2004. To cope with this loss of funds, the institution made equitable cuts campus-wide. Dean-level support safeguarded most key features of the learning communities, including continuation of ID 108, but program size was cut by some 150 students for fall 2003.

In this period of retrenchment, two low- or no-cost program improvements were made in the ID 108 classes. Challenge added a new leadership emphasis, offering students in the ID 108 classes the opportunity to experience service-learning, become peer advisors, participate in "Challenge Chats" with UNC leaders and former Challenge students, and create other projects of their own design. During spring 2003, the first group of Challenge leadership students conducted a formal survey of their peers to see whether improvements were needed in the ID 108 class or the *Staying on Track* guidebook. Students made a poster presentation of their findings at the annual campuswide Undergraduate Research Day. Survey respondents recommended that the ID course format be made more consistent across sections, the guide be converted to a workbook with more hands-on applications, general education be better explained, and connections between faculty and the advising center be strengthened.

At the same time, the Class Act ID 108 sections introduced strategies to help students become more intentional learners, and efforts were made to increase interaction between students and faculty. As part of the first strategy, students received training in the cognitive skills needed to integrate knowledge from their three clustered classes. The ID 108 instructors provided students with techniques for collaborative small group projects and used self-reflective papers and group rubrics to evaluate student participation and growth in cognitive skills. The second strategy involved small groups of students interviewing instructors from their linked classes about success strategies for each class, with other small groups interviewing the instructors about the faculty members' own educational journeys and areas of expertise. The groups then shared what they had learned with the entire ID class.

Refinements will continue. For example, the relatively flat academic performance of ethnic minority students in the learning communities continues to be a subject of conversation, as does the Ascent students' feelings that they do not build strong connections with their professors. Likewise, students' lackluster enthusiasm for the course (as evidenced by lower mean scores on recommending the course to others) continues to be explored. These student responses are offered in a context in which learning community participants consistently achieve at higher rates academically than non-participants. Despite these and other concerns, and because administrators of UNC's five programs are willing to review program offerings critically and make needed adjustments, there is optimism that the learning communities will be sustained. Additional strengths include sound leadership, dean- and faculty-level support, and the centrally positioned, flexibly designed first-year seminar. This class serves as a fulcrum of collaborative efforts to support student learning and success and is viewed as a key element in creating strong, coherent, and effective learning communities.

References

Guido-DiBrito, F. (2001). *Report of findings and recommendations: College of Arts & Sciences learning communities.* Unpublished manuscript, University of Northern Colorado at Greeley.

Shapiro, N. S., & Levine, J. H. (1999). *Creating learning communities: A practical guide to winning support, organizing for change, and implementing programs.* San Francisco: Jossey-Bass.

Tompkins, D. P. (1997). *Academic Advantage, Ascent, and Cluster: An assessment of three programs at the University of Northern Colorado.* Unpublished manuscript, University of Northern Colorado at Greeley.

University of Northern Colorado. (2003). *2003-2004 catalog.* Greeley, CO: Author.

Appendix A

ID 108. Undergraduate Studies and the Liberal Arts
Generic Syllabus
One-credit hour
University of Northern Colorado

Taught as a co-requisite for English 122 for participants in the Academic Advantage, Ascent, Cluster, and/or Freshman Challenge Programs.

Objectives:
- Students will gain an understanding of the goals, traditions, culture, philosophy, and value of the liberal arts tradition, with discussion of the general education program, academic majors and minors, and specialized program emphases.
- Students will learn to use the university resources (including the libraries and computer labs) that are essential tools for their academic pursuits and will be introduced to other services that will enhance their academic and personal success.
- Students will explore the academic and personal values that are central to their development as individuals and as new members of a community of lifelong learners.
- Students will practice the skills necessary for academic and personal success including critical thinking, problem solving, writing, and individual and/or collaborative oral presentation.
- Students will reflect upon and analyze academic, cultural, and personal experiences through in-class and out-of-class journal assignments designed to clarify their understanding of individual and institutional priorities.

Outline of Course Content:
The Liberal Arts Tradition—The Idea of a University
- Understanding the liberal arts tradition as distinct from educational programs designed for specific professions or vocations
- Benefiting from the goals and content of the general education program
- Choosing from among possible major and minor areas as related to vocational and personal goals
- Considering academic and extracurricular options: Emphasis areas within majors, cultural center programming, cultural events, and special on-campus presentations (including speakers, films, and/or musical or theatrical performances)
Resources for the Transition from School to University
- Using academic resources for course-related projects: the libraries and computer labs
- Understanding the potential of advanced technology (e-mail, Internet resources)
- Using student services offices for support during transitional periods
- Building relationships with faculty, advisors, and peers
Academic Values and Priorities
- Exploring issues involving freedom, responsibility, and self-knowledge as related to academic standards and expectations
- Understanding the campus culture: Analysis of individual, social, and community similarities and differences as expressed through campus events (e.g., plays, speakers, musical performances) and publications (e.g., *The Crucible, The Mirror*)
- Understanding points of conflict: Analysis of topics related to cultural, social,

and political diversity; areas of personal confidence and insecurity; interpersonal relationships; current issues in higher education

Personal Insights Into and Contributions to the Academic Community
- Publicly presenting collaboratively gained conclusions to an audience of your peers
- Privately reflecting in written form on personal priorities and action plans
- Finding ways to be of service to the community: options for on-campus and off-campus involvement

Proposed Texts:
- Boyer, Ernest L. *College: The Undergraduate Experience in America.* Harper & Row, 1987.
- Chaffee, John. *The Thinker's Guide to College Success.* Houghton Mifflin, 1995.
- Lawry, John D. *College 101: A Freshman Reader.* McGraw, Hill, 1992.
- Moffett, Michael. *Coming of Age in New Jersey.* Rutgers University Press, 1989.
- *The Chronicle of Higher Education*

Method of Evaluation:
Letter grades—A through F

Course Requirements:
- Weekly out-of-class journal entries (to include critiques of several on-campus presentations selected from assigned options)
- Weekly in-class journal entries and/or quizzes based on assigned readings and class presentations
- One or more collaborative oral presentations
- One or more individual oral presentations
- Library and computer lab assignments
- One or more short analytical papers

Class Act ID 108 Syllabus

Required Texts:
- *UNC Catalog-2002-2003*
- *Staying on Track ID 108*
- *Learning Dynamics* by Ford and Ford
- Daily planner

Attendance:
Attendance is required because this class meets only once a week. Large Class Act meetings (Professional Panel, PLACE workshop and Major Fair) may substitute for class meetings.

Objectives:
- To facilitate the transition into the University environment
- To establish connections with others in the University
- To understand personal needs and use the resources to meet those needs
- To learn about the University culture and expectations
- To practice critical thinking, problem solving, and oral communication skills
- To access essential resources such as the library, computer labs, and student affairs
- To formulate a four-year plan

- To recognize the demands of the teaching profession
- To identify the requirements of the PTEP program
- To prepare for the PLACE test

Campus Resources:
Students will identify campus resources and their services to enhance their success at the University.

Assignment: (See attached worksheet and quiz.)
You will be in a group for this exercise. Your group will need to go to each location, pick up a piece of literature from that area, and find out how that resource can help students. There will be an in-class quiz about this information that your group will work on together. Everyone in your group will receive the same grade.

Campus Activity:
Students should attend a campus event. The event must be either academic or cultural.

Assignment:
You must attend a campus event and write a one-page reaction paper.

Library Workshop:
Students will attend a library workshop so that they will know how to find resources for their research for all classes.

Assignment: (See attached Library worksheet.)
Students will find an article that can be used for an assignment in one of the linked content classes.

Webster:
Students will learn how to find personal information, registration dates, open class listings, and how to register. They will also look up University expectations on issues such as plagiarism, incompletes, and student's rights and responsibilities.

Assignment: (See attached Webster worksheet.)

Career Services:
Students will visit Career Services to assist them in choosing a major and career that are compatible for them. This will also help them learn about job opportunities.

Assignment:
Arrange for the ID class to go to Career Services.

Advising:
Students will meet with their ID instructor or an advisor in the Arts and Sciences Advising Center to discuss their major choice and their Four-Year plan. IDLA students should meet with Pat Doherty.

Assignment:
Students will take the four-year worksheet from their *Staying on Track* booklet to the advising sessions and have the advisor sign it after each session.

Major Fair:
There will be a Major Fair at which the five colleges that comprise UNC will present

what majors their college offers and what job opportunities are available with various majors. Students are required to attend this event and find out about two majors or areas of concentration in the IDLA major. This will assist in their future planning. Class may be dismissed for this event.

Assignment:
Credit will be given by bringing an attendance receipt from the fair and writing a one-page reaction paper. If you are unable to attend this fair, you will write a 500-word paper describing two different majors or concentrations in the IDLA major (course requirements and job opportunities) and your evaluation of which would be most suitable for you.

Four-Year Plan:
A plan developed the IDLA major to ensure that students meet the requirements for the major, concentration, and PTEP. The plan will cover courses for all four years. Students should recognize that there is flexibility in the plan, especially in general education courses.

Assignment:
Pat Doherty, an advisor for the IDLA major, will come and present for this class session. Students will turn in one copy of the plan for a grade and keep one for their file.

Extra Credit:
Seminars are offered on campus on various topics throughout the semester through the Center for Human Enrichment (Cornerstone workshops) and the College Transition Center. Many of these are on topics (e.g., study skills, test taking) that students will find helpful. Fliers will be distributed with the times and topics.

Assignment:
If you attend one of these seminars, have the presenter document your attendance. Send me an e-mail message telling what the seminar was about and your evaluation of it. You will receive 10 points extra credit for each seminar you attend (up to 50 points extra).

Professional Readings:
Students will discuss assigned reading from *Learning Dynamics*. They should identify the most significant issues for educators presented in the reading, and come to a conclusion on how to apply what they have learned from these readings. This will stimulate students thinking about issues in the profession.

Assignment:
You will be assigned to a group that will present a panel discussion of an assigned reading from *Learning Dynamics*. This panel will present to the class a summary of the reading, discuss the most significant issues for educators presented in the reading, and come to a conclusion on how to apply what your group has learned from this reading. Each member of the group will be required to speak during the presentation and assist in developing the presentation. The group should develop either an overhead, poster, PowerPoint, or handout to assist the class in understanding the reading. The presentations will be about 15 minutes in length.

Interview:
Students will interview a teacher for firsthand insight into this profession. This will assist them in their decision about pursuing the teaching profession.

Assignment:
You will develop a set of 10 questions to prepare you for the interview. Then you will give a brief

oral presentation about the most significant insight gained from your interview. An addressed and stamped thank you note (unsealed) must be turned in to receive credit for the interview.

Professional Panel Presentation:
A panel consisting of a principal, a veteran teacher, a student in the PTEP program, and a professor from the PTEP program will present their insights and take questions for all members of Class Act. This late afternoon session will be videotaped for those who cannot attend at that time.

Assignment:
Students will receive an attendance voucher at the close of the panel. If they cannot attend, they will need to check the video out in the library and write a one-paragraph response.

Volunteer Opportunities:
Students will receive a list of volunteer opportunities to work with children in the Greeley schools and community. This provides early interaction with children before the students' admission to the PTEP program.

Assignment:
For extra credit, students will write a one-page reflection on their volunteer experience. Students are encouraged to keep this to add to their professional portfolio. (See attached guideline for writing a reflection for a portfolio.)

Place Workshop:
Professionals will present to all members of Class Act in a late afternoon session. Students will learn about the PLACE test and how to prepare. They will be encouraged to form study groups. The session will be videotaped for those who cannot attend at that time.

Assignment:
Students will receive an attendance voucher at the close of the panel. If they cannot attend, they will need to check the video out in the library and write a one paragraph response.

Content Standards:
Students will locate the Colorado Content standards for their three linked general education classes and print them out. They should understand how these standards are addressed in their current classes and how they might teach to the standards in the future (www.cde.state.co.us).

Assignment:
Each student will be assigned one standard from each discipline in their learning community and identify how it is being addressed in the current class. Students will also offer a suggestion on how that standard might be addressed in an elementary classroom. Students are encouraged to work together, but each student will be responsible for writing a 100-word paragraph for each standard (for a total of three 100-word paragraphs minimum).

Appendix B
Human Resource Support for Learning Communities Programs

University of Northern Colorado
Organizational Chart for 2001-2002

Dean
College of Arts and
Sciences

Associate Dean
College of Arts and
Sciences

Full-time A&S Advising
and LC Director

.92 of full-time Administrative
Support

Full-time Adminstrative Support

Work-study
Student

Work-study
Student

Full-time Learning Community
Coordinator (Academic Year
Appointment)

.70 of full-time Learning
Community Coordinator
(Academic Year Appointment)

Full-time Advisor and Learning
Community Coordinator
(Academic Year Appointment)

Full-time Advisor and Learning
Community Coordinator
(Academic Year Appointment)

Building Integrated Learning Experiences at a Bi-National, Commuter Institution

Maggy Smith, Dorothy Ward, Cathy Willermet, and Diana Guerrero

The University of Texas at El Paso

Chapter 14

In 1996, the University of Texas at El Paso (UTEP) was designated as a Model Institution for Excellence (MIE) by the National Science Foundation. This designation carried with it a multi-year, multi-million dollar award to transform the institution and the way students made their transition to the college experience in UTEP's areas of academic strength and prestige, the Colleges of Science and Engineering. The MIE award's enormous investment in the first year of college for students who intend to major in science or engineering has as its hallmark a number of initiatives combined into a single program for entering students: Circles of Learning for Entering Students (CircLES). Central to CircLES are two components: learning communities and the first-year seminar. Faculty and administrators in science and engineering believed that students would succeed if they became immersed in the introductory issues of their disciplines within the context of a set of courses that also introduced them to college survival skills. Over time, through some trial and error, this set of courses became the first-year seminar, an introductory course in engineering or science, and a mathematics or English course. From this beginning, a university-wide passion for serving entering students emerged. The institutional strategies in place for the first-year seminar and learning communities are the subject of this chapter.

Since 1996, the first-year seminar has evolved into a credit-bearing course with instructor-selected, variable academic content in which college transition skills are taught. The University has adopted the first-year seminar as part of its core curriculum and has engaged in an aggressive effort to enroll all first-time students in learning communities for at least one semester, with the goal, as Cross (1998) states, of "making college a more holistic, integrated learning experience for students" (p. 4).

The chapter begins with a description of The University of Texas at El Paso, the first-year seminar, UNIV 1301 – Seminar in Critical Inquiry, and the seminar's role in learning communities at UTEP. As the learning community initiative has been refined to best serve UTEP students, a variety of learning communities have been offered; this chapter discusses those. Last, the chapter describes the formative and summative assessments in place.

The University of Texas at El Paso (UTEP)

The University of Texas at El Paso is a Hispanic-majority (73% in fall 2003), research-intensive institution located on the U.S.-Mexico border. The institution's total fall 2003 enrollment was 18,500 students; 2,500 of them were first-time, first-year students. Eighty-five percent of the students were non-residential, commuter students, and more than 80% worked part- or full-time. The University's non-traditional, bi-national population is characterized by an average undergraduate age of 26. Many of UTEP's undergraduates have family support responsibilities and are the first in their families to attend college (49.7% in fall 2002). El Paso is an economically disadvantaged city, with fewer than 40% of its residents having earned a high school diploma. The University plays a major role in the intellectual and socio-economic development of West Texas, and its mission is to provide quality educational programs to the residents of El Paso and its surrounding region. Student demographic data and the institution's mission, as well as an institutional concern for improving first-year student retention and success outcomes, provided the impetus for UTEP's deliberate approach to transforming the first year of college for all entering students.

In 1998, UTEP's first-year retention rate was 62%, but it dropped to 45% for the second year. Research demonstrated that UTEP students face transition demands that are simultaneously academic, personal, social, and intellectual. UTEP students come with high academic expectations and from a widely diverse academic base. Many come with limited academic proficiency, few college survival skills, and few role models. For example, the average combined SAT score of the fall 2002 entering class was 902 out of a possible 1600, yet 91% of those students indicated that they were well prepared for college. Almost all of the entering student class expected to make a "B" average in the first semester of college. In actuality, 47.5% of the entering class made a "B" average the first semester.

UTEP's plan was to help students meet their high academic expectations and to create an environment in which entering students would learn how to succeed at being a college student. The decision was made to ensure that this environment would include modified curricular and co-curricular experiences. In that context, and with the success of the MIE initiative already becoming evident, UTEP developed a rationale to address the first year of college—the Entering Student Program (ESP). ESP brings together departments from across campus (e.g., Recruitment, Admissions, New Student Orientation, Academic Advising, University Studies, and the Tutoring and Learning Center) with the goal of developing a set of services to form a comprehensive approach to the first year of college. Following two successful years of ESP (as indicated below), and with the goal of sustaining and institutionalizing those efforts, UTEP restructured organizationally and formed the University College. This new administrative unit housed the ESP departments, plus University Studies (the unit that oversees the first-year seminar and learning communities), Financial Aid, Student Assessment and Testing, the Registrar's Office, and the Visitor and Information Center. At the same time, an Office for Enrollment Evaluation and Technology was also created. The University College provides an administrative structure for academic and student service activities that support entry into college, encompassing processes for student enrollment as well as academic initiatives.

The First-Year Seminar: UNIV 1301 – Seminar in Critical Inquiry

At UTEP, the first-year seminar and learning community courses are linked in process and, in many cases, content. Most important, the first-year seminar and administration of the learning community program are situated in the same academic department on campus—University Studies, which is housed in University College. This placement provides an ideal environment for dialogue among faculty and administrators regarding achieving the goal of explicit intellectual intersections among the courses. The three-credit-hour University Studies first-year seminar (UNIV 1301) addresses academic success strategies through variable disciplinary themes. UNIV 1301 sections have such diverse discipline-based themes as Voices of Change: Social Protest in the Sixties (history), Fictional Women Detectives (English), and Nuclear Enviroethics (geology). Some of the themes reflect UTEP's location on the U.S.-Mexico border: Business Environment in the Borderplex, Environmental Issues in the Border Region, and U.S.-Mexico Border and the Power of Place.

Each section of the first-year seminar is taught by an instructional team consisting of an instructor, a librarian, and a peer (upper-division student) leader. Though the theme for each section varies according to the instructor's academic discipline and area of expertise, all sections of the first-year seminar must address the same five goals. Each section is designed to (a) strengthen students' academic performance and facilitate their transition to college, (b) enhance students' essential academic skills, (c) increase student-student and student-faculty interaction both in and outside of the classroom, (d) encourage students' self-assessment and goal clarification, and (e) increase students' involvement with UTEP activities and resources. (See Appendix A for UNIV 1301 goals and objectives.)

UTEP's Learning Community Initiative

Structure of Learning Communities

The learning communities program is designed to provide a structure through which students may form academic and social communities with their peers, strengthen their academic performance, make interdisciplinary connections, and develop a sense of belonging on campus. To this end, it provides a variety of models. Some are designed as pre-major (i.e., introduction to the major) or career interest for specific disciplines (e.g., pre-science, pre-engineering, pre-education, and pre-law majors). Others are designed for special interests (e.g., Inter-American Program, English for Speakers of Other Languages students). Still others are available to the general student population and do not have a specific focus, but they link together first-year core curriculum courses. Learning communities are built with the level of English or mathematics courses appropriate to meet the needs of students based on their placement scores in those subjects. Communities are also built when faculty members express an interest in linking pre-existing courses thematically. The three models described above are offered each fall and spring semester. A fourth model, currently offered only in the summer, is SmartSTART, a bridge program designed to provide optimum support for entering first-year students who are at risk. Figure 1 shows the range of learning community options for first-year students.

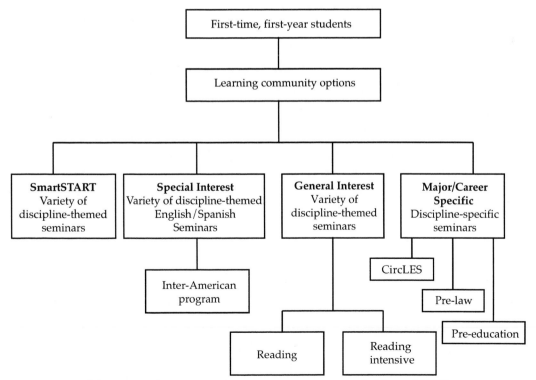

Figure 1. Variety of first-year learning community options available at UTEP.

Pre-Major Seminars: Learning Communities for Specific Disciplines

The longest standing UTEP learning community program—CircLES—co-enrolls groups of students in science and engineering in two or more courses. The goals of CircLES are to increase retention at the institution and in the major, improve academic performance, and add value to a student's education through the creation of an environment where students make connections with the University, the colleges, faculty, upper-division students, and their peers. All first-time, first-year students entering UTEP as science or engineering majors are required to enroll in a learning community in their first semester. Each fall semester, CircLES links four classes: (a) first-year seminar, (b) mathematics, (c) composition, and (d) an introductory course in either science or engineering. In the CircLES program, students continue to be in linked courses in the subsequent semester unless they are enrolled in Calculus II and are officially admitted into the science or engineering field of study.

The first-year seminar in CircLES is thematically linked with other courses in the community (e.g., Scientific Revolutions in a science community or Problem Solving and Design in Engineering in an engineering community). The goals of the first-year seminar are to aid students' transition to college by enhancing their academic skills and developing their sense of belonging to the University community. It is also designed to enhance learning in other courses by intentionally integrating the curricular content. Science and engineering assessment data for 1998-2001 cohorts (see Figure 2) show that approximately 80% of CircLES students returned the second year, while the overall one-year retention rate for the University for the same time period was approximately 69%.

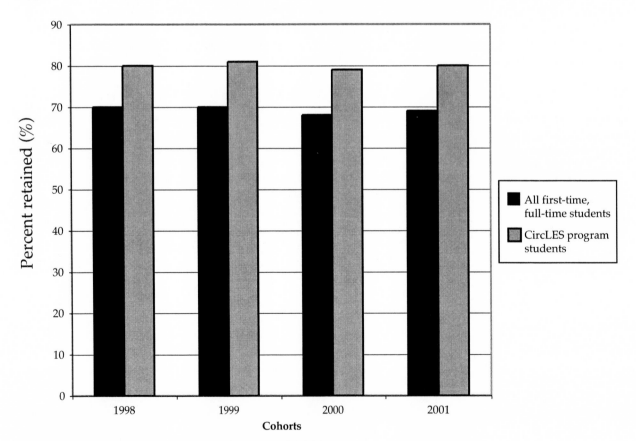

Figure 2. UTEP one-year retention rates, 1998-2001.

The other two major or career-specific learning communities—pre-education and pre-law—link first-year seminar sections with discipline-related themes to one or more additional core curriculum classes. Like CircLES, the first-year seminars in the pre-education and pre-law learning communities are intended to help students make connections with the University, the colleges, faculty, upper-division students, and their peers.

The variable content first-year seminars are integrated into learning communities in a variety of ways. Some instructors view their first-year seminar as the "glue" that holds the learning community together. These instructors, often in consultation with the team of learning community instructors, link ideas and assignments in the first-year seminar to the other courses in the cluster. This often occurs by linking first-year seminar assignments (e.g., note taking, examination preparation, study skills, and essay writing) to content in the lecture class. In other cases, the instructor connects some content ideas or an assignment to the lecture course. In this model, the first-year seminar amplifies the content of the lecture class and is used as a means of helping students work with college lecture material. It gives the seminar instructor an opportunity to use purposeful material for teaching note taking, study skills, test taking, and communication with an instructor.

For example, one UNIV 1301 class entitled Law for Beginners is the hub for the pre-law learning community. The UNIV 1301 instructor (also the coordinator for UTEP's Pre-Law Institute) pairs the seminar with a variety of disciplinary courses because, she says, pre-law students can have majors from environmental science to political science or English. Her section has been paired with UTEP's required courses in political science and history. "I use the syllabus from the professor with whom I am paired to find case law that works hand in hand with the course of study in the other class. Our course materials, therefore, are created specially for each class and are simply a packet of court cases relevant to the topics discussed in the other class" (Shelli Soto, personal communication, September 25, 2003).

Special Interest Seminars: Learning Communities for ESOL Students

Learning communities for the Inter-American Program are available for students whose Secondary Language English Proficiency (SLEP) test scores place them in the lower-level English for Speakers of Other Languages (ESOL) courses. This learning community model links a first-year seminar taught in Spanish and English with an ESOL course and/or a special section of a core curriculum course (e.g., history, psychology, or math) that is also taught in Spanish and English. In this learning community model, the integrative focus of the first-year seminar is to assist with development of the students' English language proficiency. The first-year seminar also aids international students with their transition to U.S. higher education by familiarizing them with University policies and procedures. In addition to addressing language proficiency and transitional issues, the first-year seminar in this learning community model can also help integrate academic content. For example, a first-year seminar with the theme of Physics in Everyday Life is linked with a math course. The seminar instructor sets up online simulations to help students understand the law of gravity and requires students to analyze the simulation using math skills learned in their linked math course.

General Interest Seminars: Learning Communities for the General Population

Students who are unconditionally admitted to the University may choose to be in a learning community that links the first-year seminar with English composition and a core lecture course (e.g., anthropology, history, sociology, psychology). Again, there is variability in how the first-year seminar serves as an integrator within the learning community, but most seminar instructors work to make meaningful connections with the content of the other linked courses. For example, in one learning community that linked the first-year seminar with a composition and history course, the seminar reiterated the writing process introduced in the composition course, including peer reviews and multiple drafts. To link with the history course, the first-year seminar instructor asked students to outline 10 pages of the history text to practice active reading and outlining skills. The students also brought their lecture notes from the history class to the first-year seminar where they compared note-taking strategies. Finally, this first-year seminar instructor chose the required novel for her seminar to fit with the period of history discussed in the history course.

SmartSTART: Learning Communities for Provisionally Admitted Students

In summer 2002, UTEP piloted another focused learning community—the SmartSTART program. This four-week, summer, residential, living-learning community program targeted entering START (Success Through Academic Readiness Today) students. These students are residents of Texas who are provisionally admitted to the University. A major goal of SmartSTART is to move students as quickly as possible from developmental courses to college-level work.

UTEP typically admits about 600 new START students each fall term. In 2002, START students were encouraged to begin their college career earlier by participating in the SmartSTART summer bridge program. Students in the federally funded Upward Bound, College Assistance Migrant Program (CAMP), and Talent Search programs were also invited to participate in SmartSTART.

SmartSTART students were placed in the appropriate learning community based on their test scores in math, reading, and writing. Then they were co-enrolled as groups of 20 to 25 students in a reading, writing, or math course in the morning and a first-year seminar course in the afternoon. The program scheduled students' activities, filling the day with classes, supervised study time, and required co-curricular activities. They also attended mandatory tutoring and evening enrichment programs. Evening activities ranged from examining time-management strategies to enjoying movie nights, working with information and computer technology, talking about personality and learning styles, discussing gender communications, dealing with diversity, managing finances (e.g., money management, financial aid), and navigating the institutional system. This tight schedule was designed to help them learn how to manage the demands of college life (e.g., studying, free time, living with friends). These experiences helped reinforce the content of the first-year seminar.

Instructors for the summer SmartSTART learning communities met weekly as a group to share experiences and to discuss student progress. In the SmartSTART learning communities, the first-year seminar's integrative role focused more on academic success skills than linked course content. For example, the first-year seminar addressed test-taking skills in preparation for exams in the math course and focused on time management skills to assist students with assignments in their other SmartSTART courses.

The strengths of this program were its two-semester learning community sequence and the intense academic advising that students received. Having successfully completed the summer program, students were placed in a learning community for the following fall semester. This follow-up learning community included an English or math course, a core curriculum course such as history, and a Supplemental Instruction (SI) section led by a peer leader from the Tutoring and Learning Center.

The real draw to the SmartSTART program was the laptop computer. Each student enrolled in the program was assigned a laptop computer to use for the academic year, subject to their maintaining a satisfactory GPA. For a number of reasons, the residential component was removed from the summer 2003 program. The program was expanded to six weeks, and the learning community portion was retained.

UTEP currently has resources to accommodate approximately 100 SmartSTART students, but plans are underway to increase the capacity of the program to accommodate most of the START students entering UTEP for the first time. However, one of the major challenges for the institution is getting students to take placement tests early enough to identify and recruit them into the SmartSTART Program.

Integrating the First-Year Seminar

Instructors Working Together

To foster a greater integration of curricular ideas, content, and activities among the courses in the learning communities, the learning community instructors attend a specially designed instructor development workshop (See Appendix B for a sample workshop agenda). Faculty teams are encouraged to meet at least once before the semester begins and to communicate regularly during the semester. Instructors are encouraged to describe the learning community in each of their syllabi. Additionally, they are asked to share syllabi, plan assignments, and coordinate assignment and examination schedules.

Instructors who confer with one another often find that they can link at least one assignment, such as a research paper, between the lecture and composition classes or between two or more of the linked classes. For example, in a learning community that linked history, composition, and the first-year seminar, the composition and first-year seminar instructors discovered that they both assigned interview essays, one for writing skills and the other for career exploration. While the specifics of each assignment differed somewhat, the instructors agreed to allow the students to conduct a single interview and use the same material for both essays.

Eight faculty members report jointly to University College and academic departments (i.e., communication, English, history, language and linguistics, mathematics, physics, sociology, and teacher education). Faculty members with joint appointments build their linked courses from dual perspectives, as representatives of their discipline and as representatives of University College, where an emphasis on teaching the abilities related to college success is the focus. Thus, a natural linkage exists in the Entering Student Program for intentional bridging that integrates learning across curricular and co-curricular experiences.

Instructors who link their classes express satisfaction with their students' engagement with the courses and with their overall learning community experience. Some faculty members have also related that they have modified their teaching methods by incorporating techniques that work in the learning communities into their regular classes.

Students Working Together

As part of the first-year seminar, students learn about forming study groups. These lessons are put to good use in large lecture classes, which are linked to learning communities. Students in learning communities often choose to sit together in the large lectures and form study groups. Having been prepared by the first-year seminar instructor to collaborate in study groups, students indicate that they find the practice to be an effective study strategy, one they retain all semester long. In addition, students form social bonds that improve their study activities as well as their connection to campus life. This is particularly important on a campus such as UTEP's where students often come to college having no role model at home to coach them on successful college survival skills. Many of these students also maintain their high school friendships with young people who may not be attending college. To connect students more closely to campus, one first-year seminar instructor assigned an activity journal allowing students to report on campus events they attended. The first-year seminar itself develops a sense of community, but this effect is multiplied because the course is part of a larger learning community. The students indicate that they form close ties through additional interactions in their other learning community courses. Other instructors report that their students are attending campus events in groups. The results from a pilot survey administered to a sample of the 2002 fall cohort (both learning community and non-learning community students) indicate that students in learning communities make friends more easily with their classmates than students who are not in learning communities. They also report contacting each other outside of class and studying together in greater numbers than students in stand-alone classes. Though these results are preliminary, they are certainly promising. Anecdotally, many students have reported that they make their own learning communities the following semester by intentionally registering for the same classes with other learning community students.

Learning Community Growth

UTEP's learning communities program has grown quickly: More than 1,400 students (55% of the entering student class) registered for 63 learning communities in fall 2003. Of the 63 learning communities, 17 were in the CircLES Program, accommodating 408 students in pre-majors of science or engineering. While some entering students are required to participate in learning communities (e.g., pre-science and pre-engineering majors, START students), learning communities are voluntary for the remaining student population at the moment. UTEP has not yet expanded learning communities beyond the first semester, with a few notable exceptions in science, engineering, and SmartSTART.

One reason for the growth of learning communities at UTEP is the University College's use of prescribed scheduling, which lends itself to fairly intrusive placement of first-semester students in learning communities. This initiative emerged in response to two major institutional issues. First, many UTEP students come to college and are placed in a developmental reading course. Using an interactive prescribed scheduling module, designed by the Information Technology department, advisors are able to choose learning communities based on students' reading scores. By placement into classes that are appropriately linked, students at high academic risk are prevented from registering for intensive reading courses such as history or sociology. Second, UTEP wanted to expand the institution's afternoon course availability and use campus facilities more fully throughout the day, especially as enrollment numbers increase. Prescribed scheduling allows the large number of students who attend New Student Orientation to be advised and registered into sets of classes that meet their academic needs and make better use of the institution's afternoon course offerings.

Assessing to Improve Student Experiences

The University has several mechanisms for collecting assessment data used to improve learning community efforts.

UNIV 1301 End-of-Semester Feedback Form

First-year seminar students complete this assessment of the seminar's goals and objectives and evaluate how well their particular section of the first-year seminar meets those goals. Students who successfully complete the seminar consistently report that, as a result of the course, their academic skills have improved and they feel more comfortable at UTEP. They also report the seminar taught them how to succeed at UTEP.

UNIV 1301 End-of-Semester Feedback Form for Seminar Instructors and Peer Leaders

The instructional team members are asked to comment on their semester's experiences with the first-year seminar. Their end-of-semester perspectives are compared with those of first-year seminar students to identify areas that may need attention by program administrators or that can be addressed in instructor training workshops. Some of the workshop sessions, based on instructor and peer leader feedback, include cooperative learning activities, classroom assessment techniques, and introducing time management strategies using syllabi from students' courses.

Learning Community End-of-Semester Survey

First administered in fall 2002 as a pilot, this survey was completed by a sample of learning community students ($N = 97$) and non-learning community students ($N = 188$). Though the results are preliminary, they are promising. Learning community students reported statistically higher involvement than non-learning community students in the following activities ($p < 0.01$):

- Participating in group work during class time
- Attending voluntary peer-led study groups outside of class
- Contacting classmates outside of class (in person, by telephone, e-mail, discussion boards, electronic chat)
- Discussing their grades and assignments with their instructors
- Working on assignments that linked ideas from more than one of their courses (interdisciplinary work)
- Using skills learned in one course in another course
- Forming new friendships with students in their classes

One-Year Persistence Rates

The persistence rates of first-time, full-time, first-year students are reported annually to the Texas state legislature. This important benchmark is used to track annual trends and long-term progress in increasing the academic success of first-year students. The persistence rates of first-year seminar students are also tracked for program use (see Figure 3). While the results do not differentiate between students who are enrolled in a first-year seminar in a learning community and those who are enrolled in an independent seminar section, the results do show that students who successfully complete the first-year seminar have a one-year retention rate that is considerably greater than that of the seminar non-attempters and non-completers for the same time period.

One important future assessment project is to conduct a classroom assessment of faculty who teach first-year students in learning communities—not only the first-year seminar, but especially core curriculum and other gateway courses. According to Tinto (2002), choosing faculty carefully is critical for the success of learning communities and first-year seminars. Examining students' completion rates and the grade distribution of students in a class, along with other factors, will give the institution a snapshot of faculty performance in the first-year classroom. With this information, the institution can make informed decisions about the delivery of its academic programs for entering students.

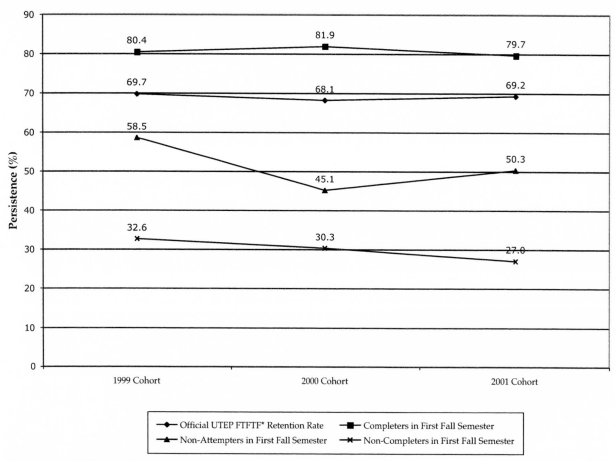

*First-time, full-time first-year students.

Figure 3. One-year persistence rates for first-year UTEP students in relation to fall seminar participation, 1999 – 2001. Students who completed the seminar successfully in spring and summer semesters are not included in the seminar group retention rates, but they are included in the official institutional rate. From Center for Institutional Evaluation, Research, and Planning (11/02), University College Dean's Office.

Learning Community Program Challenges

Linking Course Content

Because UTEP's learning community program is growing quickly, the initial emphasis has been on linking classes and co-enrolling students; less emphasis has been placed on developing theme-based learning communities or linking course content through shared assignments. However, regular workshops for learning community instructors facilitate the intentional integration of material across disciplines and encourage better collaboration among learning community faculty. Instructors are beginning to work together more often to link assignments, visit one another's classes, and make explicit interdisciplinary connections in their own classes.

Instructors of the large lecture courses as well as those who teach smaller sections of English, mathematics, and the first-year seminar are also collaborating on course content and assignments. For example, in a learning community that linked a large lecture course in anthropology with a first-year seminar, the seminar instructor and the anthropology professor worked together to prepare the learning community students for an examination in anthropology. The anthropology professor came to the first-year seminar class and discussed test-taking strategies with the students, and together the instructors worked with the students, in the first-year seminar class setting, on essay exam preparation strategies.

Publicizing Learning Communities to Entering Students

Entering students receive learning communities information with their recruitment and admission packets. However, most students are recruited into learning communities during their new student orientation or advising sessions. A peer leader from the first-year seminar and four orientation leaders who have been students in a learning community perform a 10-minute, high-energy, multimedia presentation (i.e., video and skit performances) during orientation. During this presentation, the students describe learning communities, what they gained by being in them, and what students can expect from these linked classes. These same students are highly visible during registration recruiting students, registering them for learning communities, and helping them build the rest of their class schedules.

Publicizing Learning Communities to Instructors

In departments that contribute large numbers of course sections to learning communities (e.g., English and math), sections are designated by departments rather than by instructors. In other departments, where instructor assignments are made early in the scheduling process, instructors are contacted personally by the learning communities coordinator and invited to participate in a learning community. Whether they are selected by the department or contacted personally by the learning communities coordinator, instructors are generally enthusiastic about the opportunity to participate, if they can manage their involvement with their other responsibilities. Many of these instructors have expressed an interest in teaching in a learning community because they feel the students benefit when they form a social and academic community, and the instructors themselves benefit from the opportunities to make connections with instructors in other disciplines.

Funding in a Tight Budgetary Climate

UTEP's learning community program is partially funded through a U. S. Department of Education Title V grant. UTEP plans to institutionalize budgets for the program over the next three years. Costs include salaries for the coordinator of learning communities and a scheduling assistant and funding for professional development workshops and promotional materials. The institution is seeking new ways to reward participating faculty both individually and publicly, because it recognizes that successful learning communities are those that recruit, train, and retain strong faculty leaders who serve as role models in the program. At UTEP, the faculty themselves must develop a strong sense of community in order to promote and sustain the learning communities. At the moment, financial incentives for participating in either the first-year seminar alone or in the learning community program have been put on hold. The existing rewards include certificates of appreciation and an annual Entering Student Program celebration during which a high-profile award is given to two individuals who are each recognized as an "Outstanding Advocate for Entering Students." While letters of support and materials on learning community models and assessment are provided for faculty members for their tenure review, at an institution such as UTEP, faculty participation in programs such as the first-year seminar and learning communities is largely recognized as service to the institution and not as scholarly work or as more significant teaching responsibilities. To remedy this, University Studies, a unit of University College, is set to receive its own faculty lines to share with other academic departments and is preparing criteria for faculty teaching in the first-year seminar and learning communities that will profile and evaluate their work for institutional purposes (e.g., tenure, promotion, merit, and awards).

Future Directions: Maintaining Effectiveness, Increasing Efficiency, Striving for Sustainability

UTEP made a considerable initial investment in its first-year programs because of the administration's belief in the importance of helping students make a successful transition to the University and providing interventions that increase students' opportunities for academic success. Grant money—from federal and private sources—also provided significant financial support for program development. But the recent economic downturn has affected state and grant funding for public colleges and universities nationwide. Significant state budget reductions have forced UTEP to look for ways to cut costs without reducing academic effectiveness. Key changes to the first-year program have resulted from this effort, specifically the merging of two programs and two advisory committees. This merger was planned but the budgetary climate accelerated the process. It is anticipated to be an efficient merger that will not diminish, but enhance, effectiveness.

Since their inception, University Studies (i.e., the department that provides administrative oversight for the university-wide first-year seminars and learning communities) and CircLES, which provided administrative oversight for science and engineering first-year seminars and learning communities, have operated separately, though cooperatively. While assessment data demonstrated the effectiveness of both programs, the dual administration resulted in significant duplication of effort and a lack of efficiency. Not only did the two programs have separate staff, they also had separate instructor/peer leader recruitment and training efforts, different instructor/peer leader requirements and rewards, and separate program assessment efforts. After considerable discussion and planning, which included the participation of key representatives from both programs in the National Learning Communities Project Summer 2003 Institute, the two programs merged in fall 2003, expanding and somewhat re-structuring UTEP's Entering Student Program (ESP). This merger provides one administrative unit with a single reporting line to the dean of University College, eliminates program duplication, increases efficiency and effectiveness, and makes long-term sustainability of UTEP's Entering Student Program more likely. The merger also reduces campus confusion regarding program features and responsibilities.

This union has also brought about a rethinking of program advisory committees. The first-year seminar and learning communities had separate advisory committees to help with decisions of design and assessment. Though both committees consisted of administrators, faculty, and staff from across campus and shared some members, the two committees operated independently of each other. Rethinking the role of the advisory unit, largely as a result of the merger, has led to the creation of a single advisory committee. The Entering Student Program Advisory Committee has representatives appointed by the deans of all seven colleges and by the vice president for student affairs. Plans are being discussed to include representatives appointed by the vice presidents for institutional advancement and finance and administration. As liaisons, the members serve a dual role: (a) On the committee, they represent programmatic concerns specific to their college majors; and (b) in their colleges, they promote the efforts of the Entering Student Program. This single advisory unit also places visible programmatic emphasis on the integration of the first-year seminar and learning community efforts.

As noted above, the instructor development workshops conducted for first-year seminar and learning community instructors have been combined. This change is due, in large part, to instructor feedback received on workshop evaluations. In the past, all first-year seminar instructors and all learning community instructors, both novice and experienced, had a one-day workshop. On workshop evaluations, instructors pointed out the duplication of effort and the increased demand on their time the two separate workshops created. These separate faculty development days also contradicted the message of the first-year seminar as an integrative course in the learning community. In response, instructor development is now conducted on a single day, and the first-year seminar and learning community sessions are largely integrated.

Programmatic changes also resulted from student comments on the first-year seminar's end-of-semester feedback form. Students frequently recommend more major-specific first-year seminars. In response to this student feedback, the pre-law and the pre-education learning communities were created, increasing discipline-specific strands of learning communities to four, with pre-science and pre-engineering already in place. Each of these learning communities (described previously in this chapter) includes a first-year seminar whose academic theme reflects the discipline (e.g., Law for Beginners, Effective Teaching and Educational Policies in a Multicultural Environment). Through the Entering Student Program Advisory Committee, other colleges will be encouraged to help create and support learning communities specific to their disciplines. With newly articulated goals and an expanded Entering Student Program, integrating learning and building community among all first-year students at UTEP will hopefully be a natural outcome.

References

Cross, P. K. (1998). Why learning communities? Why now? *About Campus, 3*(3), 4-11.
Tinto, V. (2002, April). *Moving beyond access.* Keynote speech presented at the AACRAO National Conference, Minneapolis, MN.

Appendix A
University 1301 Goals and Objectives

Goal 1. To strengthen students' academic performance and facilitate their transition to college

Objective 1.1 Students will explore one or more academic topics to become aware of and practice the habits of scholarship.

Objective 1.2 Students will become familiar with major UTEP academic policies and requirements.

Objective 1.3 Students will examine personal and social transition issues affecting college success, including topics such as academic expectations, high-risk behaviors, and relationships.

Goal 2. To enhance students' essential academic skills

Objective 2.1 Students will engage in critical-thinking/problem-solving activities.

Objective 2.2 Students will practice oral, written, and electronic communication skills.

Objective 2.3 Students will conduct library and electronic research.

Objective 2.4 Students will examine and develop academic survival and success strategies (e.g., note-taking, active reading, time management).

Goal 3. To increase student-student and student-faculty interaction both in and outside of the classroom

Objective 3.1 Students will meet at least twice with the instructional team to discuss academic progress and transition to UTEP and to explore options for improvement.

Objective 3.2 Students will participate in group activities and learn more about group roles and facilitation skills.

Goal 4. To encourage students' self-assessment and goal clarification

Objective 4.1 Students will participate in at least one activity to assess learning styles and relate them to college tasks.

Objective 4.2 Students will participate in at least one career assessment activity that examines the student's interests, abilities, and values.

Goal 5. To increase students' involvement with UTEP activities and resources

Objective 5.1   Students will attend/participate in social, cultural, and intellectual events at UTEP.

Objective 5.2   Students will become aware of and use selected academic and student support resources.

Appendix B

University Studies Instructor Workshop
Spring 2004
Saturday, November 22, 2003

8:00 - 8:30	Breakfast
8:15 - 8:30	Welcome Dean of University College
8:30 - 9:00	Theme Design: Identifying a Learning Community Theme (Icebreaker)
9:00 - 9:10	Break
9:10 - 10:40	Developing Strategies for Transferring Skills Center for Effective Teaching and Learning
10:40 - 10:50	Break
10:50 - 11:20	Helping Students Read Effectively
11:20 - 11:50	Student Health Center: A Campus Resource
11:50 - 12:40	Lunch
12:40 - 2:20	Developing Shared Assignment
2:20 - 2:30	Break
2:30 - 2:50	Service-Learning Opportunities Institution for Community-Based Teaching and Learning
2:50 - 3:00	Conclusion Workshop Evaluation

Chapter 15

Learning Communities and Integrated Seminars as Sites for Addressing the Divided Self

Kathleen Byrnes, Marylu Hill, and John Immerwahr

Villanova University

When I was with my friends, my mind was occupied with our talking and laughing, exchanging kindnesses, reading good books together, now joking, now being serious, disagreeing without animosity as one might disagree with one's own self (and finding that our rare disagreements seasoned our usual concord), teaching and learning from one another, sorely missing those who were gone and welcoming with you those who came. These and such like signs coming from hearts that loved one another, through mouth and tongue and a thousand gracious gestures, were the kindling of a fire that melted our minds together and made the many of us one. St. Augustine (401/1960 2.8.16)

St. Augustine paints an idyllic picture of a learning community, where he and his friends are "teaching and learning from one another." Typical of Augustine, the community he describes is not a purely intellectual one. He values not only the serious intellectual exchange, but he also stresses the interpersonal relationships built on laughter, sharing, and mutual support that make "the many of us one."

College students do form communities of friendship and mutual support, but these communities are not always built around the teaching, learning, and reading of good books required of them. Too often, student communities are formed around bonds that have little to do with their formal academic lives. The result, speaking again in Augustinian terms, is a divided self where students' lives are fragmented between their academic pursuits and their social development. At Villanova University, the creation of a number of first-year student learning communities addresses these issues. In this chapter there is a brief history of the origin of the program, followed by a discussion of the current configuration and plans for the future.

Villanova University's Mission and Learning Communities

Villanova University is an Augustinian, Catholic university located in the western suburbs of Philadelphia. Villanova's current full-time undergraduate population is 6,434 students, including 1,557 first-year students, the majority of whom live on campus. The University is composed of four undergraduate colleges: Arts and Sciences, Engineering, Commerce and Finance, and Nursing. The University's Carnegie Classification is Master's I.

The origin and continuing support for the learning community effort at Villanova University grows directly out of the University's mission, which states that Villanova seeks to develop the "total person: intellectually, emotionally, spiritually, culturally, socially, and physically." Indeed, the Villanova community "seeks to reflect the spirit of St. Augustine by the cultivation of knowledge, by respect for individual differences, and by adherence to the principle that mutual love and respect should animate every aspect of University life" (Mission Statement, n.d.).

Villanova offers programs for students and faculty from all faith traditions. At the same time, Villanova stresses the goals inherent in its Catholic and Augustinian character, and many members of the community have come to Villanova precisely because they hold to those values. Augustine sought a unity, as he said, of "heart and mind," and he saw community as playing an important role in nurturing that unity.

The Genesis of Learning Communities at Villanova

At Villanova, the idea of student learning communities evolved to meet a number of needs. Two concerns were of particular importance: (a) the need for a more intense academic experience and (b) the desire for more intentional delivery of co-curricular programs. First, Villanova started to experience a dramatic improvement in the level of academic preparedness of incoming students in the late 1980s. This improvement was linked to Villanova's increased national visibility after the 1985 basketball championship. The strategic policies of a new University president starting in 1988 helped to build decisively on Villanova's emerging sense of national presence, resulting in the markedly different student base it has today. At that time, several faculty leaders and administrators became convinced that the traditional first-year curriculum was not sufficiently challenging for students. In those days, an incoming Villanova student would typically be enrolled in five different introductory courses. Often, these courses would be characterized by lectures rather than discussion and by tests rather than papers. Many felt that Villanova was fostering a mechanistic and passive approach to learning and that the campus did not provide as rich an intellectual environment as it might. Villanova chose to create a more vibrant campus intellectual life where students would be engaged as active learners.

In order to achieve this, Villanova began an extended program of curricular reform. One important piece of that reform effort was the institution of the Core Humanities Seminar (CHS) in 1992. This two-semester, interdisciplinary seminar is required of all first-year students, with enrollment in each section capped at about 16 students. Faculty, recruited from the various humanities disciplines, guide students as they read significant texts from the Western tradition. The course has a strong emphasis on learning to read, think, and write critically.

The first semester of CHS includes reading and discussing texts by Augustine, portions of the Bible, and, at the instructor's discretion, some combination of texts by authors such as Plato, Sophocles, Euripides, Chaucer, Dante, Machiavelli, and Shakespeare. The second semester follows the Augustinian and humanistic themes of the first semester as they play out in the modern and contemporary world. The instructors stress an interdisciplinary approach, and the classes are run as seminars, not as mini-lectures. The structure of the course, drawing on a variety of readings in the humanities and often emphasizing concepts outside the instructor's home discipline, requires that the professor model for the students what it means to be a lifelong learner. Although CHS was originally created for Liberal Arts and Science students, shortly after it was instituted, the three professional colleges (i.e., Business, Engineering, and Nursing) required it for their students as well. Today, all first-year students at Villanova take CHS.

While some of the sections of Core Humanities are taught by regular full-time tenured or tenure-track faculty members from the various departments, it quickly became obvious that it was also necessary to recruit a group of faculty dedicated to this course. The eventual strategy was to recruit a contingent of post-doctoral fellows through a national search process which, as the program has developed, has become increasingly competitive. These faculty members are new Ph.D.s coming from prestigious national and international institutions. They typically come to Villanova for three years (often while they are finishing their first book), and most have gone on to tenure-track jobs at other institutions or, in some cases, at Villanova. The post-doctorates bring an enthusiasm and freshness to the course, with a commitment to maintaining academic rigor.

In general, the instructors for Core Humanities are selected on the basis of the following criteria: They must have completed their doctoral degrees in the humanities. They must show an interest in interdisciplinary thought. They are strong teachers or clearly demonstrate the potential for becoming excellent teachers. They are supportive of the mission of the University. They are interested in connecting their work with the thought of St. Augustine, and they are supportive of the concept of learning communities. Insructors receive an orientation for Core Humanities at the beginning of the school year and, throughout the year, participate in discussion groups and symposia on academic and pedagogical development. The director and assistant director of Core Humanities routinely do classroom evaluations of new faculty, in addition to the student class evaluations administered at the end of each semester.

The second ingredient for the learning communities arose from the growing need to provide a better delivery system for co-curricular programs, especially those facilitating students' personal and interpersonal development. Traditionally, Villanova had many commuter students, but in the last 10 years as the University began to change from a local and regional school to a more national institution, the student population became largely residential. The character and needs of the students also evolved in several significant ways. The Division of Student Life at Villanova shared the academic goal of creating a more stimulating academic environment outside the classroom, but the Division of Student Life also wanted to find a way to deal with the issues that emerge in a resident student population. Professionals in the Division of Student Life sought to develop a higher level of intentional programming to deal with typical student concerns (e.g., homesickness, time management, decision-making about relationships, alcohol). Yet, Student Life experienced the dilemma familiar to student life professionals elsewhere: It would develop an excellent program on time management to offer in the residence halls, but only the students who were already good time managers would attend. The Student Life staff members were looking for an alternate delivery system that would create a greater receptivity for programming.

Putting It All Together

University administrators decided it was time to create a structured learning community at Villanova that addressed both the academic and student life concerns. A team attended the Annual Conference on The First-Year Experience in South Carolina in 1996 in order to refine the plan being developed at the time. The resulting proposal was a collaborative endeavor between Student Life and Academic Affairs, the latter focus being within the Core Humanities department. The proposal and the resulting program combined forces to provide a richer intellectual environment and one more support to students in their overall development. This program, called "The Villanova Experience" or VEXP, was piloted in the 1996-1997 academic year with 160 students. From the beginning, the following have been some of its defining characteristics:

- Students are offered the opportunity to apply for the program in the summer before the their first year.
- All accepted students are housed in the same residence hall, with mixed genders by floor or wing.
- All the students are assigned to a specially designated section of Core Humanities Seminars associated with the program and with other students from the residence hall. As much as possible, there is a complete overlap, so that only those students in the CHS classes are those living in the residence hall and vice versa.
- The students in each CHS class are also scheduled for a "Fourth Hour" outside the normal class schedule, called the "Villanova Experience Seminar." The Fourth Hour classes are typically held in the residence hall lounges, usually in the late afternoon or early evening.
- Each Fourth Hour is led by a staff member facilitator, typically from either Student Life

or Campus Ministry. The Fourth Hour has a curriculum based largely on the content of a nursing course titled "Healthy Lifestyles," but also includes issues unique to the first-year student's transition to college. Attendance at the Fourth Hour is required by the CHS.

Villanova Experience seminar facilitators are selected from faculty and staff at the University. In most cases, they have a minimum of a master's degree and multiple years of experience in working with college-age students, including work with groups and facilitation. The coordinator of the program (i.e., the assistant vice president for Student Life) solicits and interviews the candidates. The majority of facilitators are professional staff from the Division of Student Life, though professional staff members from Campus Ministry as well as faculty from the Nursing College are in the pool and are selected on a regular basis.

In the summer, half-day training opportunities are offered for the facilitators. The components of the training include:

- Introduction to learning communities at Villanova
- Components of the Villanova Experience Program
  - Core Humanities Seminar (CHS)
  - Villanova Experience Seminar
  - Residential component
  - Additional co-curricular programming expectations
- The Villanova Experience Seminar
  - Annotated syllabus guideline
  - Topics/resource manual
  - Coordination and collaboration with CHS faculty/class
  - Budget

The first week of the semester, an additional 90-minute training program for faculty, facilitators, and student facilitators is scheduled. During this time, the teams (i.e., faculty, facilitators, and student facilitators for each section) have planning time to assist them in coordinating their efforts through the semester. Periodic meetings are also held throughout the year with these groups. Each Villanova Experience facilitator receives a $600 annual stipend at the end of the year. The student facilitators and the faculty are not monetarily compensated for their participation.

Early Reactions From the Students

The formal evaluations of the program will be discussed in a later section, but the initial anecdotal feedback from students was positive. Since the students were taking a small discussion-oriented class, living in the same residence hall, and also taking a Fourth Hour together, they got to know each other well. Many of the instructors felt that the class discussion was much more uninhibited and the students seemed to be spending much more time discussing the class material outside the classroom.

The response from students the first three years was so positive that ultimately the program has made one of the least popular residence halls into a major success. There is one residence hall on campus that has a number of attractive features (including its own cafeteria, gym, and swimming pool) but is also located rather far from the areas where most first-year students live. As a result, the hall was quite unpopular. To make it more attractive, it was used to house the Villanova Experience. Many of the older students on campus said that this would be a disaster, and some who had younger siblings coming to Villanova told them not to sign up for the program. Yet, the results were outstanding. The students love the building, and the hall has gone from a less desirable to a coveted place to live.

Early Lessons: The Great Divide

While laying the groundwork for this first learning community, a critical need arose for yet another type of learning community—one that would build bridges between faculty and staff professionals. The great value of those early conversations was the effort to find ways to talk to each other. Initially, the widely divergent perspectives brought to the enterprise by faculty and Division of Student Life staff members were particularly striking.

Responses on an annual survey administered each year illustrate the roots of this divide between faculty and staff perspectives. As part of Villanova's orientation each August, each faculty member takes a survey asking how many of the listed activities they participated in when they were undergraduates. It starts with a list of questions culled from the Division of Student Life:

- Were you a resident advisor?
- Were you a member of a fraternity or sorority?
- Did you work with the career services center?
- Did you work with student government?
- Were you a member of a student club or organization?

Responses reveal that many of the new faculty had very low involvement with student life professionals at their own undergraduate institutions. As the conversations developed, some faculty expressed the assumption that Student Life offerings were light-weight and anti-intellectual. By contrast, many of the Division of Student Life staff were highly involved with these activities and found them very valuable. In effect, the two groups have different understandings of the purpose of undergraduate education. While these differences have previously existed, in the past they were often submerged. In the Villanova Experience, both groups were asked to work together, dealing with the same students, and the differences between perspectives became dramatically apparent to both groups.

One question that arose was what students should be doing in the Fourth Hour. In one early meeting, an influential faculty member said, "A Fourth Hour? That will be great. Perhaps students could use the extra time to discuss how current events apply to our course material." The Division of Student Life staff members were thinking that the Fourth Hour might be used for a session on Myers-Briggs Type Indicator as a way of understanding diversity or for a session on decision making about sexuality and relationships. What was interesting was not that each had a different view, but that each was surprised to learn what the other person was thinking. Instead of being resolved after the first year or so, these tensions set a dynamic that continues to this day. Part of the reason for the continued tension is that many of the Core Humanities sections are taught, as mentioned earlier, by post-doctoral students on three-year contracts. So while the Division of Student Life staff members became used to dealing with the issues, each new group of faculty members has to start over again. Thus, the process is an ongoing dialogue, with new voices being added to the discussion periodically.

The Villanova Experience Today

The academic year 2003-04 was the eighth year of the Villanova Experience program. As of 2003-2004, the program serves some 240 residential students, plus 30 commuter students, and 15 transfer students annually. As the program has evolved, the learning objectives have solidified. Students ideally will meet the following learning objectives by the conclusion of their first college year:

- Enhanced critical thinking and writing abilities through the intensive work in the Core Humanities Seminar
- Communication with at least one professor and professional staff member of the university who can serve as a resource for the student
- Time spent in their residence hall discussing classroom readings, themes, and assignments with fellow residents
- Improved understanding of academic integrity and why it is an important community value
- Knowledge of campus resources available to assist them with academic concerns in order to attain academic success
- Increased ability to be self-sufficient in personal maintenance tasks and to be independent problem solvers
- Knowledge of the basic obligations of community membership and understanding how those obligations are reflected in the University's values and expectations for student behavior
- Exploration of the basic principles of personal health and wellness and increased understanding of behaviors that constitute health risks among college students

The Fourth Hour curriculum has also evolved. Its primary goal is to address the needs of first-year students holistically as they make the transition to college life academically and socially. Thus, the Fourth Hour combined with the Core class seeks to cultivate both intellectual curiosity and personal development, while fostering a strong sense of academic and social community. The following is a list of topics covered by most facilitators:

- Making the transition to college (e.g., goal setting)
- Participating in team-building activities (e.g., "low ropes" course)
- Developing academic integrity
- Being active in the classroom, becoming a successful student
- Living in community and getting along with a roommate
- Becoming aware of diversity and celebrating differences
- Clarifying values and making ethical decisions
- Building relationships: friends, peer pressure, navigating the social scene
- Communicating across gender lines
- Beginning and sustaining romantic relationships
- Developing effective time management skills

In addition, at least one Fourth Hour class each semester must be integrated with the corresponding CHS theme and planned in conjunction with the faculty member. Examples of such integrated sessions include symposia on current events, debates, and most recently, a game called "The Augustine Game, or What Would Augustine Do?" created by a group of VEXP faculty and facilitators. Each class will also engage in some cultural activities outside the residence hall (on or off campus) from going to a play to exploring China Town in Philadelphia to experiencing South Philadelphia and Pat's cheese steaks. Activities are encouraged, and each section has a class dinner at some point in the semester.

Typically, faculty members and facilitators also work out some joint programming, such as a trip to a museum or attendance at the Shakespeare Festival or the Renaissance Fair. On occasion, the faculty member will attend the Fourth Hour session, and usually the facilitator attends a couple of the CHS classes. Often, the facilitator can act as a resource person for the faculty member in dealing with student problems that might arise. For example, if a student is doing poorly in the class, the faculty member might ask the facilitator to help assess if something is going on outside of class (i.e., roommate problems, stress) and tap into appropriate resources.

As the VEXP has evolved and attempted to respond to faculty concerns that the program was not academic enough, it has explored various routes to inculcate more co-curricular academic involvement. Initially, a colloquia series was implemented and led by faculty from across the University on "cross-over" topics that spanned the gap between the classroom and what is perceived as "real life." Thus, one week would feature a discussion on the sociology of making friends led by a sociology professor, while another week would feature a political discussion on current events. However, attendance proved to be an issue unless the topic was strictly academic. Faculty members were reluctant to require attendance, and unless the topic was viewed by the students as completely fun, they were unlikely to attend on their own initiative. Greater success occurred when each class was encouraged to choose an event, like a guest lecturer or field trip, based specifically on their course syllabus and theme. Since such events were tied into the individual class, both faculty and students felt the events served a clearer purpose, thus effectively eliminating the attendance issue.

As VEXP moved toward other learning community models described below, it was found that one of the most effective ways to create academic community is through the use of shared texts. Since the VEXP is not centered on a shared syllabus for all VEXP sections, one shared reading has been implemented this year for all VEXP sections which is, in turn, linked with an introductory movie to serve as a community-wide event. Finally, the theme of the shared reading gets picked up again in the St. Augustine section of the Core Humanities class. For example, this year all VEXP sections read the story of the Garden of Eden in *Genesis*, with an emphasis on the question of free will. The students then watched the movie *Scotland, PA* during the first week of classes. At mid-semester, they returned to the theme of free will in their reading of St. Augustine.

Spinoff Models From the Villanova Experience

Like many schools, a one-size learning community does not fit all. Although the Villanova Experience is considered a success, varying faculty and student interest led to the development of other models for first-year learning communities. All use the basic components of the Villanova Experience: students being in community both in and out of class. The earliest spinoff was a model of the Villanova Experience for commuting students. Thirty students are enrolled in two designated sections of CHS and attend their Fourth Hour together. Fewer than 10% of first-year students are commuters, so they have felt disconnected from other students as well as from campus. This program helps students find each other and facilitates connection to Villanova in and out of the classroom. Most recently, the academic component of the VEXP for commuters was expanded by creating two commuter sections with two professors teaching the same Core Humanities texts at the same time. The sections share a common time slot, and once every three weeks the sections meet together for a large academic lecture and discussion. The two sections also share the same facilitator (i.e., a Student Life professional, like all the other VEXP sections) and meet periodically as a large group in the Fourth Hour as well.

The next spinoff was the Visions of Freedom program, now called Politics and Freedom Learning Community. A group of faculty members decided that they wanted to have a learning community with a strictly academic focus. As mentioned above, despite general guidelines (particularly in the Ancient, Medieval, and Renaissance portion of Core) for which authors or genres should be covered in the CHS, CH classes do not follow a set syllabus. Each Core professor creates his or her own set of course readings based on the general guidelines. However, in Politics and Freedom, a group of five faculty members created a completely common syllabus, so that all five sections are reading the same texts at the same time. These students (approximately 72) reside in one of the smaller residence halls. The five sections come together for a common lecture once every two weeks, in addition to one-to-two lectures from outside speakers. The academic content of the course focuses specifically on issues surrounding political philosophy and notions of community, so the community in the hall creates a small laboratory to discuss some of the same issues that are raised in the class. As with many the residential learning communities, the level of informal conversation in the residence hall dramatically increases in terms of academic content when such programs are in place. For example, the Politics and Freedom resident assistants routinely report clusters of students engaged in late-night discussions of democracy, politics, or other such topics over pizza in the lounge. This year, the students have created political parties within the hall, along with a press and a constituency.

No formal Fourth Hour classes are connected to the Politics and Freedom Learning Community; however, the residence hall staff supports various co-curricular activities relevant to the topic including guest speakers, bus trips to New York to see a play, or museum visits to view exhibits related to the course material. Students in this learning community have the opportunity to explore important issues in conversation with classmates, hall mates, and CHS professors. Faculty and Residence Life staff meet regularly to plan joint programming that brings ideas from class into the students' co-curricular activities.

Another spinoff is the House Masters Program. It also revolves around the Core Humanities seminar and houses students in two small residence halls. This model grew out of the following dilemma. From the perspective of creating a learning community, it would be best to have all the students in an entire residence hall learning from a common syllabus in their CHS class. At the same time, most faculty members objected to the idea of a common syllabus across sections taught by different instructors. Individual faculty members expressed the view that their own individual classes would be most effective if they taught the material that they themselves found most useful. This was particularly true in CHS. The course was not intended to cover a specific content; instead, the emphasis is on fostering writing, discussion, and intellectual growth. As such, instructors tended to develop an individualized theme for their courses and to choose readings (from within the course parameters) that worked most effectively with those themes.

To address the concerns of the faculty, the House Master learning community was created, and it designated an individual faculty member as a "house master." Since many of the CHS faculty members teach three sections, with almost 50 students in total, all 50 students could live together in a single residence hall. Indeed, there is one hall that holds precisely this number. These students all have a common syllabus and a common teacher. Typically, the faculty member also offers some programming through the residence hall. This might be something as simple as an evening when the faculty member stops by the residence hall to help students with papers or a trip with students to a museum or play off campus. The house masters also work closely with the Residence Life staff on issues that come up in the hall and are welcome to take part in various hall social functions. It is worth noting here that the close coordination that occurs between the faculty member, the resident assistants, and the learning community coordinators has made a critical difference for the success of these House Master communities. In addition, it is a model of teamwork for faculty and Student Life professionals working in other learning communities.

Wanting to explore the possibility of building a learning community around a first-year course other than Core Humanities, the students from a large section of the introductory philosophy course have been housed together. The Philosophy Learning Community is the most minimalist learning community in terms of coordinated programming efforts between faculty and the Division of Student Life. Approximately 75 to 90 students are enrolled in the three-credit course that meets twice a week in a large lecture and once a week in small discussion groups. The faculty member meets periodically with the Residence Life staff in the building to coordinate themes being discussed in class with themes for co-curricular programming. This learning community is designed only for the fall semester.

In the 2001-2002 academic year, the Office of Residence Life piloted the Leadership Learning Community. In this community, students are housed together in one building and are enrolled in a non-credit leadership course that meets weekly for 75 minutes. The course is taught by members of the Student Life and Residence Life staff. The weekly leadership classes engage students in discussions and experiential learning activities designed to further students' understanding of leadership and community development.

Assessment

Various assessment tools have been used to measure the success of the VEXP and other learning communities. Initially, student satisfaction surveys gauged the strengths and weaknesses of the program, and learning community students consistently reported more contact with their faculty members than those not in a learning community. The students also reported an environment more conducive to studying in the residence hall that translated into more hours spent studying in the halls. In addition, students indicated a higher level of satisfaction with the residence hall community and with their adjustment to Villanova in general compared to the first-year students in non-learning community residence halls. Other supporting data such as fraternity and sorority rush figures and hall violations data (both of which were lower than other first-year residence halls) would suggest that the learning communities were accomplishing their community-building goals. However, quantitative data analysis, including tracking grade point averages of learning community participants against nonparticipants, has not yet been conducted.

Two other assessment tools have been implemented for the class of 2004: the College Student Expectations Questionnaire (CSXQ) and the College Student Experiences Questionnaire (CSEQ). However, the data relevant to learning community participation have yet to be analyzed.

Challenges

At national conferences on learning communities, lack of faculty buy-in is frequently mentioned as a problem and, in one way or another, Villanova has experienced this as well. Some faculty members are not interested in the learning community approach at all. These faculty tend to assume that learning communities are either too time-consuming (which in itself is a critical issue, especially for junior faculty who must publish aggressively to secure tenure) or not academic enough in their focus. The first objection was addressed by reassuring faculty that there are multiple levels of commitment, from minimal to strong involvement, and not everyone is expected to be able to make the same sort of commitment. The second objection tends to arise from the perception that the learning communities are strictly Student Life initiatives, even though once faculty see the opportunities for an enhanced academic experience through learning communities, this perception is reevaluated.

Some faculty members liked the idea of a learning community but did not value the time spent on transition issues and student development. They were encouraged to create their own learning communities, based on different models. For the most part, they have built their learning communities on CHS, as seen above. Politics and Freedom and the House Master models have been very successful, both from faculty and student viewpoints.

Plans for the Future: The 100% Solution

Villanova is now exploring the "100% solution." The plan is to expand learning community efforts dramatically. In the past, learning communities were created before working with the housing office to make sure all those students would be housed together. Also, the fact that all first-year students are taking CHS allows the creation of universal learning communities. For 2004-2005, plans are to ensure that all students will be housed with their CHS classmates. There will then be a universal platform to build a variety of different learning communities, depending on the level of instructor interest. But the critical baseline will already be established—housing students with their classmates from Core Humanities—which promotes deeper conversations and a humanistic approach to community. With this baseline in place, all the learning communities should create a positive impact on the first-year student experience at Villanova.

References

Mission Statement. (n.d.). Retrieved June 30, 2004, from http://www.heritage.villanova.edu/mission.html

St. Augustine. (1960). *Confessions.* (J. K. Ryan, Trans.). New York: Doubleday. (Original work published 401 CE).

A Learning Community Focused on Peer-Facilitated Research, Writing, and Critical Thinking

Kay Tronsen

Washington State University

Chapter 16

Young's (1992) critique of education describes a fragmented experience that causes students to focus on discrete, separated chunks of information at the loss of an understanding of the social and community aspects of knowledge. Those who work in the Washington State University Freshman Seminar[1] want first-year students to consider themselves part of a community of knowledge, even as novices. The questions that drive the pedagogy of the WSU Freshman Seminar program are: "What image of humanity is inherent in [higher education]?" and "How do learners fit into this idea of inquiry?" (Young, 1992, p. 26).

The WSU Freshman Seminar learning community program operates from a belief that students are responsible for their own learning and that students should be engaged in the learning process through active and collaborative work. First-year students in the seminar program are invited to make connections with peers, faculty, and other campus resources. The primary learning objectives center on enhancing the students' critical thinking skills while introducing students to and engaging them in an intensive research process. Assessments conducted on the program, as described below, suggest that these foci correlate at a statistically significant level to improved adjustment to college, greater intellectual confidence, and a number of other desired learning outcomes. The seminar course, one of two courses in each learning community link, is guided by undergraduate peer facilitators who report to graduate students and consult frequently with the faculty member in their paired course.

This chapter begins with an overview of both the Freshman Seminar program and the Freshman Seminar course, followed by curriculum details of the seminar course including a discussion of the facilitators—both the graduate students who form the leadership body and the peer facilitators who manage the classroom. WSU's emphasis on peer facilitation is fairly unique among learning community programs. As such, this instructional model is the centerpiece of the current discussion. The chapter concludes with a discussion of assessment and its role in supporting the WSU Freshman Seminar learning community program.

History

Washington State University is a public, land-grant research institution located in the heart of wheat fields in Pullman, Washington, about 90 miles south of Spokane. The Pullman campus has 15,451 undergraduates. The mission of the University is to "enhance the intellectual, creative, and practical abilities of individuals, institutions, and communities that we serve by fostering learning, inquiry, and engagement" (Washington State University, 2003, p. 3).

The Freshman Seminar program began in 1996 with the approval of the University's Faculty Senate in recognition of the intellectual and cultural transition needs of first-year students at WSU. A cooperative effort of both Academic Affairs and Student Affairs, the Freshman Seminar program, as part of the General Education Program, is funded through the Office of the Provost and provides academic credit for the Freshman Seminar course granted by the Office of General Education. Administrative responsibility rests with a coordinator in the Student Advising and Learning Center (SALC) in the Division of Student Affairs.

While the broad goals envisioned by the designers of the Freshman Seminar program support University efforts to increase retention and graduation rates, the underlying motivation is to create a set of opportunities to address many of the informational needs of students and to help them adjust their expectations to the realities of college life. Based on national learning community research and undergirded by Chickering and Gamson's (1987) "Seven Principles for Good Practice in Undergraduate Education," the program was created to offer the following benefits:

- Greater intellectual interaction (student-student, faculty-student, faculty-faculty)
- Greater curricular coherence and integration of knowledge
- Greater understanding of issues which cross subject matter boundaries
- Earlier encounters with diverse perspectives
- Increased opportunities for active learning
- Significant opportunities for student-peer facilitation and faculty development

In addition to increasing retention and graduation rates, the program's explicit focus on the research process is consistent with the University's role as a research-intensive institution and its mission to involve undergraduates in collaborative research efforts.

Structure

WSU's learning community program co-enrolls a group of 15 students in a section of the Freshman Seminar and one other general education or introductory course in the major; the latter is referred to as the shared course. Each section of the Freshman Seminar meets immediately following its shared course, which usually has a much larger enrollment. In the Freshman Seminar, students research a topic from the disciplinary perspective of the shared course, using the research process as an introduction to the type of academic endeavors they will be involved in across disciplines and throughout their career at the University. The shared course faculty members identify major themes to emphasize in their courses, and students choose one of these overarching themes as a starting point for selecting a research topic. The seminar research culminates with the final project in the form of a multimedia presentation.

The Freshman Seminar serves as an integrative point for the students to engage content as a means to an end instead of an end in itself. They encounter the questions important in a discipline, experience the processes of researching in that discipline, and then spend time with the shared course faculty as they navigate the research process (Weimer, 2002). As one shared course faculty member expressed it:

> Freshman Seminar helps students understand the relationship between the highly specific, focused nature of research topics and a broad overview of the field. Often students enter WSU with a notion that taking a course means mastering certain content. Freshman Seminar helps students to see that a field of inquiry has a life of its own, that it is more than a mere collection of facts.[2]

The Freshman Seminar course allows students the opportunity to investigate an aspect of the shared course curriculum in more depth than is typically possible during an introductory course and to use that process to reflect on the overall requirements of university-level work. The work students do in the seminars provides new insights and considerations of the larger content they explore in the shared course. This heightened intellectual interaction is the key to the program.

The seminar course is a two credit-hour elective, and each semester 19 to 26 sections (serving 250 to 300 students) are offered. The course is typically led by two undergraduate facilitators. Shared course faculty come into the seminar course at pivotal points in the semester to provide support for brainstorming and give feedback on the proposal, the research process, and the project development. Participating faculty members, who teach the shared course, receive a small stipend for their work in the Freshman Seminar program.

The research focus of the Freshman Seminar program and course provides a purposeful venue for faculty to be involved with the students in a small, informal setting. This structure allows professors the opportunity to interact with students at a deeper level than typically possible.

> As a shared-course faculty member, I believe Freshman Seminar provides opportunities for participants to develop research and technological skills, to critically evaluate information, and to learn about teamwork. Due to the smaller group sizes and informal settings, I am better able to interact with the students, and help them to make the most of these opportunities.

Peer facilitators meet with the faculty at the beginning of the semester and then periodically throughout the semester, discussing the research as it develops and arranging visits to the seminar courses. The peer facilitators attend the shared course with the seminar students until the topic is chosen and the process of research is well underway. As another shared course faculty commented, "I've especially enjoyed getting to know the peer facilitators. It's an unusual twist on the ordinary student-faculty relationship: We are allies with the same problems to solve."

To introduce the University's library system to seminar students, a librarian is assigned to each seminar for the semester and also receives a small stipend for her or his work. Librarians provide additional research support for the peer facilitators, create a resource guide once the students choose a topic, and give feedback on the proposal and final project. Assessments indicate that links to the shared course faculty and librarians help students build alliances across campus, learn to work with faculty on issues of mutual interest, and learn the library system from a member of the staff who is familiar with the purpose of the seminar project and understands the unique challenges faced by incoming students. Librarians also indicate benefits of participation:

> The librarians really enjoy their work with FS [Freshman Seminar] because it allows us a chance to get to know students better over the course of a semester and to work with a focused topic as it develops. Our involvement with FS allows us to introduce the library and its resources to first-year students in a positive, non-threatening environment.

Another librarian indicates that the benefits to students are matched by the benefits to the library:

> To succeed during their first year in college, students need to be able to effectively manage the research process. FS introduces students to that process and to what is expected of college students in terms of the location, evaluation, and presentation of information. Working with FS students provides librarians with an opportunity to help them make a successful transition to the more complex information environment of a research university, and to ease any "library anxiety" that might keep them from asking for our help throughout the course of their academic career. It also allows us to work directly with first-year students for an extended period of time in order to evaluate how they tend to conduct research,

what sort of typical questions they have and resources they use, and to continually improve the services that we provide for undergraduate students.

Curriculum

Learning Outcomes

The seminar program has a concise list of learning outcomes that are communicated openly to students in the course syllabus (Appendix A). At the end of the semester, the learning outcomes are used to gauge performance against intent. The learning outcomes for the Freshman Seminar program are an outgrowth of the overarching interest in critical thinking and research and are centered on four concept areas: (a) individual and collaborative learning strategies, (b) oral and written communication skills, (c) information literacy and knowledge of the academic research process, and (d) technological fluency. Under each of these main areas are target outcomes. The learning outcomes are pivotal to discussions of assignments and activities and are used to guide changes.

The Syllabus

All sections of the Freshman Seminar course follow a cross-disciplinary, committee-designed syllabus that provides the facilitators with the "mountain peaks" of the semester: elements such as topic emphasis (e.g., visual communication or writing an effective thesis), assignment and project due dates, and special activities (e.g., presentations). (See Appendix A for a sample syllabus.) The research process provides opportunities for discussing important transition topics, including academic dishonesty and appropriate use of resources. In addition to their work with the librarians and shared course faculty, students generate research ideas through guided reading, class discussion, and brainstorming in both face-to-face and online environments.

Collaborative work forms the bulk of the seminar classroom processes with the class dividing into small groups that focus on particular aspects of the larger research project. Each small group is responsible for writing a thesis and for designing part of the web site associated with the research project. Group contracts are negotiated by small groups in each section in order to establish individual and group responsibilities and behavioral expectations. Each research team designs an author's page, conducts reflections on the research project, and writes a proposal including an annotated bibliography, all of which are submitted in the WSU-created online course management system called the Bridge. Research teams also compose rough drafts, use standard scholarly quantitative and qualitative research methodologies, and offer a formal presentation of their research.

Final Project

The culminating event of the semester for the seminar program is the Research Symposium in which all seminars come together in an academic fair environment to present their projects to the wider community. This invitation event is attended by shared course and other faculty, administrators, staff, and students and is publicized through campus and community media. During the Symposium, which is held on central campus, students use state-of-the-art technology to display their research projects in a highly visual forum. The comments of one shared course faculty member demonstrate the powerful impact of the experience on student learning and success:

In response to "what do students need to succeed during their first year of college," they simply need some successes. In addition to all the skills they learn during FS, they also have the opportunity to experience the successful completion of a collaboratively conceived, researched, written, and web-designed project. I remember attending my first FS expo and being thoroughly impressed with the sophistication of their web presentations, but more importantly, being impressed by the topics they selected to research, and the level of research per se. Many students literally beamed with pride as they explained their projects to me. I can't think of a better way of creating an environment that fosters successful collaboration and meaningful work. What a wonderful way to begin one's academic life here at WSU.

Peer Facilitators

Peers are used in a variety of helping contexts including tutoring, classroom instruction, and mentoring programs (e.g., Falchikov, 2001; Ender & Newton, 2000). Whitman and Fife (1988, p. v) acknowledge the "potent force" of peer instructors, but both they and Boud, Cohen, and Sampson (2001) see such leaders as under the direction of traditional faculty members in the classroom. Despite substantial evidence in support of peer-assisted learning, Hamid and Gardner (2001) note that only 10% of first-year seminars employ peer instructors—alone or in collaboration with a faculty or staff member. WSU's Freshman Seminar learning community program is one of the few first-year programs in the country formed around peer instruction. The peer facilitators are guided by graduate facilitators, and for the seminar course they work within the parameters of a highly structured program syllabus. The facilitation model provides a certain amount of freedom within those parameters. Graduate facilitators, who supervise a group of peer facilitators, offer suggestions, use their experiences to help guide the work in the classroom, and give peer facilitators freedom to try ideas as they remain mindful of the program's goals. The shared course faculty members also experience a facilitative role in the seminars. During their meeting with seminar students, they do not lecture; rather, they participate equally in the discussion, ask questions, and share their experience and knowledge.

Peer Facilitator Duties

The peer facilitators are charged with inserting themselves into the students' efforts without taking responsibility for them. More specifically, they are asked to build rapport with the students; explain the research process, syllabus, and class expectations; elicit discussion; and be involved in the online learning environments. The comments of one peer facilitator suggest what a delicate balancing act this is:

> To me, the hardest thing about Freshman Seminar is being able to let students go and see where they end up. It's so hard not glancing at the syllabus or the course schedule without worrying about what needs to get done and by what date that I think we fall behind on letting students discover things for themselves. ... We often forget, in the midst of deadlines, that the important breakthroughs come in subtle and unobservable ways. ... I guess that is what it comes down to. We have to let go of our students. Much like parents, we have to forget about what needs to get done and trust that they will work. Sometimes, the hardest thing to do is let go of their hands, perhaps because we like the security of knowing they are on task.

The course syllabus directs the "what" of the flow of instruction while the peer facilitators provide much of the "how." They are also responsible for establishing contact with the shared course faculty and librarian as well as working closely with their graduate facilitator, who collaborates with the peer facilitator as they adjust the classroom activities to meet the needs of each seminar section.

Training

Selection and training of peer facilitators is a lengthy and multi-step process. Potential peer facilitators apply to the program and participate in an initial screening and interview. Peers who make it through this first round enroll in a two-credit peer leadership course and a one-credit research course taught by librarians. The peer leadership course is centered on first-year experience research with a focus on facilitation, learning environments, and critical thinking. They are exposed to various aspects of Freshman Seminar by observing the seminar course and by meeting current facilitators who visit the leadership course as part of discussion groups or panels. During these class sessions, the instructors observe and evaluate potential facilitators prior to their selection and entry into the classroom as facilitators. Upon completion of the course, applicants participate in a second round of selections. A successful candidate begins as a facilitator the following semester, typically in the fall. The peer facilitators are hired for 10 hours per week to facilitate one seminar. They meet with their graduate facilitator individually and with a small facilitator group or cluster weekly. For their participation in the seminars, facilitators receive an hourly wage.

Recognition and Rewards

Administrators in the WSU Freshman Seminar work to build a supportive community in a variety of ways, including recognizing outstanding facilitators with awards and encouraging their input into the program. When facilitators' questions and concerns arise, administrators ensure that the facilitators see the impact of their ideas on the program.

The efforts of shared course faculty and librarians are recognized during an Appreciation Lunch and Dessert where faculty and librarians interact informally with peer and graduate facilitators. Shared course faculty and librarians also engage in conversations about their experiences in Freshman Seminar by brainstorming ideas for improving the link with the shared course. These program participants are also invited to engage in project evaluations and are asked to attend student presentations at the Research Symposium.

Challenges With Peer Instruction

Despite best intentions, comprehensive training, and the efforts of graduate facilitators, on rare occasions an undergraduate does not succeed as a facilitator. Interventions include in-seminar observations and conversations with the student, the shared course faculty, and graduate facilitator. The most serious problem occurs when the facilitator refuses to become engaged themselves in the research project and, by extension, in the learning process. While the peer facilitators are supposed to encourage students' ownership of their projects, they cannot be disinterested in the topic or the process themselves. This disinterest becomes readily apparent to the students. Another issue, albeit a rare one, is immaturity—when a facilitator cares about the class only as it reflects on him or her. Intensive screening and exhaustive ongoing training are critical to identifying and nurturing students with potential.

Although peer facilitation is viewed as a strength within the program, its use is perceived by some outside the program as a weakness. Biases toward teacher "expertness" and authority raise questions about using peer leaders in a two-credit course. Assessments based on the mission and strategic goals of the University and desired learning outcomes have been important in answering concerns about the use of peer facilitators to organize first-year student academic work. Anecdotal evidence also suggests that peers have a powerful impact on learning. A former seminar student reflected on his own peer facilitator:

It was interesting, because she always questioned my answers, and it especially made me mad when she challenged the answers I felt most confident about, but this sort of questioning forced a type of retrospect which made me and my classmates reconsider some answers which we would have deemed concrete, and this added a more in-depth look into our FS topic.

Graduate Facilitators

The WSU Freshman Seminar program employs five graduate facilitators (GF) each year who receive teaching assistantships and tuition waivers. They are selected based on their teaching experience, mentoring or facilitation experience, and positive attitude toward working with undergraduates. The graduate and peer facilitators are supervised by the coordinator of the Freshman Seminar program, who maintains oversight of all program components. Graduate facilitators are responsible for overseeing five seminars, which involves being available to the peer facilitator during the hours the seminar course is being conducted and visiting the course when appropriate. Graduate facilitators meet weekly with each peer facilitator and lead weekly small group meetings of the peer facilitators from their cluster of five seminars. They also meet weekly with the other graduate facilitators and administrative staff. As one graduate facilitator notes, the collaborative nature of the work is both the most challenging and rewarding aspect of the position:

> I think that the most challenging part of being a GF is managing time. There are a lot of responsibilities involved in being a GF in the Freshman Seminar program and to add the responsibilities of being a graduate student (especially while completing coursework), there never seems to be enough time … which leads on to what I believe are the most rewarding aspects of being a GF—working collaboratively within the learning community [with each other, PF's, librarians, and shared course faculty] to make a difference in the first-year experience of students.

The Integral Role of Online Learning in Freshman Seminar

The Freshman Seminar takes place in computer labs. With the seminar syllabus embedded in the Bridge, the course is developed specifically as an interactive and collaborative space, offering personal spaces, activity areas, and public forums. Because the Bridge is used in other classes at WSU, the students' experience in Freshman Seminar prepares them for their online work in other courses. The online environment also offers opportunities to invite shared-course faculty to take part in threaded discussions and gives students the chance to explore technological innovations, such as document sharing.

The final project, as described above, is a web-based presentation of their research. Many of the assignments are submitted online in the Bridge space and lead to conversations about the use of visual communication and web technology in higher education.

The Future of the Freshman Seminar Program

Along with portfolio assessment (described below), three sections of the WSU Freshman Seminar incorporating service-learning were piloted in fall 2003. Anecdotal evidence suggests that student enthusiasm for this approach is high. In addition, an effort to strengthen intellectual links between the shared course and the seminar course has led to a pilot project where students in five sections of the seminar course read a book recommended by the shared-course faculty that serves as a basis for discussion and research topic selection. Plans are also under way to increase opportunities for recognition of shared-course faculty and librarians.

Assessment

Retention

At the end of its first semester in fall 1996, the program was already making substantive progress toward furthering WSU's mission of improving student academic performance. First- to second-year retention rates of Freshman Seminar students typically have been higher than those of other first-year students (see Figure 1).

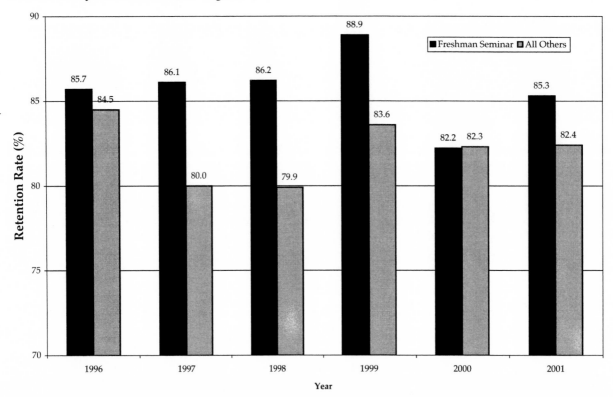

Figure 1. First- to second-year retention rates as related to seminar participation, fall 1996 to fall 2001.

The WSU Center for Teaching, Learning, and Technology (CTLT) has also completed several studies on the Freshman Seminar program. An overview reveals the following:

- A study investigating the effect of Freshman Seminar on students' academic adjustment to college found that seminar participants who struggled more academically in high school earned higher grades in all their courses than a matched group of non-seminar students.
- A study on the effects of Freshman Seminar and student retention found that a higher percentage of seminar students returned to college the semester following the seminar than a matched group of non-seminar students.
- The Goals, Activities, and Processes (GAPS) formative assessment was administered to 941 students during the 2000-2001 academic year. GAPS investigates processes taking place in technology-enabled courses. The 2000-2001 study compared the effects of technology, as it was implemented in the Freshman Seminar, and indicated that seminar students scored significantly better on desired learning outcomes than students in other WSU on-campus courses (Brown, Myers, & Roy, 2003). Specifically, students in Freshman Seminar were sig-

nificantly more likely to experience prompt feedback from instructors/peers on course activities, spend more time on task, discuss course topics outside of class, learn in new ways, and share their ideas and respond to the ideas of others.

- The 2000-2001 GAPS also investigated the way the peers facilitated electronic communication in Freshman Seminar. Seminar students scored significantly higher on most indices of student engagement than students in other WSU on-campus courses. Specifically, students in Freshman Seminars were more likely to ask for clarification, discuss ideas with other students, work on assignments with other students, ask other students for comments on their coursework, discuss course concepts with the instructor, make use of their unique abilities, and create their own understanding of course content.

- A study investigating the effects of Freshman Seminar on student integration on campus found that seminar students were less likely than non-seminar students to report feeling isolated from other students.

- A qualitative study examined the way seminar students perceived the value of technology on their learning. Students identified three major areas in which technology had a positive impact on their learning: (a) knowledge of web design and information organization, (b) Internet and library research skills, and (c) use of technology to communicate with instructor and peers.

- A return-on-investment (ROI) study, conducted in 2002, analyzed the costs and benefits of the Freshman Seminar program. The increased rate of retention of Freshman Seminar students is associated with an estimated ROI of 96.7%. In other words, the increased student retention associated with students' participation in the Freshman Seminar program resulted in increased revenues to the University that are twice the cost of the Freshman Seminar program (Bothell & Henderson, 2003). As noted elsewhere in this monograph, a single intervention, such as the WSU Freshman Seminar Program or any other learning community program, cannot be given sole credit for increasing retention rates and associated revenues. The return-on-investment argument is, therefore, used with great caution here.

While the studies above have not yet been replicated over multiple semesters, program administrators have a high degree of confidence that results would remain fairly consistent across time. Characteristics of enrolled students and the core components of the program have not changed markedly since these studies were conducted.

Critical Thinking Rubric

As part of the University-wide Critical Thinking Project, the Freshman Seminar program has adapted the University's critical thinking rubric for use in the Freshman Seminar (see Appendix B). The rubric has a multimedia focus that incorporates the visual components of the research presentation and highlights four critical thinking components: (a) focus, (b) multiple perspectives (including the student's own), (c) analyzing arguments, and (d) logical reasoning. Design of this version of the rubric was the product of a yearlong series of workshops, discussions, and collaborative efforts among faculty members, administrators, graduate facilitators, peer facilitators, and other students from both the Freshman Seminar program and the Center for Teaching, Learning, and Technology. This process allowed Freshman Seminar program designers to sharpen the focus of assignments and address procedures for incorporating the rubric into other assessment efforts. All assignments are now assessed using some portion of the critical thinking rubric. At the end of the semester, the rubric is used by mixed groups of faculty, librarians, administrators, and facilitators to evaluate final projects.

Portfolio Assessment

In 2003, the WSU Freshman Seminar implemented portfolio assessment into the seminar courses. Students collect evidence of their learning throughout the semester and then write a reflective piece about their learning in the program as related to established learning outcomes. The two-fold intent was to create additional venues for students to take responsibility for their academic work and to decrease the peer facilitators' responsibility for judging student work. Program administrators and graduate facilitators recognized an inconsistency between the call to have these upperclass undergraduates serve as guides through the seminar process and the teacher-authority role of "grader" they took on at various points. This inherent tension in peer facilitator roles became apparent as students fixated on points and grades during the semester. As Entwistle (2001) notes, the complex combination of teaching and assessment in the learning environment greatly influences the way students perceive their role in the class and leads to what the author refers to as either surface learning or deep learning. WSU recognized that deep learning often could not take place in an environment where points mattered most. The portfolio is intended to allow students to judge their own level of accomplishment.

Conclusion

In 2004, the WSU Freshman Seminar program moved into its ninth year. The intent at its inception, and throughout its history, has been to demonstrate that active, engaged learning focused on authentic projects that are the primary responsibility of undergraduates can lead to transformation in student learning, in the library, and in the academic lives of first-year and continuing students, faculty, and staff.

Notes

[1]The First-Year Seminar Program is a linked learning community program in which each link is composed of a two-credit seminar course intended to introduce students to the intellectual expectations of college and one general education or pre-major course. Groups of students are co-enrolled in both courses in the link.

[2]The author would like to thank the following for allowing their quotes to appear in this chapter: Ryan Laughlin, personal communication, July 29, 2003; Mike Takayoshi, personal communication, July 28, 2003; Nick Parsons, personal communication, July 27, 2003; Geoff Gilmore, personal communication, July 31, 2003.

References

Bothell, T. W., & Henderson, T. (2003). Evaluating the return on investment of faculty development. In C. Wehlburg & S. Chadwick-Blossey (Eds.), *To improve the academy: Vol. 22. Resources for faculty, instructional, and organizational development* (pp. 52-70). Bolton, MA: Anker Publishing.

Boud, D., Cohen, R., & Sampson, J. (2001). *Peer learning in higher education: Learning from and with each other*. London: Kogan Page.

Brown, G., Myers, C. B., & Roy, S. E. (2003). Formal course design and the student learning experience. *Journal of Asynchronous Learning Networks, 7*(3). Retrieved October 7, 2003, from http://www.aln.org/publications/jaln/v7n3/v7n3_myers.asp.

Chickering, A. W., & Gamson, Z. F. (1987). Seven principles for good practice in undergraduate education. *AAHE Bulletin, 39*(7), 3-7.

Ender, S. C., & Newton, F. B. (2000). *Students helping students: A guide for peer educators on college campuses.* San Francisco: Jossey-Bass.

Entwistle, N. (2001). Promoting deep learning through teaching and assessment. In L. Suskie (Ed.), *Assessment to promote deep learning* (pp. 9-19). Washington, DC: American Association for Higher Education.

Falchikov, N. (2001). *Learning together: Peer tutoring in higher education.* New York: Routledge-Falmer.

Hamid, S. L., & Gardner, J. N. (2001). Summary and recommendations. In S. L. Hamid (Ed.), *Peer leadership: A primer on program essentials* (Monograph No. 32) (pp. 97-101). Columbia, SC: University of South Carolina, National Resource Center for The First-Year Experience and Students in Transition.

Washington State University (2003). *Washington State University 2003-3004 catalog.* Pullman, WA: Author

Weimer, M. (2002). *Learner-centered teaching: Five key changes to practice.* San Francisco: Jossey-Bass.

Whitman, N. A, & Fife, J. D. (Eds.). (1988). *Peer teaching: To teach is to learn twice.* (ASHE-ERIC Higher Education Report No. 4). Washington, DC: Association for the Study of Higher Education.

Young, R. (1992). *Critical theory and classroom talk.* Clevedon, Avon, England: Multilingual Matters.

Appendix A
Washington State University
Freshman Seminar, GenEd 104 Syllabus
Fall 2003, 2 credit hours

Course Description

While one of the goals of the Freshman Seminar course is to support your transition to college by assisting you in strengthening your critical thinking and computer skills, we are focused on giving you a unique opportunity to value yourself as a learner and engage in a process that will enable you to develop strengths in a variety of ways that will see you through many other courses in your college career. Through collaboration with your peers, faculty, and librarians, you will develop a better understanding of the expectations of the University. Under the guidance of experienced peers, you will develop a web-based research project on a topic connected to the shared course. Learning is a process and these outcomes help us to help you describe that process. We look forward to getting to know you this semester.

Required Materials

- A three-ring binder
- Readings as announced in seminar

Learning Outcomes:

Through Freshman Seminar activities you will strengthen:
Individual and collaborative learning strategies by
- Understanding the academic expectations of the University including critical thinking needed to be successful as a student and academic integrity when using resources
- Assuming responsibility and ownership for your own learning
- Practicing self-awareness and reflection of your own learning processes
- Developing and applying team standards/rules; working effectively and efficiently in a team or group

Oral and written communication skills by
- Writing for a variety of audiences and purposes
- Employing critical thinking to identify, produce, and support an effective and challenging thesis
- Presenting an effectively designed web-based project to the academic community with confidence and knowledge

Information literacy and knowledge of the academic research process by
- Performing all stages of the research process, from the initial topic selection to the final adjustment of the thesis based on evidence and feedback
- Locating information in a variety of print, non-print, and electronic sources and critically evaluating those sources
- Analyzing the information you have gathered to develop and test a hypothesis
- Using feedback provided by faculty and peers to revise and defend your thesis
- Recognizing that knowledge changes as a result of ongoing research, creating new questions

Technological fluency by
- Participating appropriately in an online educational environment

- Demonstrating the ability to construct a web page and apply other technological tools
- Developing an ability to communicate arguments through a visual medium

Evaluation and Grading

Your graduate facilitator together with your peer facilitator and hypernaut* will determine your mid-term and final grades for the Freshman Seminar. Your peer facilitator will keep track of your participation in both the face-to-face and online environment.

Although your peer facilitator and hypernaut will be primarily responsible for responding to your daily work (i.e., Bridge activities, assignments, personal commentaries), your graduate facilitator, being *the instructor of record*, has the final say in all grading decisions.

*Peer associated with the seminar who helps students and instructors with the technical aspects of the course.

Descriptions of Assignments, Activities, and Class Processes

THE BRIDGE

The Bridge is an online learning environment with many tools to supplement your face-to-face classroom interaction. The Bridge is also used in many other classes at WSU.

Threaded Discussions

You will be asked to take part in threaded discussions throughout the semester using the Bridge. These assignments will give you the opportunity to share your ideas and thoughts and give feedback and reactions to your peers. In your responses to your peers, you should summarize important points, ask for clarification, ask for examples, and identify connections you have with their answers. ** **Hint:** You might want to type your responses in Word first so that you can check your spelling, and in case the Bridge decides to shut down or kick you out, you have your work saved in Word.

Personal Running Commentary

You will be provided private space on the Bridge that only you and your facilitators can access. These commentaries are a reflection on the learning process as you go through the semester. They are intended to encourage you to reflect on your own learning and to help build a resource fund for you to draw from as you prepare your mid-term and final portfolio for the class.

RESEARCH PROJECT – Course Assignments

The activities and assignments that you will participate in this semester lead to your Final Project. The research will be presented in a web-based presentation. The project will be evaluated using the Multi-Media Critical Thinking Rubric (MMCTR) by an invited group of academic colleagues from the University. The assignments are briefly described below and you will receive handouts with more details:

Author's Page (Part 1):

This assignment is designed to introduce you to FrontPage as well as give you a chance to introduce yourself as an author and scholar.

Author's Page (Part 2):

Toward the end of your seminar experience, you will have a chance to add reflections about the research to your Author's Page.

Group Proposal:

In your class/subgroups, you will write a proposal for your project. Your group will present this to the shared course faculty, peer facilitators, and graduate facilitator in order to gain feedback and ideas for the topic. The proposal will include a storyboard of the design of the web page, an outline of the research, and an annotated bibliography.

Content Draft (Part 1):

The content for the first draft of your web page will be submitted using the Document Tool on the Bridge.

Content Draft (Part 2):

The members of your group will combine individual research writing into one draft of your web page and submit it in Frontpage.

Presentations:

You will have the opportunity during the semester to practice your public presentation skills. You will present your project mid-semester as part of a process called the Review Panel as well as more formally toward the end of the semester, either in your shared course or in front of an audience in your seminar. You will also do a more informal presentation during the Research Symposium at the end of the semester.

PORTFOLIO

In recognition of our goals to promote learner-centered experience, you will compile a collection of your work in Freshman Seminar in a portfolio that will include a reflective essay and the evidence of your growth as a learner. This portfolio will be worth 60% of your final grade (see below). You will be given an assignment sheet that will help you to develop this portfolio. You will turn in a smaller version for your mid-term grade and receive feedback to enable you to prepare the final portfolio.

FINAL GRADES

Portfolio	**60%**
Final Project	**40%**

Fall 2003

Week 1	**Day 1**	Intro to Freshman Seminar Intro to Bridge Introduce theme idea	Assignment: Bridge: Introduce self Discuss first thoughts of theme
	Day 2	Decide on Theme	Assignment: Bridge: Discuss possible topics
Week 2	**Day 1**	Labor Day	Assignment: Bridge: Discuss possible topics
	Day 2	Intro to Frontpage Begin author's page pt.1 Assign articles	Assignment: Bridge: Discuss possible topics Read articles

Week 3	Day 1	Finish author's page pt. 1 ***Author's page pt. 1 due***	Assignment: Bridge: Discuss possible topics Finish articles
	Day 2	Faculty visit Discussion of readings Free-write	Assignment: Bridge: Discuss possible topics
Week 4	Day 1	Select research topic(s) Develop research question(s)	
	Day 2	Form subgroups Assign proposal	
Week 5	Day 1	Explore library resources (Library visit)	Assignment: Collect 4 sources to bring to next class
	Day 2	Research: Gleaning information from sources; citing sources	Assignment: Create bibliography in Frontpage
Week 6	Day 1	***Proposal Due*** Faculty visit – discuss proposal, assign content draft	Assignment: Begin 1st draft of content
	Day 2	Research writing: Incorporating info from sources Plagiarism workshop	Assignment: Continue writing
Week 7	Day 1	Visual communication	Assignment: Find visuals for web page
	Day 2	***1st draft of content due*** Peer review of writing Discuss writing – revise	Assignment: Begin 2nd draft of content
Week 8	Day 1	Discuss writing – How do the drafts fit together? – Storyboard	Assignment: Visit Writing Center
	Day 2	Build skeletal structure of web page	
Week 9	Day 1	Merge content and web page incorporating visuals	
	Day 2	***2nd draft of content due*** Work on research project	
Week 10	Day 1	Present to review panel	
	Day 2	Review panel feedback Work on research project	

Week 11	Day 1	Work on research project	
	Day 2	Work on research project	
Week 12	Day 1	Veteran's Day	
	Day 2	Work on research project	
Week 13	Day 1	Work on research project Assign author's page pt. 2	Assignment: Begin author's page pt. 2 (Reflection)
	Day 2	Author's page pt. 2 (Reflection) **Web page complete**	
THANKSGIVING BREAK			
Week 14	Day 1	Practice presentation Assign reflective essay	**Outside evaluations**
	Day 2	**Research symposium**	**Outside evaluations**
Week 15	Day 1	Debrief the symposium Receive outside evaluations	
	Day 2	**Reflective essay due**	

Appendix B
Multimedia Critical Thinking Rubric: Freshman Seminar Fall 2003

The rubric identifies four critical thinking skills. Students are scored along a continuum from emerging skill level to mastery for each one.

1. Focus.

2	4	6
Emerging	Developing	Mastering

Jump directly into their argument without any introductory summary of important aspects of the topic to contextualize it. Present aspects of the topic incorrectly, as just information, and/or without a focused thesis. Distract their audience with multimedia elements that maybe interesting in themselves but are tangential or not explicitly, textually connected to their argument.	Contextualize their argument with an introductory summary of important aspects of the topic. Focus their thesis in an academic argument—rather than just providing information—making clear the important aspect of their topic to their thesis. Draw in the viewer with multimedia elements that further clarify the important aspects of their topic.

2. Multiple Perspectives.

2	4	6
Emerging	Developing	Mastering

Address only a single perspective, failing to address differences of perspective among sources, or address a variety of perspectives without taking a stand of their own. Limit their argument to only one or two contexts*, avoiding interactions and/or conflicts among contexts. Present multimedia elements in ways tangential or not explicitly, textually connected to the perspectives presented in the text.	Address diverse perspectives drawn from outside sources and explain how these perspectives interact or conflict to create the issue being discussed, while taking a stand on their own perspective. Connect to a variety of contexts*, explaining the interactions and/or conflicts among those contexts. Improve the viewers' understanding of the various perspectives being presented textually through the use of multimedia elements.

*Examples of contexts: political, cultural, ethical, theological, educational, economic, scientific, social psychological, technological, ecological, historical, personal experience, local, and global.

3. Information Literacy.

2	4	6
Emerging	Developing	Mastering
Rely on a single source or unreliable source(s), such as dot-coms, personal web sites, or academic abstracts. Mimic the perspectives of their sources without reflection ("plug and chug") or deny evidence without adequate support. Fail to distinguish among fact, opinion, and value judgments. Present multimedia elements inaccurately or for shock value. Authors don't look closely enough at the source of the multimedia to know what it represents, or they provide disturbing or provocative multimedia without explaining what makes those multimedia applicable to their presentation.	Use a variety of reliable sources to provide sufficient evidence to support the claims they make, and they justify the authority of sources when necessary for an academic audience. Examine the reasoning of sources and explore their relevancy to the authors' argument. Distinguish clearly among fact, opinion, and value judgments. Present multimedia elements accurately and relevantly. The multimedia represents what they say it represents, and if they use any disturbing or provocative multimedia, they provide support for its use.	

4. Coherence.

2	4	6
Emerging	Developing	Mastering
Limit discussion to individual responses to sources, not drawing conclusions or exploring possible implications. Assume a great deal in the claims they make, failing to provide sufficient reasoning to support and/or connect claims to each other. Link the pages so that navigation seems arbitrary, unconnected to the logic of the written and multimedia content. Present multimedia elements, such as fonts, colors, images, and audios, inconsistently across the pages of the site. The differences make it seem that the pages are not even part of the same site.	Draw conclusions and explore implications of contexts, assumptions, and evidence. Reflect upon the claims they make, unpacking assumptions and providing sufficient reasoning. Guide the viewer with links that complement the logic of written and multimedia content. Unify their multimedia elements across the pages of their site. There can be variety as long as it is complementary—without the text the pages should still clearly be part of the same site.	

Leslie Bessant (B.A., Emory University; Ph.D., Yale University) is a professor of history at Ripon College. In addition to serving as the coordinator of the college's First-Year Studies Program from 1997 to 1999, he has led study-abroad programs in Zimbabwe and Tanzania. His scholarly research focuses on the social and agricultural history of colonial Zimbabwe.

Glenn Blalock is an associate professor of English, co-director of the University Core Curriculum, and coordinator of the First-Year Writing Program. He earned his Ph.D. from the University of North Carolina-Chapel Hill, specializing in composition/rhetoric and in American literary culture. He has been at Texas A&M University–Corpus Christi since 1999 and has been involved with learning communities and writing-across-the-curriculum initiatives since 1989.

Rennie W. Brantz attended Doane College in Nebraska and completed his Ph.D. in modern German history at The Ohio State University. He has been teaching history at Appalachian State University since 1973. In 1990, he became director of Appalachian's Freshman Seminar program, which over the last 13 years has grown from 24 to 62 classes, added a summer version called SummerPreview (1992), started a peer leader program (1996), and created numerous faculty development strategies. The seminar has become the anchor course in Appalachian's Freshman Learning Communities program. Brantz has received several teaching awards, international study grants, and in 1997 was named an "Outstanding First-Year Student Advocate" by the National Resource Center for The First-Year Experience and Students in Transition.

Cathy Brinjak is an instructor in the Academic Services Department at Slippery Rock University of Pennsylvania and is serving as the interim director of the Academic Advisement Center and coordinator of the FYRST Seminar course.

Kathleen Byrnes is assistant vice president of student life and coordinates the Villanova Experience program at Villanova University.

Nannette Evans Commander is director of Freshmen Studies and an associate professor at Georgia State University. She oversees the Freshmen Learning Community Program, University Service Learning Program, and State Scholars Program in the Office of Undergraduate Studies. Having served as a faculty advisor for the Strategic Thinking and Learning Community, she has participated in the curriculum development of the first-year seminar course since the inception of the Freshmen Learning Community Program in 1999. She holds a Ph.D. in educational psychology and has a joint faculty appointment with the Office of Undergraduate Studies and the Department of Educational Psychology and Special Education. A faculty member since 1989, her scholarly interests are learning and cognition, student success, and retention.

Nikki Crees is assistant director of Freshman Learning Communities in General Studies at Appalachian State University. She holds a master's degree in higher education administration from Appalachian State University and a bachelor's degree in industrial relations from the University of North Carolina–Chapel Hill. She worked briefly in Appalachian's Learning Assistance Program before beginning her work with Freshman Learning Communities in 2002. She teaches in Appalachian's award-winning Freshman Seminar program.

Pat Doherty coordinates the Class Act learning community and advises students in the Arts & Sciences and the Interdisciplinary Studies Liberal Arts Advising Centers at the University of Northern Colorado. She has also taught English and ID 108 in several learning communities.

Phyllis Endicott retired in July 2002 after 23 years of service to the University of Northern Colorado. In 1992, she became director of the Arts & Sciences Advising Center and program manager of the Freshman Challenge Program. In 1993, she took on the coordination of the new Academic Advantage program, and in 1998 she was appointed director of all UNC Learning Communities. Before her assignments in the College of Arts & Sciences, Endicott worked for 13 years at the Center for Human Enrichment, UNC's federally funded student support services program. There she taught English composition, tutored in the Writing Center, coordinated the curriculum, and directed the first computerized writing lab at UNC. Endicott holds a B.A. in English from Wellesley College and an M.A.T. in Secondary English from Harvard Graduate School of Education. Currently, she is employed as the Writing Lab instructor at UNC's Center for International Education.

William J. Fritz has been a geology professor at Georgia State University since 1981. He was appointed associate provost for undergraduate studies in 2001 and has oversight responsibility for all enrollment services (registrar, undergraduate admissions, student financial aid, student advisement, freshmen studies, international student and scholars services, and cross-functional enrollment management group). He has been responsible for enrollment management at a time of great change at Georgia State University. In 1999, he implemented Freshmen Learning Communities within the College of Arts and Sciences, which later led to a university-wide initiative.

Skye Gentile received her undergraduate and graduate degrees in Communication at California State University, Hayward. She has been the General Studies Lead Instructor for three years and worked with the freshman learning communities from their inception. Gentile also teaches at Chabot Community College. She has pioneered service-learning for Hayward's learning communities and is working with learning communities and service-learning at Chabot. She continuously creates workshops, establishing partnerships with community organizations for both colleges. Her interests rest in assessing student learning, portfolio construction, diversity in teaching style, and helping teachers create classroom climate conducive for collaborative learning.

Beth Glass is assistant director of freshman seminar at Appalachian State University. She holds a master's degree in college student development from Appalachian State University and a bachelor's degree in mathematics from the College of William and Mary. Prior to coming to Appalachian, she taught secondary mathematics in Danville, VA at both the junior high and high school levels. She served briefly as assistant coordinator for Appalachian's Student Support Services TRIO program before beginning her work with Freshman Seminar in 2001. She teaches both Freshman Seminar and Peer Leader Seminar while working to create opportunities for faculty and student development.

Diana Guerrero is director of enrollment, evaluation, and technology for the University of Texas at El Paso's University College dean's office. Her work involves student assessment issues and the use of technology to improve enrollment processes. She earned a master's degree in educational psychology and guidance from The University of Texas at El Paso, has received UTEP's Distinguished Achievement Award for Service to Students, and has served as vice president for enrollment management, admissions, and financial aid for the American Association of Collegiate Registrars and Admissions Officers (AACRAO). She was a contributing author for AACRAO's *The Admissions Profession: A Guide to Staff Development and Program Management*, the *Handbook for the College Admissions Profession*, and wrote the foreword to *Becoming A Leader in Enrollment Services*.

Sandra S. Harper is provost and vice president for academic affairs and professor of communication at Texas A&M University–Corpus Christi. She earned her Ph.D. from the University of North Texas, specializing in the college teaching of speech communication. Prior to coming to Texas A&M University–Corpus Christi in 1998, Harper served as the vice president for academic affairs at Oklahoma City University and the dean of the College of Arts and Sciences at McMurry University. She has been involved in core curriculum reform since 1990 and is a member of the national implementation team for the American Democracy Project.

Alicia B. Harvey-Smith is dean of learning and student development on the Catonsville campus of the Community College of Baltimore County. She earned a Ph.D. from the University of Maryland – College Park in education, an M.S. from Johns Hopkins University in counseling and guidance, and a B.S. from Morgan State University in business administration. Her dissertation was entitled *The Adoption of the Learning Paradigm in Student Affairs Divisions in Vanguard Community Colleges*. She is the author of several articles and essays as well as the text, *Getting Real: Proven Strategies for Student Survival and Academic Success*.

Jean M. Henscheid is a fellow with the National Resource Center for The First-Year Experience and Students in Transition at the University of South Carolina and managing editor for *About Campus*, a periodical published by Jossey-Bass. She served as associate director of the National Resource Center from 1999 to 2001 and directed the Freshman Seminar Program at Washington State University between 1994 and 1999. She authored the monograph *Professing the Disciplines: An Analysis of Senior Seminars and Capstone Courses* for the National Resource Center and, with Dorothy Fidler, authored *Primer for Research on the College Student Experience*. She received her Ph.D. in education from Washington State University, conducting research on residential learning communities and the first college year. For the past decade, she has been active in the national learning communities movement, most recently serving as a fellow and web editor for the National Learning Communities Project.

Marylu Hill is assistant director of the Core Humanities program and an assistant professor in the Core Humanities department at Villanova University.

John Immerwahr is associate vice president for academic affairs and professor of philosophy at Villanova University. Over the years, he has also served as a senior research fellow at the Public Agenda (a non-profit research and education institution founded by Daniel Yankelovich and Cyrus Vance in 1975). His recent research with the Public Agenda has dealt primarily with public attitudes toward higher education, including "Great Expectations: How the Public and Parents View Higher Education," "The Price of Admission: The Growing Importance of Higher Education," and "Taking Responsibility: Leaders' Expectations of Higher Education." His publications in philosophy primarily focus on 18th century philosophy (especially the work of David Hume), and he has also written a number of articles on teaching philosophy.

Jodi Levine Laufgraben is associate vice provost and director of periodic program review at Temple University. Since 1994, she has directed Temple's Learning Communities and Freshman Seminar Program. She recently implemented a common reading program for first-year students.

In her previous role as assistant vice provost for University Studies, she was responsible for University Studies, the academic home for students deciding on a major. In addition to her administrative responsibilities, she is an instructor in Educational Leadership and Policy Studies, teaching courses on educational administration, research design, action and collaborative research, and personnel. Nationally, she is involved in several projects. She serves on the National Advisory Board for the National Resource Center for The First-Year Experience and Students in Transition, is a fellow for the National Learning Communities Project, and was a principal investigator in the Restructuring for Urban Student Success Project. Her publications include the monograph *Learning Communities: New Structures, New Partnerships for Learning* (published by the National Resource Center for The First-Year Experience and Students in Transition), *Creating Learning Communities* (with Nancy Shapiro, published by Jossey-Bass), and the recently released *Sustaining and Improving Learning Communities*, from Jossey-Bass.

April Longwell is an instructor in the Academic Services Department at Slippery Rock University of Pennsylvania. She is also director of orientation and serves as the coordinator of the learning community clusters.

Sharon McMorrow coordinates the Ascent and Cluster learning communities and the Supplemental Instruction Tutoring Program at University of Northern Colorado. She has also taught English and ID 108 in Ascent and Cluster and tutored in the University Writing Center.

Diane Mockridge (B.A., City College of New York; Ph.D, Duke University) is a professor of history at Ripon College. She served as coordinator of the college's First-Year Studies Program from 2000 until 2002. She has also led study-abroad programs in Florence, Venice, and Rome. Her research focuses on medieval hagiography and gender roles in medieval and early modern Europe.

Sally K. Murphy is general education coordinator and professor of communication at California State University, Hayward. She earned her Ph.D. from the University of Minnesota in 1986, specializing in conversation analysis and forensics. Prior to coming to CSU, Hayward in 1990, Murphy taught at the University of Pittsburgh and George Mason University. She has been involved in learning about learning and curriculum reform since 1987. She is a fellow with the National Learning Communities Project.

Joel Nossoff has been director of New Student Programs at the University of New Mexico since 1994. He was assistant dean of Undergraduate Studies at California State University–San Bernardino (1988-1994), and director of the Minority Engineering Program at California State University–Los Angeles (1978-1988). He has initiated and directed first-year seminars at all three campuses. At UNM, he directs the FLCs. In 2003, he was honored as an "Outstanding First-Year Student Advocate" by the National Resource Center for The First-Year Experience and Students in Transition.

Deano Pape (B.A., Central College of Iowa; M.A., Central Missouri St. University) was hired as instructor and director of forensics when he came to Ripon College in 1997. He was promoted to assistant professor in 1999. Pape now serves as director of Communicating Plus, a communication across the curriculum program that features training and support in the areas of written communication, oral communication, problem solving, and critical thinking. The program includes the Communicating Plus Center, a collaborative learning environment on campus. In addition, he serves as the current coordinator of First-Year Studies, working with faculty in the implementation of the Ripon FYS Seminars. Pape's scholarly interests include film criticism and computer-mediated communication.

Joni Webb Petschauer is director of Freshman Learning Communities in General Studies at Appalachian State University. She holds a master's degree in history from the University of North Carolina–Chapel Hill and a master's degree in student development from Appalachian. Her career experiences include working with Appalachian's Upward Bound project and 13 years as the institution's Learning Skills Coordinator. In 1991, she began teaching Freshman Seminar as well as co-leading the annual week-long training program for new course instructors. She co-authored with Cindy Wallace the "Instructor's Manual" that accompanies *P.O.W.E.R. Learning*, Robert Feldman, McGraw-Hill, 2000 (1st ed.); 2002 (2nd ed). She consults with campuses about improving access to higher education and developing and improving comprehensive first-year programs.

Andrew Piker is an associate professor of philosophy and chair of the Department of Humanities. He earned his Ph.D. from Vanderbilt University and specializes in business, medical, and professional ethics, as well as ethical theory. He has also taught at Kent State University and East Carolina State University and served as a co-director of the Core Curriculum Program at Texas A&M University–Corpus Christi.

Howard N. Shapiro became Iowa State University's first vice provost for undergraduate programs in 1998. The undergraduate programs that report to the vice provost include University Career Services, Honors Program, Instructional Technology Center, International Education Services, Student Outcomes Assessment, Center for Teaching Excellence, University Studies, and the Program for Women in Science and Engineering. The vice provost also works closely with each of the colleges. Shapiro has been a faculty member in mechanical engineering at Iowa State University since 1975, when he came to the university after receiving his Ph.D. in mechanical engineering from Ohio State University. He teaches and does research on energy utilization, thermodynamics, refrigeration, and industrial efficiency. Shapiro was a co-founder of Project LEA/RN, now a campus-wide program for faculty and staff to study teaching and learning in order to enhance student achievement in their courses. He is also the co-author of *Fundamentals of Engineering Thermodynamics*, presently in its 5th edition, which is the most widely used engineering thermodynamics text.

Maggy Smith is a full professor of English and dean of the University of Texas at El Paso's University College. She earned a Ph.D. in communicating and rhetoric from Rennselaer Polytechnic Institute and has taught writing and rhetoric courses at all levels at a number of institutions of higher education for more than 20 years. As dean of the University College, she oversees all of UTEP's enrollment departments as well as retention and first-year programs. Recently, she co-authored a book chapter with UTEP's president Diana Natalicio on helping first-year students succeed in research universities.

Diana Suhr is a statistical analyst in the Office of Institutional Research and Planning at the University of Northern Colorado. She has also taught classes in educational psychology and mathematics.

Randy L. Swing is co-director and senior scholar of the Policy Center on the First Year of College, located at Brevard College in Brevard, North Carolina. During the Center's first three years, his work focused on developing and disseminating new tools and techniques for evaluating the efficacy of first-year programs. His leadership roles include contributing to two national surveys of first-year students, *Your First College Year* (YFCY) and the *First-Year Initiative* (FYI) benchmarking survey. Until 1999, Swing worked for 20 years in various first-year programs at

Appalachian State University. Most recently, as founding director of the Assessment Office, he developed and initiated a longitudinal, campus-wide assessment program with focus on learning outcomes. Prior to earning a doctoral degree in higher education from the University of Georgia, he earned his M.A. and Ed.S. degrees in student development from Appalachian State University and a B.A. in psychology from the University of North Carolina–Charlotte. He serves on the review boards for the *Journal on Excellence in College Teaching* and *Innovative Higher Education* and is a fellow of the National Resource Center for The First-Year Experience and Students in Transition. Swing's current work includes a large-scale project to establish "Foundations of Excellence in the First College Year" with the Council for Independent Colleges and the American Association for State Colleges and Universities.

Kay Tronsen is coordinator for the Freshman Seminar Program at Washington State University. She received an M.A. in English, composition and rhetoric, in 1999, after teaching English in the public school systems. She is currently finishing a Ph.D. Her experience includes teaching English to first-year students at WSU and serving as graduate assistant to the director of composition in the English Department at WSU. Her awards include the Jerard TA Distinguished Teaching Award, English Department, WSU, 1998-1999; A.J. Staples English Department Award, California Baptist College, 1990-1991; and the President's Award for Excellence in Writing, California Baptist College, 1991.

Dorothy Ward is an assistant professor in the Department of English at the University of Texas at El Paso and is currently chair of the University Studies Department and director of UTEP's Entering Student Program. She earned a Ph.D. in English from the University of North Texas and has taught at institutions of higher education for more than 20 years. Most of her professional career has focused on first-year students. As director of the Entering Student Program, she collaborates with key University staff and administrators to develop and coordinate academically centered initiatives that strive to improve entering student success and retention. As chair of University Studies, her responsibilities include administrative oversight for the University Seminar (UNIV 1301: Seminar in Critical Inquiry), including the training and supervision of instructors and peer leaders. In 2000, she was recognized with UTEP's Outstanding Advocate for Entering Students Award and in 2001, with the Distinguished Achievement Award for Teaching Excellence.

Cathy Willermet is assistant director of the University Studies Department at the University of Texas at El Paso. She coordinates UTEP's learning communities program, markets learning communities to entering students, and leads workshops encouraging instructors to make connections across disciplines. She earned her Ph.D. from Arizona State University in physical anthropology, and co-edited *Conceptual Issues in Modern Human Origins Research* with archaeologist Geoff Clark. She teaches the first-year seminar as well as upper-division courses in anthropology.

Amanda Yale is an associate professor and has served as the interim associate provost for enrollment services at Slippery Rock University for the past two years. She has been a member of the faculty for 15 years as director of the Advisement Center and coordinator of the FYRST Seminar course. She completed her dissertation studies and research on the first-year seminar course.

Dan Young received his Ph.D. in education in 1993 and has been on the faculties of the University of Washington, the University of Tennessee–Martin, and the University of New Mexico. In addition to developing first-year programs, he has developed masters and teacher education programs. He directs the FIG, LLC, FISC, and experiential learning programs at UNM.

Titles on Improving the Teaching and Learning
of First-Year College Students

Monograph 34. Service-Learning and The First-Year Experience: Preparing Students for Personal Success and Civic Responsibility. *Edward Zlotkowski, Editor.* Produced in association with Campus Compact. This monograph combines a research-based argument for the value of service-learning in the first year of college with a practical discussion of the issues related to implementation. Readers will find program and course models from a variety of disciplines, curricular structures, and institutional types. Connecting service-learning to the broader issues of the first college year, this monograph allows readers to examine where and how learning best takes place. 167 pages. ISBN 1-889271-38-1. $35.00

Monograph 32. Peer Leadership: A Primer on Program Essentials. *Suzanne Hamid, Editor.* This volume focuses on the use of peer leaders in the first-year seminar classroom and also includes examples of undergraduates fulfilling a variety of academic and social support roles on campus. Topics include a historical overview of research on peer leadership and information on emerging leadership trends; a discussion of recruitment, selection, and training for successful programs; recommendations for effective program management; practical examples from a variety of campuses; and comprehensive appendices, including sample applications, contracts, job descriptions, training agendas and syllabi, team-building activities, and evaluations. 155 pages. ISBN 1-889271-36-5. $30.00

Monograph 29. Solid Foundations: Building Success for First-Year Seminars through Instructor Training and Development. *Mary Stuart Hunter and Tracy L. Skipper, Editors, Joseph B. Cuseo, Major Contributor.* This volume focuses on the critical issue of instructor training as a method for improving the delivery of the first-year seminar as well as all first-year courses. Topics include a research-based rationale for implementing an instructor training program, uses of student development theory in approaches to college teaching and learning, group-learning pedagogies, and assessment tools for the instructor training program. 132 pages. ISBN 1-889271-30-6. $30.00

Monograph 26. Learning Communities: New Structures, New Partnerships for Learning. *Jodi H. Levine, Editor.* Learning communities have become one of the most widely used structures for achieving both academic and social integration of new students. This monograph describes various successful models, links theory with examples of good practice, and describes how learning communities can facilitate faculty development. In addition, chapter authors outline strategies for dealing with logistical concerns and provide comprehensive resource listings and recommendations for building learning community programs. 180 pages. ISBN 1-889271-27-6. $30.00

Learning Interdependence: A Case Study of the International/ Intercultural Education of First-Year College Students. *David J. Bachner, Laurence J. Malone, and Mary C. Snider.* Challenging the notion that study abroad programs are best suited for "mature" students, faculty and administrators at Hartwick College designed an intercultural, interdisciplinary course for first-year students, spanning an entire academic year. The book includes information on program development and student outcomes, with an appendix featuring syllabi from six courses based on the model. 203 pages. ISBN 1-889271-35-7. $30.00

Use the order form on the next page to order any of these titles from
the National Resource Center.

Use this form to order additional copies of this monograph or to order other titles from the National Resource Center for The First-Year Experience & Students in Transition.

Prices advertised in this publication are subject to change.

Item	Quantity	Price	Total
Monograph 39. *Integrating the First-Year Experience*		$35.00	
Monograph 34. *Service-Learning & The First-Year Experience*		$35.00	
Monograph 32. *Peer Leadership*		$30.00	
Monograph 29. *Solid Foundations*		$30.00	
Monograph 26. *Learning Communities*		$30.00	
Learning Interdependence		$30.00	

| | | | Shipping & Handling | |
| | | | Total | |

Shipping Charges:

	Order Amount	Shipping Cost
U.S.	$0 - $50	$ 6.50 US
	$51 - $150	$10.00 US
	over $150	$15.00 US
Foreign	For orders shipped outside of the United States, customers will be billed exact shipping charges plus a $5.00 processing fee. Fax or e-mail us to obtain a shipping estimate. Be sure to include a list of items you plan to purchase and to specify your preference for Air Mail or UPS Delivery.	

Name _____   Department _____

Institution _____   Telephone _____

Address _____

City _____ State/Province _____ Postal Code _____

E-mail Address _____

Select your option payable to the University of South Carolina:

❏ Check Enclosed   ❏ Institutional Purchase Order   Purchase Order No. _____

Credit Card: ❏ *VISA*   ❏ *MasterCard*   ❏ *DISCOVER*

Card No. _____   Expiration Date _____

Name of Cardholder _____

Billing Address _____

City _____ State/Province _____ Postal Code _____

Signature _____

Mail this form to: National Resource Center for The First-Year Experience & Students in Transition, University of South Carolina, 1728 College Street, Columbia, SC 29208. Phone (803) 777-6029. FAX (803) 777-4699.
E-mail burtonp@sc.edu Federal ID 57-6001153.